Wildfowler

Shooting, Yachting, and Sea-Fishing Trips

Wildfowler

Shooting, Yachting, and Sea-Fishing Trips

ISBN/EAN: 9783337034368

Printed in Europe, USA, Canada, Australia, Japan

Cover: Foto ©Andreas Hilbeck / pixelio.de

More available books at **www.hansebooks.com**

SHOOTING, YACHTING,

AND SEA-FISHING TRIPS,

AT HOME AND ON THE CONTINENT.

SECOND SERIES.

BY

"WILDFOWLER," "SNAPSHOT."

In Two Volumes.

VOL. II.

LONDON:
CHAPMAN & HALL, 193, PICCADILLY.
1877.

TABLE OF CONTENTS.

SHOOTING ON THE CONTINENT.

CHAP.		PAGE
XXXVI.—SHOOTING IN FRANCE—*Continued*		1
XXXVII.—GAME-PRESERVING IN FRANCE. PART I.		6
XXXVIII. ,, ,, PART II.		12
XXXIX. ,, ,, PART III.		19
XL. ,, ,, PART IV.		27
XLI.—HIRING A SHOOTING IN BELGIUM		34
XLII. ,, ,, ,, *Continued*		42
XLIII.—UNEARTHING FOXES FOR THE BRITISH MARKET.		49

YACHTING.

XLIV.—OUR OPENING CRUISE		59
XLV.—THE PLEASURES AND TRIBULATIONS OF AN ENTHUSIASTIC CORINTHIAN		65

SEA-FISHING AND SEAFOWL-SHOOTING EXCURSIONS.

CHAP.	PAGE
XLVI.—Old Shoreham	77
XLVII.—From Brighton to Worthing	88
XLVIII.—Littlehampton	99
XLIX.—Bognor, Middleton, and Barn Rocks	110
L.—The Blackwater (Essex)	124
LI.—Beachy Head	134
LII.—The Northern Watering-Places of Kent	147
LIII.—The South-East Coast	160
LIV.—Portsmouth	169
LV.—Seaham Harbour and Bay	180
LVI.—Off the Shipwash	191
LVII.—Eastbourne and Selsea Bill	204
LVIII.—Off the Tyne Bar	214
LIX.—Sunderland	224
LX.—The Wallet, Orfordness, and the Deben	234
LXI.—Off the Tees Mouth	244

Table of Contents.

CHAP.	PAGE
LXII.—Jersey	255
LXIII.—Holyhead	267
LXIV.—The North-East Coast of the Isle of Wight	278
LXV.—Kingstown	289
LXVI.—Sea-Fishing at Kingstown and Dalkey	296
LXVII.—The most available Stations	301

SHOOTING ON THE CONTINENT

(*Continued.*)

CHAPTER XXXVI.

SHOOTING IN FRANCE—*Continued.*

As to the dogs the professional shooters use, they are of no particular breed. In fact it seems that any kind of dog will do for them, provided they have sufficient nose to lead them up to game. They don't care whether they point, stand, crouch, or run in; but by dint of killing a lot of game to them, and enforcing orders, the men come to such a thorough understanding with their animals that lucky is the game that escapes them both. Of course their dogs are thoroughly well broken to retrieve any distance, by land or water, whatever may be their other qualifications. Those *chasseurs de profession* who live in a hare country, have their dogs generally high on legs, and of a breed but faintly traceable to any peculiar race. Some look like harriers, some like sheep-dogs, some like half-bred setters and lurchers; but they are one and all swift and courageous. Many hares are caught by these dogs and brought to their masters, even if the hares have not been fired at. Greyhounds might more advantageously be employed, but such a proceeding is not allowed in France; the law does not allow the use of greyhounds for the pursuit of game, but, like all other ill-applied or useless laws, this one is evaded. Evidently it had been made to prevent hares from being coursed at all; but as the legislators (evidently not much versed in sporting knowledge) have only mentioned greyhounds in the forbidding clause, of course the police can but stick to the *word*—not to the *spirit*—of the law; and if a dog possessing all the speed of a greyhound, without his outward appearance, is brought to play his part in the field both gendarmes and *gardes-champêtres* look on with astonishment, but do not prosecute; for do not books say that a greyhound has small ears? Well then, so long as the coursing dog has not small ears he is beyond the pale of the law. The consequence of this is that, by interbreeding greyhounds with long-eared harriers, pointers, or setters, a race of dogs *with pendulous ears* is obtained, and these are incited to course, showing occasionally a turn of speed that reflects great credit on their breeding: these dogs have, at the same time, retained sufficient nose to find their game themselves. Such dogs in England would be called lurchers; in France they are classed among the *chiens de chasse*; which elastic denomination includes, as its name implies, all dogs employed in the pursuit of game, but whether in a legitimate or illegitimate manner is another thing to determine.

The number of French professionals who employ these hare-catchers is almost incredible. I met in my rambles one of these individuals who bred such dogs for sale, and who kept a couple for his own use. I was astonished at first, when I knew nothing at all about all this, at the way in which this man, who was reputed such a destroyer of hares, worked out his programme. His dogs were never by him. One of them might be seen trotting along the off-side of a hedge, and the other inspecting minutely the interior organisation of some stray bushes in the open; while their master, fully a hundred yards away from them, was walking quite unconcernedly, just as if beating the field on "his own hook." Suddenly one of the dogs would spring a hare. If puss came within range the sportsman (?) tried to bundle her over; if not, he would stand by and let the dogs work up to the hare, kill her, and bring her to him. But if anyone was close by he invariably fired off a barrel, so as to have a reason to allege for his dogs chasing the hare; and, if questioned, invariably asserted that he had wounded it; this, in nine cases out of ten, was false, as he well knew. I convinced him once by examining thoroughly a hare that his dog had brought back, and, as he insisted that he had wounded it, I got it skinned there and then by a keeper; and then he revealed to us the dodge, and acknowledged that he owed his reputation as a killer of hares more to the speed of his companions than to his own skill. He said that he fired a barrel as an incentive to the dogs, who always redoubled speed then, on the idea that the hare was wounded; and the noise of the explosion served also, at the same time, as a blind to the passers-by on the road, or to other sportsmen who might have been within sight. He told me that not a hare out of a dozen escaped the two dogs he had with him, unless there was some strong covert at hand, or when the fields were much cut up and divided by hedges; otherwise, in a perfectly open plain, he was so sure that a hare once started would come into his bag, that he would take any odds about it. He did not consider it unsportsmanlike at all; in fact his ideas of sport were very limited, being confined to the well-known axiom, " the more the merrier," not considering how they were got. I hinted that such dogs must have been awkward customers to manage when they got close to some good preserve ; but there again his ideas differed from mine, as he thought it very jolly to get other people's game without having to pay for it. However, all this game-shooting, or game-catching, or whatever it may be called, only keeps the professionals' pots boiling. As it is with our own professionals, their harvest season is in the middle of winter ; then they are everywhere, and kill or take everything. If there is a little snow they set lark-snares. I have known one hundred dozen larks taken by a man and his little boy in one day. Of course, if partridges *will* come where the snares are set, and *will* catch themselves, nobody can reasonably expect that the snare-setter will set them free. He just gives them a twist of the neck, and puts them out of sight.

Then come the wildfowl. The seashore gets lined with professional shooters, who keep up an incessant firing all day and during part of the night. Rivers, streams, rivulets, and marshes are well looked after. Every inch of the shore or ground is well beaten, and at night the fowlers resort to their huts with their call-ducks, as I have described in a former chapter. Professionals are often, at the same time, poachers. There are but few among them who do not keep ferrets ; and when the season is propitious and the weather favourable, they are not always to be found at home of a night. Howbeit they drive a comfortable trade ; and what with the game they catch and kill, their poaching expeditions, their breeding of dogs and ferrets, and their dog-breaking for the *chasseurs bourgeois*, they live very comfortably and are very jolly.

And, by-the-way, the French poacher offers a great

contrast to his English brother. The British poacher is almost invariably a great big surly man, addicted to strong drink and swearing; the French poacher is a pleasant, chatty, sober, laughing sort of fellow, who, if occasion presents itself, will entertain you with the recital of some of his excursions on your *own* ground, and think the story almost as good as the excursion itself. If you happen to meet at the market town in England a poacher who has been on your estate, he will point you out to his mates, and scowl at you—much to your wonder, as very likely you don't know him.

Not so with his French *confrère*. In a similar case he will raise his hat or *casquette* to you, and smile a pleased smile, just as if you were one of his acquaintances. And if his friends and neighbours ask him who you are, he will say: "Ha! he is a jolly fellow! I go shooting or ferreting on his ground occasionally, and although he does not know it" (this with a wink), "it is just as well to be polite with him when one meets him; I might some day want him to remember me favourably. Well, here is his health; and may he for a long time keep the —— shootings, and always have them as well stocked as they are now."

CHAPTER XXXVII.

GAME-PRESERVING IN FRANCE.—PART I.

ALL officials in the pay of the French Government are virtually gamekeepers. They don't always choose to act in that capacity, but they may and ought to. Custom-house officers, tax-collectors, soldiers, all Government *employés* (besides gendarmes, *gardes-champêtres*, and private keepers) may prosecute, at the Government's expense, any poacher whom they may have found at work in his illicit calling. Even private individuals may prosecute, but there must always be at least three witnesses to the offence. All prosecutions are carried on by the *procureur*, so that there are positively no *direct* expenses attending a private gentleman's prosecution of a poacher caught on his ground. I have purposely written *direct* in italics, because there are other costs besides the direct ones attending a prosecution which none the less draw on your purse—I mean your loss of time and your lawyer's fees. You may do without one, that is if you know the language well, but at the best it is very awkward. As a rule, even French owners or lessees of shootings employ a lawyer to attend the case on their behalf. However, the point now under consideration is the fact that almost everybody in France is virtually, if not actually, able to enforce the preserving of game. At first sight, then, one might reasonably expect that game in France, having such a number of protectors, ought to be well preserved, and, as a natural consequence, ought to be abundant. Quite the reverse is the case, though, for a very simple reason, viz. that the game-protectors are very often the best and most successful poachers. It is a fact patent to anyone who may have had some experience of French management that, from the highest to the lowest, everyone poaches more or less, and none more than the officials whose direct duty it is to see that no poaching occurs. Every sportsman knows that the greatest poacher in a village is the *garde-champêtre*. How can it be otherwise? The poor fellow is badly paid, over-worked, and made answerable for everything that goes amiss. I will take, for instance, one that I came to know some years ago. He was a man in the prime of life, about forty, strong and hearty. His commune was a large one, measuring, I should say, ten square miles, comprising the usual lands, marshes, and woods. He had to see that the poor of the village did not plunder their richer neighbours' fields, or orchards, or gardens; that no thief from the neighbourhood made a raid on the property of the commune in the dead of the night; and when harvest was nigh at hand, or in full swing, night and day he was on duty watching over the crops. Besides these, he had other duties—warning trespassers, arresting vagabonds, watching for wire-hangers, seeing that any shooters on the land were duly provided with a *permis-de-chasse* (shooting-licence); moreover, that they had the right of shooting over the particular fields where he had seen them; whether this right had been granted verbally (in which case he had to accompany the supposed delinquent to the owner's house, and ascertain the truth of the sportsman's statement); or, if said sportsman had exhibited a lawful lease or paper entitling him to shoot on the land, the *garde-champêtre* had to see if the name mentioned on the permission agreed with the one mentioned on the shooting-licence. Furthermore, said licence must be subjected by him to a strict scrutiny ; for, unlike our own, the French licence specifies in its margin all the particulars that may tend to the identification of the bearer—such as his age, his height, the colour of his hair and his eyebrows, of his eyes, of his beard (if any), the *style* of his nose (whether it be straight, large, small, upturned, or *ordinaire*) ; it also states whether bearer's mouth is large, or small, or middling-sized; the general form of his face, and any deformities or peculiarities in his gait, countenance, or personal appearance that might constitute a clue to his identity. No wonder that the French *permis-de-chasse* is decidedly an imposingly large document, measuring exactly 16 inches in length by 13 inches in breadth.

The *garde-champêtre* of whom I write had to see that all those shooting on his commune were *en règle*, and he had to see that they did not break through hedges, and did not walk through the clover-fields, or through the vineyards when the grapes had not been collected : all these constitute offences, punishable by fines; for, as some great French writer has well said: "The French peasants won't mind if you say that you don't believe in God, so long as you don't break through their hedges or interfere with their harvests— that they can't forgive." So they are always very particular in impressing on the *garde's* mind that all those trespassers must be brought to account. Fortunately, the fines for that sort of offence are insignificant, and the best plan is to submit if one has been guilty. I was caught a good many times, and was fined two or three francs each time. The reader can see by all this that the *garde's* life was anything but an enviable one. For all his duties he received sixteen pounds a year and a wretched thatched cottage. I have said thatched, out of courtesy, but the fact is that, when it rained, an umbrella was of paramount importance within the *garde's* dwelling. Nor is his a peculiar case. Few keepers are better off. Now, can anyone expect that those men will remain honest long? Is it likely? Sixteen pounds a year does not go far, even in France, towards keeping a wife and a flock of children. *Gardes-champêtres* are always a prolific tribe. The consequence of all this is that the man becomes a poacher. By his very profession he is always alone in the fields night and day; he can go wherever he likes. However honest a man may be, when he becomes pinched, and meets with temptation—strong temptation—together with the almost absolute certainty of never being discovered, he is apt to fall. And so they do. Ninety-nine *gardes-champêtres* out of every hundred are poachers. The one who is not a poacher need not be praised on that account, because he would most likely have been one if he could, but something quite unconnected with his own free will has prevented him.

I have said intentionally that the *gardes* feel almost secure against being detected; some have been caught, however, but with a great deal of trouble; for who is to catch the delinquent? The gendarmes would not do it if they were set to it, for the *garde-champêtre* belongs in some degree to their fraternity—"*les loups ne se mangent pas entre eux*;" besides, the tables might get turned some day. If a gendarme has been prevailed upon to lie in wait for the "official poacher," he will take good care to let him know all about it, so that the fellow won't show himself, and the gendarme will tell you the next morning that your suspicions were quite unfounded, and, of course, he will decline acting any further in the matter, so that you will be left to your own devices.

Now, your prosecution to be valid must rely on the fact of the keeper having been caught in the *very act of poaching* —*i.e.* actually setting wires or firing at game. This, I contend, is not an easy matter, for you must bear in mind, that whereas a single gendarme's testimony would have been sufficient to convict the fellow, you must have at least two witnesses besides your own testimony when you act on your own account. A man who is so minded can always hide himself without being detected. It is quite another thing for three persons to be hidden within sight of the same spot, and yet remain undiscovered by the poacher. However, it has been done, and may be done again. But too many precautions cannot be taken; because the *garde* who intends coming out at night to poach on a certain field will hang about the whole afternoon, if not the whole day, at some distance from the place, to make sure that no one is keeping watch, so that it becomes almost an utter impossibility for the intending watching party to get to their posts without being perceived by the man or his confederates—generally his own children—whom he places, when evening sets in, around his hiding-place until his little business is over.

Now this fact of confederates being placed in ambush would convict any other man, but not the *garde-champêtre*. His line of defence is obvious and overwhelming—viz. he knew that a poaching expedition was intended for that night by a party of men, and, as he could not keep watch everywhere at once, he had called in the help of his youngsters or of his friends. What can be said to that? Again, supposing the man himself is met with a few hares hidden under his blouse, once he perceives that he has been seen he will walk straight up to you, and lifting up one side of his blouse, he will show you the game, and tell you mysteriously that "he has found them caught in wires," and that he will be sure next night to catch those who had set them. The fact is those *gardes* are as bold as brass, and the man before you is the real culprit.

CHAPTER XXXVIII.

GAME-PRESERVING IN FRANCE.—PART II.

POACHING, with the class of which I wrote in the preceding chapter, is not only a trade, it is a passion which nothing can stop in a man who has such frequent opportunities of practising it. Therefore, after being cautious and watchful for a little time, soon your man will venture on his tricks again.

There is, however, one thing on which I would caution the sportsman—it is not to let his own keepers know anything of the expedition he projects against the *garde-champêtre* till he actually sets out with them for the night; for, if his keepers get wind of it, they will let their *confrère* know it directly. Their point of view of the affair is simply this : You are their master, that is true ; they eat your bread and receive your money, no one can deny that. You may be a very nice man into the bargain, but you are not one of their class, you are not a peasant. You are a man of the town, and as such only fit to feed and fee them, and be robbed and plundered to all the extent allowed by the law. And if Jean Marie, the *garde-champêtre*, poaches on your ground, why, he only does what they wish they could do themselves, and what they perhaps do also. Besides, Jean Marie belongs to the village ; he has been to school with them; he is perhaps related to them—therefore, in all conscience, I ask you: Do you think they will willingly let Jean Marie run blindfold into a trap? Not likely! Keep, then, your own counsel. For the same reasons above mentioned, if you send only your keepers to see about poachers, they will scare the men, but they will not catch them. They are men of substance in their little way, owners of their own houses and gardens; members perhaps of the municipal council; why should they run the risk of a broken head, being shot at, or otherwise maltreated, all for your interest, for you who are not of their clique? Some will say: Why not have men from a town as keepers, then? For this reason, simply. It is true that Frenchmen who live in towns despise peasants as much as the peasants hate them; so far, then, the speculation would be a good one; but the men of the town won't leave the town's *cafés*, theatres, balls, &c. Everyone knows the love a Frenchman has for all these amusements. For him, to be a keeper, would be little less than transportation. He may, under pressure of circumstances, undertake to fill the post, but he soon gives it up. He misses his people; he finds no sympathy with his neighbours (quite the other way); then he is not accustomed to a country life. He does not care about rising at four in the morning, or passing a few nights watching for poachers. The damp tells directly on his constitution, and if he stick to his work he soon breaks down; so that lessees of shootings are completely in the hands of the peasants, both as regards poaching and "keepering."

Owners of shootings have generally better keepers; these are old servants of the family. From generation to generation they have served in the same household; they make common cause with their masters; what is his is theirs. For their own sakes they won't let him be plundered. These make good keepers. I am sorry to say that this class of men is fast disappearing in France. So many changes happen nowadays in the best-regulated families, that circumstances break, in a short time, that which two centuries could not have put asunder. Some families of servants have been for many generations bound, so to speak, to one family. Some unlucky day the young heir wastes his substance, discharges his servants, and goes abroad; the servants take some other situations, but the charm is broken. They "annex" all they can; their reverses have been a caution to them, and in their turn they do their best to ruin their new masters. As far as shooting is concerned, I think I can say with confidence that the most difficult thing a sportsman experiences is finding a trustworthy keeper, whether it be in France or in England. Well, then, do not put any confidence in your keepers. Ascertain yourselves how things go on if you wish them to be properly attended to. "*Ce qu'on fait soi-même est bien fait*," is a very true maxim. Anyhow there is no one to blame then but one's own self, and in that case the recriminations are generally of a gentle character.

I assisted once at the detection of a poaching *garde-champêtre*; and to this day I cannot help laughing at the discomfiture of the private keepers when the poacher was found to be the government keeper, and their own well-beloved relation (he was brother-in-law to one and cousin to the other). This is how it came to pass: I had been asked by a friend to come over for the passage of ducks; he had some very fine marshes, and the sport being always of a first-class nature, I most willingly went over to his place. I found him in a rather gloomy mood; he had that very evening, quite accidentally, he said, discovered some "wires" in a hedge near his largest wood. Now nothing in the world could have possibly annoyed him more, for he was a most passionate "beagle-man," and of course he was enraged at this premeditated attempt on the lives of his hares. "I have had," he said, "much trouble to stock that wood. It had been so frequently hunted and *battued* previously to my taking the shootings, that there was hardly a hare to be seen in it or about it; and now that it is in a flourishing condition those 'beastly' fellows must set nooses. The worst of it is that those wires not only catch the hares, but also may catch the dogs. Now large dogs may be caught by the legs, but beagles get more frequently caught by the neck, and it is a serious matter to me. I would not have one of my beagles strangled for twenty pounds."

"Remove the wires," I said.

"It would not answer," he replied, "because we do not know where they are all set; and if we left but one or two it would be as bad as ever. No; we must catch the man, and insist upon his telling us where he has placed all his nooses; even if I must promise to let him off, which, by the way, I should not think of doing."

"What! after your promise?"

"Promises be hanged!" he retorted. "Do you think I am going to stand on etiquette with a blackguard of that kind? Let me just catch him, and see if he does not pay dearly for it."

"Do you suspect anybody?" I asked.

"No," he said; "that is the worst of it. I am at a loss to make out who it can be, or, for the matter of that, how many there may be; but it does not signify, for I am determined to go in force and make it out this very night. I have sent word to my keepers; they will be here directly;

and I shall go with them. We will take our guns in case of resistance, and woe be to the poachers if they show fight."

"I should not advise you to," I remonstrated; "you might act rashly on the impulse of the moment."

"You are right, perhaps—I shall be careful."

"Well, I think I will go with you too," I said.

And so it was agreed.

By-and-by the keepers arrived, wondering what they had been summoned for; and when told of the arranged expedition they showed some uneasiness; however, there was nothing for them but obedience.

Accordingly, at about three o'clock in the morning, we all set out. It was bitterly cold, and very dark. We walked on in silence for about half an hour, then tall trees loomed before us in the morning fog. We were close to the wood.

"Here is the place, my lads," said my friend to his men; "go you yonder and hide behind those trees. We will remain here."

The men obeyed, and we were left alone. We crouched in the dry ditch beside the hedge, and waited in silence. The stillness was positively oppressive, and the darkness quite as intense as when we had left the house.

We had been waiting about an hour and a half; the gray light of dawn was just appearing behind the hills, when my friend, nudging my elbow, pointed with his finger through a tuft of grass that grew at the side of the ditch. He made room for me, and I quietly crawled forward and looked through. A man, in brown velveteen trousers, blue blouse, and an old *kepi*, was stooping by the hedge about thirty yards away from us. His being so near us almost startled me. He had come so noiselessly that his presence seemed like a miracle. He looked down and felt with his hands in the hedge quite composedly, like a man who does not fear being interrupted. When he had done he came towards us leisurely enough. He never saw us till he placed his foot on the other side of the ditch, and stooped over us to look at a noose. Then he made, indeed, a jump; but we were up in a crack, and the tic-tac of my friend's gun soon brought him to his senses.

"If you move a step, I fire," said my friend.

Of course he did not mean it, but it had the desired effect. By this time the two keepers ran to the scene of action, and their consternation knew no bounds when they saw who it was that had been captured.

"Why, So-and-So," they exclaimed, "is that you?"

"You knew it precious well, you *canailles*," he said, shaking his fist in their faces; "but I shall make you smart for it!" and he reviled them in good round terms.

However, we marched him off home, and there he gave up half-a-dozen wires and two hares. His case was clear. The very least he could get for the offence was five years' detention; however, my friend weighed the matter in his mind, and I advised him to be lenient.

"You will only get the whole village about your ears," I said, "if you get him taken up and convicted."

So he made him sign a paper in which was stated what he had done. The keepers and I witnessed the document, and my friend magnanimously let him off.

The man was so gratefully astonished that he was ever after the most persevering of watchers on my friend's behalf. But the most comical part of the business is yet to come, and here it is: Somehow, the affair got bruited, and it came to the ears of the *procureur*, and this official actually wanted to prosecute my friend for having shown mercy to the man! Decidedly, France is not always a very pleasant place to live in. However, the fellow was dismissed from his official employment. He is now keeper to my friend, and a better one he never had.

CHAPTER XXXIX.

GAME-PRESERVING IN FRANCE.—PART III.

NEXT to the *gardes-champêtres* come the gendarmes. Everybody knows that these men have invariably been in the army for some considerable period. They are, as a rule, honest and strict, but are considered by the French as a "stuck-up" body of men, in this wise, that they do not mix with their neighbours. The reason for this is that, having been so long under military discipline and in military accoutrements, they have, imperceptibly to themselves, come to divide mankind into two classes—one, the military portion of the community, the other comprising the *pekins*, or *bourgeois*. The latter, in their eyes, are little more than simpletons, whom it is their duty to watch over and prevent from running into mischief. This official feeling is carried even into their private relations with the public. A gendarme always speaks to and of a civilian with more or less superciliousness. This comes from the force of habit. When a man has for twenty years been accustomed to look down with contempt upon those who are not of his "cloth," he cannot readily "lower himself" to their standard.

The *gendarmerie* (*i.e.* the gendarmes' barracks, or rather lodgings, for they are, most of them, married men with families) is but little frequented by outsiders, partly on account of the gendarmes' *froideur*, partly also through the outsiders' fear of them; for who knows but that some future day the gendarmes may have to act officially against their neighbours and quondam friends?

As far as game is concerned, gendarmes don't put themselves much out of the way to preserve it. They don't go out on purpose to see if they may chance upon detecting an offender, but they will go, if they have not any business more important on hand, to catch a poacher, if advised in time of his whereabouts. They can also search a house if its owner or one of the lodgers therein is suspected of having wires, nets, or other instruments prohibited by law. This the *garde-champêtre* can do also; but when it comes to a thorough investigation of such a matter, the gendarmes make their appearance. Their arrival in a village is invariably looked upon by the inhabitants as a calamity. As soon as the village boys have run in to announce their approach, which is never known beforehand, it is most ludicrous to see the men—if they are at home; or their good wives, if the male portion of the community be in the fields—darting indoors, hurriedly hiding whatever might be deemed contraband, and then, assuming an indifference which they are very far from feeling, they come again on their doorsteps and humbly wish the horsemen a cringing welcome. The gendarmes are then in their glory. The population is at their knees —everyone volunteers to lead them to the house they have come to honour with their presence, and everyone but the delinquent considers himself a lucky fellow at having escaped for that time. There is no mistake about it, half-a-dozen gendarmes will keep five or six thousand French people in awe, if not in order; but no one dreads the *garde-champêtre* barring the very poor people, to whom he is a regular bugbear, as he tyrannises over them, and bullies them to his heart's content. Professional poachers do not care a rap for the *garde-champêtre*, but, should they get wind that the gendarmes are about, or even that the gendarmes suspect them, that is enough—they will keep quiet for some time to come. Therefore, from all this we may come to the conclusion that, if the gendarmes would or could devote more time to the preservation of game, there is not the slightest doubt that game would be tenfold more abundant than it is now. Unfortunately, they do not attend much to this part of their business, but the little they do is most efficiently done.

Now, as men, gendarmes are polite, obliging, and honest; they are good husbands, good fathers; officially they stick to their orders with strict accuracy, and, as far as game is concerned, the greatest praise I can give them is to state that, ever since the gendarmes have been organised, not one of them has ever been known to poach. It is true that they could not do it very well, but they could manage it if they liked. Where there is a will there is a way. Therefore, let them have the praise unreservedly.

In large towns the *sergents-de-ville* (policemen) can stop any man on suspicion, and see if he has a licence to shoot game—that is, if he is at the time carrying a gun and looks as though he had been shooting. But although they can, they rarely do so. Generally, they do not even favour the *chasseur* with a glance, much less do they trouble him for his *permis-de-chasse*. The only time I ever saw a *sergent-de-ville* interfering was at Abbeville, in the department of the Somme. I was setting out for some snipe-shooting; it was just at dawn of day. I had nearly reached the last houses of the suburb previous to entering the marshes (for which Abbeville was justly famous), when my attention was attracted by the singular behaviour of a policeman. He was hidden in a corner of a yard-door, looking towards the open country.

"What is the matter?" I said to him.

"Hush! hush!" he said; "don't stop talking to me, else *they* will see you."

So I went on, and looking ahead, I perceived two men with very voluminous blouses coming towards the town, smoking their pipes, and looking very innocent. When I passed them they said good-morning to me, and grinned.

"What are you laughing at?" I said.

"Oh, nothing," they replied, and laughed still more.

I could not, for the life of me, make it out at the time; but half a minute later the policeman confronted them, and I came back to see what the row was about. The men's blouses covered about three score of snipe and other marsh birds; they were all strung by their heads on a string, and hung round the men's shoulders under their blouses. A long line, abundantly garnished with horsehair loops and rolled round a wooden framework, was also discovered in their possession. These men had evidently been snipe-snaring, and they had laughed at me when I had met them because they thought of what a fruitless errand I was bent upon, since they had scoured all that part of the marshes. They were eventually convicted, and sentenced to a month's imprisonment for the offence, and for having eluded the *octroi*. This is the only time I saw a policeman prosecuting in a poaching action. The custom-house officers who may have to do with game-preserving are the men at the *octroi*, the travelling excisemen, and the coast-guards.

For those readers who have not been on the Continent

I must explain what the *octroi* means. The *octroi* is a house built first and foremost of those which constitute the suburbs of a town. There is such a house on each road leading into the town, and in each house are Government *employés*, who inspect every cart and every basket going towards the town, and levy a tax on all articles of food, whether eatables or drinkables. Now, a man who should attempt to pass this house without declaring voluntarily all that he has at the time in his possession liable to the tax, may be mulcted in a very heavy fine. So that poachers who have been very successful in their night expeditions are in a fix as to how they are to proceed so as to bring the game into the town without getting into trouble.

If they should *declare* what game they have, the officers would ask them where they got it; if they attempted to sneak in without such a declaration, and were subsequently discovered, it would go hard with them; so that to the uninitiated it seems a puzzle how they can possibly manage it. In some places the poachers have confederates among the *octroi* men, and thus the difficulty is removed; but in other places, where the officers are not to be bribed, many very ingenious devices have been adopted, of which the following are the most in vogue: dogs are trained to carry to and fro between the poacher's house in the town and a *cabaret* outside the town. Of course these dogs are not sent on their errand save at night, and when the night is very dark, otherwise they might be seen. Some of these dogs are wonderfully trained. Instead of keeping on the opposite side of the road, when they have to pass the *octroi* house, they watch for an opportunity, when no officer is actually standing at the door, and then dart before it quite close to the building, so as not to be seen from the windows. However, notwithstanding their good training, their natural instinct, and their great swiftness of foot, they are occasionally caught by a very summary process—*i.e.* shot by the officers.

That the officers are empowered by the law to act thus is a fact. A few years ago, at a fashionable seaport, where some friends of mine resided, a tobacco smuggler lost his steed in a similar way. The man had a very swift horse and a light cart, and used to dash past the *octroi*, shouting that he had nothing to "declare." But one day the officers were informed that the individual was a *contrebandier* for Belgian tobacco and cigars. They got ready for his next appearance; some of them hid themselves with firearms at a distance from the *octroi* house, and when the cart dashed by, and the man declined to stop, those ahead jumped on the road and, with needless cruelty, shot the unfortunate horse, and then, of course, captured the man. The arrest of the *contrebandier* created but little interest at the time; but the death of his swift-footed animal brought down the censure of the people and of the press upon those who had killed it, for it was evident that the man could not have escaped the officers; and he declared himself, on his trial, that he was pulling up when he perceived the ambush laid for him, and that he besought the men not to fire on his horse. But I suppose the officers had been too well blown up by the authorities, and were so enraged against both biped and quadruped that they summarily cut short the latter's career as a sort of revenge. However, they were legally entitled to act as they did, and no doubt it acted as a preventive to others of the same trade. Women are frequently employed in carrying game within the precincts of towns. They are rarely detected; but should the officers have any suspicions, they may detain the supposed offender till a female searcher is sent for and makes her appearance, when the woman is subjected to a thorough inspection. Carts with false bottoms, donkeys loaded with firewood or straw, in the midst of which the game is safely secured, and a hundred other devices are employed, all of which are efficient enough when a few head of game are concerned; but when a regular load has been collected, nothing short of bribing the officer in charge can insure its safe *entrée* into the town; and, judging from the immense quantities sent into the markets, the bribery system must be carried on to an alarming extent. Sometimes a licensed dealer collects the game in the country with his own cart; and, of course, when he passes the *octroi* he pays for what he has, and the officers cannot say a word to him as to where the game comes from and how it was caught. But the poachers don't find this a profitable way of getting rid of their spoils; because the dealer, who knows perfectly well how they came by them, gives but a small price for the game, and the poachers dare not refuse, for fear he should inform against them.

Travelling excisemen who meet a poacher can prosecute him on their own testimony alone. These excise officers are usually in a dog-cart, knocking about on all the cross-roads on their way to village inns, where they inspect the stock-in-trade, and draw the government taxes on the liquids. They frequently meet suspected characters of the poaching fraternity, but they rarely prosecute them, because they frequently themselves take a pot-shot over the hedges. I have seen several instances of this myself.

The coastguards are very worthy fellows, and, considering the many temptations thrown in their way, deserve credit for not doing more than they do in the poaching line. Their beats are usually along rabbit downs and cliffs, where they are mostly the only human beings to be seen;

they can conveniently substitute a shot cartridge for a bullet one in their guns, and the trick is done. Nobody sees or hears them beyond an occasional sportsman or two who may chance to witness the performance, as I have now and then; but this I must say in their favour—they may occasionally shoot a rabbit, or noose one, but they do not make a trade of it. They don't destroy for the market; what they kill or catch is for their own larder and no more; therefore a real sportsman may wink at their doings, as they frequently, by their presence, prevent more earnest poachers from invading the land. Always give them leave to kill a rabbit or two when they require it, and it will be found by far the best plan. They are pleased with your confidence in them; whereas otherwise they might have killed somewhat extensively, just out of spite, if kept too much in hand. They invariably refrain from any undue use of the leave given them voluntarily, and, moreover, when they meet with any poacher coming in with the evident intention of setting to "work," they insist upon his taking his departure. And this the poacher obeys with alacrity, for the coastguard may prosecute any such offender if he choose.

CHAPTER XL.

GAME-PRESERVING IN FRANCE.—PART IV.

SOLDIERS in France may also prosecute poachers. The law invests them with that prerogative; but I never heard of any poacher having been convicted through a soldier's prosecution, or even on his testimony. On the other hand, soldiers are very often prosecuted for poaching. In fact, wherever soldiers are, there game will disappear. There is nothing very startling in that fact when one considers the composition of the ranks in the French army. As far as |poaching is concerned, the best French poachers are among the worst French soldiers. Land-owners and game-preservers dread having a camp installed near their respective properties; and when such is the case there is no preservation of game possible. The soldiers being all dressed alike, it is most difficult to identify an offender if he has not been actually caught. Naturally enough, the culprit's companions will not betray him. And again, as everyone in the mess profits more or less by the marauder's depredations, they are not likely to give a clue as to who he may be. Poaching and marauding, in the minds of the privates, are not looked in the light of thieving, but, on the contrary, they are considered rather as plucky and deserving enterprises. Such being the case, one may well imagine how poaching must flourish among the soldiers. I have known and heard of several rather startling instances of this propensity, some of which, being historical, may be referred to. For instance, during the existence of the great camp along the coast in the department of the Pas-de-Calais, the downs in its immediate neighbourhood were so completely ransacked, that when the camp broke up there was not one single rabbit left, and it had to be completely restocked. Previously to doing this the downs were thoroughly inspected and examined, and then it was found that the rabbit burrows were entirely destroyed, having been dug up with spades by the poachers until they got to the rabbits. In the course of the inspection several corpses of soldiers in their uniforms were found buried in the sand. These men had evidently met with death whilst poaching, by some sandhills suddenly crumbling down upon them, overpowering them, and smothering them. These discoveries created at first a great sensation, because it was thought that the men might have been murdered, or might have fallen in duels; but it was soon ascertained that such suppositions were erroneous. None of the remains bore traces of wounds, and the clothes showed no signs of having been pierced either by swords or by bullets; they did not even reveal traces of blood. In the camp, when the men had been missed, it had been supposed that they had made a bolt of it, and, accordingly, they had been booked as deserters. But at the time of the discoveries a thorough inquiry was instituted, and it was ascertained beyond a doubt that the alleged deserters were the very same men whose remains had been found; and it was also brought out in the course of the evidence that they were one and all incorrigible poachers and marauders; so that there was not the slightest doubt but that it was while in the act of poaching that they had thus lost their lives. Most of the bodies had spades near them, and it was conjectured that by thoughtlessly and recklessly digging out the rabbits from their holes the men had caused the fall of the sandhills.

At first, when the camp was organised, very strict orders were issued from head-quarters to prevent the soldiers from committing depredations of any kind. When any man was satisfactorily convicted he was punished very severely, according to the rules and regulations provided for his case; but his comrades took good care to avenge him on the prosecutor at the first opportunity. For instance, a keeper who had convicted a soldier was caught one night, and got such a beating that he was left for dead˙ by his assailants. Inquiries were instituted to find out who were the delinquents, but to no purpose. Another time a gang of fifty soldiers invaded the downs in spite of keepers and villagers. What could be done? Nothing. The officers were powerless, because the guilty men could not be pointed out. As men, the soldiers are not worse than any other poachers, but as gamekeepers (in title, if not in deed) they are not worth much. It is a perfect mockery to have them invested with the right of prosecuting poachers.

This power of the soldiery gives rise occasionally to most ludicrous scenes. In 1871, after the war, all the *moblots* (free-shooters and volunteers) had been discharged from their respective regiments or companies, and had returned again to their villages. The war had made the young men rather free with other people's property. *Meum et tuum*, for the time being, were meaningless words; besides, had not a Republic been proclaimed? and does not its flag bear these words—dear to every poor man—

viz. "Liberty, Equality, Fraternity?" Therefore, every man had, he thought, a right to help himself to other people's goods. Strange to say, the authorities did not consider these things in the same light, and offenders were prosecuted and punished, to their utter astonishment, just for all the world as if Napoleon had been still on the throne. This severity of the Republic's judges went a long way to make the Republic unpopular among the thieves. Game laws, particularly, were thought to have been entirely repealed from the very moment that the Republic had been proclaimed, and as during the war gendarmes and *gardes-champêtres* were too much engaged in political duties to attend to the usual routine of their work, the consequence was, that the villagers had poached to their hearts' content; but as soon as peace was signed they found out their mistake. Owners and lessees of shootings complained of their depredations, new private keepers were duly sworn in, and prosecutions began on all sides. This put a stop somewhat to the recklessness of these good peasants, but as to stopping poaching altogether in France, that will never be.

About these affairs, a friend of mine who had hired a shooting in France wrote to me as follows: "I came in for my full share of unwelcome visits; and really some of the excuses put forward by the culprits for their defence, when caught, were very amusing. One said that he had no idea whatever that he was doing wrong in watching by moonlight for a hare and shooting it on my ground. The *procureur* told him that the very fact of shooting during the night made the offence more punishable. 'I had no idea that such was the case, Monsieur le Président,' said the poacher; 'upon my honour, I thought that, as this gentleman (pointing to me) was shooting all day, I could not possibly interfere with his sport *if I went at night!*' This ingenious excuse did not prevent its author from being fined fifty francs and his gun confiscated. Another one (he was a recently-liberated *garde mobile*, and still wore his regimental jacket when caught) took it into his head that he had more right than I to sport over my land, and accordingly, when I made my appearance with a keeper on the scene of action, the *moblot* very coolly said that he was a soldier, and could and would prosecute *me* for carrying a gun during the closed season. *He* was 'wiring' for hares, and for this grave offence he was imprisoned."

Now, the Game Laws in France being somewhat strict, I think it but fair that British sportsmen should be warned against all possible contingencies. Provide yourself with a passport or some other papers, so as to be able to prove that you are respectable; then take a steamer to France. When you get there, ask your hotel-keeper the address of the *préfet* or mayor of the town; pay either of these officials a visit, and state your wishes. They will give you all necessary information concerning your shooting-licence, and where to go shooting when you have got it. If you have any private letters of introduction, either to them or some other persons of note, such as bankers, lawyers, clergymen, or doctors, you will get on splendidly. At any rate, you may depend upon being well received and honourably treated by the officials; but if you go mixing with the fellows you will meet at the *table d'hôte*, and if you take their words for granted, then, you may depend upon it, you will get into trouble, and it will serve you right. They will tell you that you can do without a licence (don't you believe it); that they know a place where you can sport without leave (it may be true, and it may not, therefore put yourself on the safe side by making sure that you will not repent it), and they will try to impress upon you that they are very grand people indeed.

I was once *invited* to a shooting excursion by a likely young fellow, and I gladly accepted his offer. We drove to the place the very next day, and we shot about in fine style. I came home delighted. At the *table d'hôte* someone asked me where I had been shooting, and it came out that the young scamp had taken me on a *réserve* (preserved grounds). It was market-day, and he knew the keepers would be in town, so he thought he could play the *grand seigneur* very cheaply, and he did, as it turned out. But it might have ended far differently had we been caught. Of course I "blew him up" when I saw him, but he only laughed fit to kill himself, and said it was the best lark he had had for a long time. He was a lawyer's clerk, at £40 a year, and the joke of inviting me so grandly to sport on his estate was, indeed, very entertaining; but, all the same, had one of the keepers turned up, I fancy the laugh would not have been on our side. He told me subsequently that once he had been caught on the grounds of a great man somewhere in the neighbourhood. Just when he least expected it, a keeper met him at the corner of a hedge. Nothing daunted, our young fellow called out to the man as soon as he saw him : "Where the d—l have you been all this time? You are a nice fellow, you are! Here have I been for the last two hours firing away, in hopes that you would turn up, and come to carry my bag and show me the best places, but I might just as well have sneezed! Mr. X." (the name of the owner) "had told me, though, that I should be sure to meet you about here."

"Well, sir," said the keeper, very humbly, "I was busy at the farm, and did not hear you till now. I beg your pardon, I am sure. Shall I relieve you of your game-bag and accompany you now, sir?"

Our young clerk took out his watch with an important air:

"Hem!" he said; "it is getting late; I don't think I shall have time to go up to the house now. I will write a note to your governor; you will be sure to take it to him, won't you?"

"Certainly, sir."

He then wrote on a piece of paper, sending his best compliments and thanks for the day's sport, despatched the keeper home with it, and then bolted. Not bad, is it? But scarcely the thing for a *sportsman* and a *gentleman*.

CHAPTER XLI.

HIRING A SHOOTING IN BELGIUM.

I HAVE several times related incidents of sport which have happened to me in Belgium, and have pointed out the low rates at which shootings may be hired in that country. I now intend giving a narrative of the success which attended the venture of an acquaintance of mine, who, taking a hint from my articles, wrote to me last year for further information and particulars, then set out for Belgium, and secured, at a trifling cost, a rare bit of ground, where he can, almost all the year round, enjoy himself with his gun.

He went direct to Ostend in July, just in the height of the season, and no doubt enjoyed himself very much there, for Ostend is a very lively place when the fashionable Continental world, east of the Rhine, takes it for its place of rendezvous.

I remember fishing one morning on the West Pier two years ago, and having for my right-hand neighbour no less a personage than the Princess of Italy, and on my left I had a grand duke; the rest were all counts, barons, and such other small fry.

As regards outdoor sports, the bathing is first-rate; there are plenty of boats for sails and rows, and those fond of sea-fishing will find a trawling trip very enjoyable. Shrimping, however, is the staple fashionable enjoyment.

Well, my friend, with a letter of introduction that I had given him, went to a lawyer in the town and explained to him his wants. The lawyer announced a shooting to let along the coast, for the sum of a thousand francs per annum. This included the use of a cottage near the sea. Imagine renting the shooting over some two thousand acres, together with the use of a small house, for £40! My friend went on the following day to inspect the ground, and found the house rather small but comfortable, whilst on the land he saw plenty of birds and hares, and in the downs found lots of rabbits. Moreover, the sea was within a stone's-throw of his house that was to be. Altogether he was delighted, and concluded the bargain by signing his agreement, and, to prevent any misunderstandings, paid a year's rent in advance.

The next thing to be done was getting his sporting license. Here a word to the uninitiated may be welcome. The shooting license in Belgium costs £1 16s., and gives the right to shoot everything in season, from one end of the year to the other. The coursing license, however, costs £3 per greyhound. This is somewhat expensive, considering that 5s. defray the tax on this side of the Channel; but in Belgium greyhounds are considered a very great luxury, and, accordingly, none but very well-to-do men think of having them. As regards the figure of the tax, it has been placed at such a high standard to please the shooters, who are there very numerous and influential, and who, as a body, detest greyhounds. The reason is, the shooters say that they have a long trudge sometimes to bag a hare or two, because when the season advances the hares get wary, and the land being mostly flat, they spy the shooters from afar, and bolt before they can get near enough for a shot. This makes shooting hares very awkward, but renders coursing all the easier, as the flatter the land the less interrupted view have the dogs, and almost every hare coursed is bound to come into the bag somehow, especially when more than two dogs are slipped at puss. The shooters are, therefore, perfect fanatics in their hatred of greyhounds, and there are more lawsuits arising from their use in Belgium than from any other sporting cause.

This was soon made patent to my friend, for he was no sooner installed in his new domicile than he found a certain animosity engendered against him amongst his neighbours when it became known that he intended coursing a good deal. He had taken out three greyhound licenses, and his leash of first-rate dogs had duly made their appearance, only to raise a perfect storm of discontent amongst his neighbours. This, however, he paid no attention to, being one of those fellows who quietly go their way, so long as they are not bothered, but when they are once roused are awkward folks to deal with.

"Some of the village fellows have resolved to poison my dogs," he wrote to me then, "but I gave them to understand that if they did I would spare no trouble to get them to prison, and I think this has settled them."

Still, there was that unfriendly feeling towards him, against which I would warn any sportsman intending to try Belgium as a field for sport.

On the other hand, the authorities always give every countenance to respectable strangers, and any complaint is sure to be well attended to.

Well, the 1st of August soon came round, and the opening of the marsh-shooting season was duly posted in the village, on the door of the town-hall. My friend's ground comprised about five hundred acres of a first-rate marsh, and there he repaired on the first lawful day. The ground is extremely flat, and but for a belt of downs would reach the seashore. There are two canals or streams running across the land, and a multitude of ditches cut it about like a chess-board. In some places the ground is boggy, and affords very good lying for snipe. The streams and ditches have always some duck or teal, and in the drier parts lots of plovers, curlews, &c., are to be met with, together with a fair sprinkling of hares, quails, and partridges.

During the month of August neither hares nor partridges could be shot, according to the law of the land, but quail, snipe, ducks and teal, plovers, and curlews were bagable. Accordingly, my friend gave a free berth to all tabooed birds and quadrupeds, and contented himself with the fare set before him. His keeper accompanied him, and carried, besides his game-bag and ammunition, the inevitable jumping-pole, which is, in these low lands, a *sine quâ non* for anyone walking across the fields. He bagged the first day over two score of birds, and was delighted with his sport.

He had asked me to join him, but I was not well at the time and could not leave England.

Every day during the whole month he met with sport; and had he sold his game, he could have paid half his rent during that time alone.

He used to vary his trips by occasionally taking to fishing—coarse fish I presume—and used to have very good fun. Besides angling and marsh-shooting, the rowing and sailing on the sea and on the streams were highly enjoyable. The sea-fishing was not much, but any amount of seafowl-shooting was to be had. There were always hundreds of birds on the sea, and several large "passages" also took place along the shore. Finding that the launching of an ordinary boat from the sands was very awkward, owing to the sea occasionally deluging it and drenching his ammunition, my friend procured a Poole canoe, and by placing his provisions and cartridges under the for'ard deck, they were safe. The shore being very shallow, he had to be content with a light draught canoe; and, for the same motive, could not use a very heavy swivel, as it would have got him and his craft aground repeatedly. His swivel was, in consequence, rather light, and carried only twelve ounces of shot. With it, however, he did remarkably well, bagging repeatedly a score of birds in the course of a day's sail over the sea.

As to using the swivel inland, that was out of the question. The Belgian laws forbid the use of such guns in all inland marshes.

The shore-shooting was simply first-rate. Of course, when only one gun sports for several miles, a shore is apt to become very much frequented by birds, and such proved to be the case to a most extraordinary extent. I have letters in which my correspondent tells me that he many times shot thirty, forty, and fifty birds in a morning, and went home out of ammunition, and positively tired of sport.

"Thousands of curlews and oystercatchers passed here on August 15 and 16," he wrote to me. "I shot forty of them in the two days with a single 4-bore flock gun, and I had a crack at them with the swivel gun, as I was coming to shore to land, flooring over fifteen at a single shot. As for seagulls, oxbirds, sandpipers, and seaplovers, at times they could be reckoned by thousands, and I shot loads of them with my double 12-bore."

This pleasant state of things lasted on the shore until the latter end of October, when the sea-fishing improved considerably, owing to shoals of fish visiting the shore. This was no sooner perceived, than the whole population of the villages near the seashore began setting their usual long lines at low tide ; and, what with digging for lugs, baiting lines, and watching for the tides, the shore became rather too lively for birds to settle on it. Still, this did not interfere with the flocks at sea, and during the whole of the season good sport was to be had there, when the weather was not so rough as to preclude an attempt at launching the canoe. At last, towards January, the flocks at sea increased so much, that the villagers, according to their annual custom, baited lines with dead fish and worms, and began hooking the birds. Several were caught in that manner. I once saw, myself, a black duck brought to shore in that style. He had hooked himself somewhere in the beak, but was otherwise perfectly uninjured. As for seagulls, they are caught very easily with a piece of cork, of the shape of a sprat, painted white or covered over with a piece of parchment, and provided with a couple of right-angled hooks at the tip. This bit of cork is tied to a long string, and when the wind blows from the shore, it is allowed to drift away to sea ; the boy or man who holds the line keeping himself out of sight, as far as circumstances will admit. As soon as the voracious gulls perceive the white piece of cork, they think it is some delicious edible, and greedily pounce upon it. Some disgorge it when they find it treacherous, but others hook themselves, and are then dragged ashore—there to have their necks twisted. These birds are killed generally for their feathers, but some of the peasants also eat them. In fact, many of them make a living out of their winter lines for birds and seafish.

One of the great drawbacks to shooting in Belgium is

that no powder but the Belgian compound is to be used. All other powder is confiscated.

As for empty cartridge-cases, although they are allowed to be imported, the duty placed on them is preposterous. I believe, however, that the great firm of Ely have established a depôt of their cartridges at Liege, from whence any number may be obtained.

As regards the Belgian powder, the best is very fair, but does not come up to the best English powder by a long way. The great proof of this is in the fact that the natives themselves try to get the English sailors who trade with Ostend to bring them some canisters from England, even if it be some inferior stuff, as is generally the case.

As regards the police of the fields, this is superintended by the rural keepers and by the gendarmes. The latter travel about on horseback, and keep to the roads. They therefore but rarely have an opportunity of capturing a delinquent, unless a man, when he sees them, loses his head, and shows, by his behaviour, that he is up to no good. One was caught thus, in the sight of my friend, through his own showing. The fellow had no license, and was trying to shoot some ducks in a stream during the frost. On perceiving the gendarmes on the road, instead of going on quietly, he began to run away. The ice broke under him in a flooded meadow, the gendarmes went to him, and he was caught. Had he kept where he originally was they would never have noticed him.

As for the *gardes-champêtres*, they are ubiquitous beings, and with their leaping-poles they go flying all over the country like leaping-frogs, and you never know when they may pounce upon you, as they wear no uniform. If, therefore, you do not know them by sight, and have no strong field-glass to detect them when they are yet a long way off, you are almost sure to be caught—that is, if you are doing anything wrong, such as sporting without a license, walking through a standing crop, damaging a fence, or sporting over the land of somebody who objects to it.

CHAPTER XLII.

HIRING A SHOOTING IN BELGIUM.—*Continued.*

WHEN the ground which is reserved is somewhat extensive, it is usual to have boards with notices stuck up here and there along its limits, warning shooters of the state of the matter.

Some of these notices are worded very queerly. So, at least, I have been told, for I do not profess to understand Flemish, but I know they all begin with "*Het is verboden;*" and that is enough for me.

Nevertheless, in spite of the notice-boards which abound all over the country, it is very easy to get leave to sport, if you only know how to set about it; and my friend confirms me in this with his own experience.

"I could shoot over ten square leagues of ground if I liked," he tells me, "and I have never had a row with anybody yet but a poacher."

This poacher, by-the-way, he caught ."calling" quails, and as this dodge is tolerably common on the Continent, and almost unknown over here, I will describe it, as it is rather clever and very amusing—that is to say, when you carry it on yourself, not when somebody is drawing all *your* birds into *his* snares. The dodge consists in setting, in a standing crop, wheat preferred, a stand-up net a foot or so high, and as long as you like. Ten yards is as much as it need be, although some use them double that length. This being done, the man lies down close to his net, and takes his *appeau*, or bird-call, wherewith he produces the well-known " Tit-titit ! tit-titit !" of the male quail. Now, quails are extremely pugnacious, especially in love matters, and no sooner is that note heard than the challenge is taken up by all the cocks within hearing. They immediately reply " Tit-titit !" and hop towards the intruder. The net being in the way, they get their necks in the meshes, and there they are, ready to be bagged and killed, or else placed in a cage. As for the hens,.they don't come to fight, but come to the " voice of the charmer," thinking that a sweetheart is calling upon them to respond to his fiery declaration. And so the whole lot are taken. A practised *appeleur* will rid a plain of quails in two or three days.

My friend did not know this dodge, and one day, hearing a quail calling close by, he went, in order to spring and shoot it, when, to his great astonishment, he stumbled over the man, who had already caught four or five birds. These were set at liberty, the net destroyed, and the man would have been prosecuted, had he not pleaded extreme distress and ignorance of the law. Thus ended the adventure; and, barring a few hares potted here and there by neighbouring shooters—to whom, probably, my friend returned tit for tat whenever occasion offered—he says that he does not think any poaching worth mentioning was carried on.

Some workmen from the large towns keep greyhounds on the sly, and go about to distant places, by excursion and cheap trains, with their dogs, during the season, and when no one is about, they like a bit of coursing. But a keeper in sight is enough to deter them, the law being extremely stringent. Besides, if they were to give poor puss a chance it would not be quite so bad; but this is not done. In short, it is not the sport that tempts the men; it is the meat. They would consider themselves dreadfully stupid if they were to come home empty-handed; but with two or three hares they are very proud. As to how they got them, that is another matter; they don't mind sending six dogs on if they have six to send; and, moreover, Belgium is the place to see lurching carried to a science. There, the greyhound that kills is *a* greyhound, according to his owner's estimation; the others are perfect curs that ought to be shot; and the way these men expatiate on their dogs' qualities is amusing.

"Did you see how my dog waited for a chance?" one will say exultingly; "ah, he is no fool, that dog of mine is not. The others pumped themselves dry, but as for him, why, he bided his time, killed, and is as fresh as a rose! Good dog!"

The greatest drawback to the rearing and preserving of game in all the flat Belgian lands consists in the presence of many birds of prey.

About spring time, the numbers that turn up are simply extraordinary, and the destruction of game proportionately great. At times, six or seven hawks, large and small, are seen together quartering the ground. They are, however, very easily got rid of. One has merely to build a small blind, anywhere near the downs, or in a favourite field of theirs, and wait in ambush therein, with a heavily-loaded gun, until they appear. I shot there, in that sort of style, about a dozen a week for a month. They sweep about just like dogs quartering their ground. They do not fly high either, but keep some three or four yards above the ground. I have often been much struck, when in my blind, at the eagerness which the whole lot manifested the moment they got wind of me. They could not make out where I was, and, presumably, thought I was "dead meat," and fit for a jolly meal. They would then come higher up on the breeze, like dogs scenting in a field, literally tracking me to my lair, until a couple of shots laid two of them low.

This sort of thing was also experienced by my friend, and I suppose that the birds must come from the Prussian forests and from the large woods in Luxembourg, where preserving is carried on in a slip-shod manner, owing to the almost impenetrable retreats where the vermin, as a body, take refuge. In the breeding season, however, they all come out to mate, and later on, they must provide food for their families; hence the relentless manner in which they sweep the fields of anything they can find.

It must not be imagined that watching for these birds is devoid of interest. When the hut has been nicely built, and has plenty of straw at the bottom, it is as comfortable a little snuggery as can be imagined ; and with the weather fine, the small birds singing everywhere around, the sun shining, and the flowers of the fields sprouting forth, one may spend a few mornings there in pleasant meditation.

I think nothing could better suit a man who has an independence than taking a direct interest in all things pertaining to a shooting.

There is always something to be done.

My friend, who, by-the-way, is a retired officer, tells me that he never was in better health or happier in his life.

"I am always doing," he declares; "but, of course, I take matters coolly, and it is very enjoyable. During the season we were out every day. When the coursing came on, we went twice a week with the greyhounds. In winter time, I went punting and sailing. On odd days, I perambulated the marsh, or walked on the seashore. In snowy weather, we had lots of shore birds. When nothing better was to be done we went twirling for larks, &c. Now that the season is over, we are looking out for all vermin, making huts on the downs, getting the ferrets in trim, and breaking my young dogs to hand. In fact, I have not a moment's idleness, and I thank my stars that my lot has fallen in such quiet latitudes."

Happy fellow!

I have, just now, mentioned twirling. Perhaps some of my readers do not know how it is practised; if so, I will enlighten them. The twirl consists of a somewhat conical and elongated block of wood of the form of an A, studded here and there, pretty freely, with bits of looking-glass, and transfixed by a rod. This rod is put in circular motion, either by mechanism hidden in the box of the apparatus, or else a piece of cord, being wound round the body of the rod and pulled suddenly, sets the twirl going round in one direction. If the pull has been strong enough, the cord will not only get unwound as the rod is revolving, but the impetus given to the twirl will be sufficiently great to ensure its going round a certain number of turns, during which the cord will be wound up again the other way round the rod, when, on the twirl giving signs of stopping, another pull will set it going again, and so forth.

As a rule, those shooters who use the cord twirl fasten the cord to their left ankle, and pull it thus, by moving their left foot backwards and forwards for each turn of the twirl. Others, disliking this tedious process, engage a boy to work the twirl, and content themselves with knocking over the larks as they come fluttering above the shining bits of glass. Finally, some shooters buy the mechanical twirl, wind it up, set it up in a field, and await the result. If a few boys are sent about the neighbouring stubble to

Hiring a Shooting in Belgium. 47

rouse the birds, they are sure to come over the twirl the moment they catch sight of its dazzling rays.

Larks, over twirls, are very easy to shoot, as occasionally they keep fluttering in the same place above the instrument, thus offering a mark that even a "muff" can hardly fail to hit. At the same time, a practised shooter never takes a deliberate aim at them, but goes on snap-shooting at a couple of birds, as long as they will flock to him. When carried on thus, it is not bad practice, and a fellow who can, without aiming, knock over ten couple of larks consecutively, at forty or fifty yards, will be a pretty fair shot at anything else.

Several versions have been given as to the cause of the attraction of twirls to larks.

Some say the lark likes to come and look at himself in the looking-glass. How could it do so, as the twirl is always in motion?

Others say that the lark takes the twirl for the sun. I fancy that they are dazzled by the flashing light, and come towards it just as sea-birds, on dark nights, will fly, with all steam on, against the flashing lights of lighthouses, and there break their heads against the glass.

The fascination exercised by a twirl on larks is most remarkable. I have seen scores sitting round the twirl, gazing at it with as much astonishment as larks' countenances could possibly exhibit. They turn their heads on one side, and look, and look, and seem perfectly petrified.

In some parts of the country, instead of twirls, the lark-shooters use live owls in a wire cage as decoys to the birds. This answers far better than the twirls, for, with the latter, after some firing has been going on, the larks are apt to give the twirl and its owner a somewhat wide berth, but when the attraction is an owl, nothing can restrain them, and they will flock from all parts to try and assail their enemy. Nothing can drive them away. Their fury is so great that all the firing in the world would not disturb them. It is almost laughable.

Both twirls and live owls are means frequently resorted to by shooters in Belgium.

My gallant friend had never tried it until he went there, and he now declares it to be very good fun; and so it is, when there is nothing better stirring.

Well, then, to resume. Here is a sportsman, who, for £40 a year (including his rent, rates, and taxes), kills between 200 and 300 partridges, courses some 60 or 70 hares, shoots 200 or 300 rabbits, besides a couple of thousand of birds of passage, ducks, quails, teal, geese, swans, snipe, plovers, curlews, oystercatchers, &c. Including the pay of his keeper, I daresay the whole lot does not cost him more than £100 or £110 a year, and surely it cannot at that price be considered dear. And, since everybody complains that no shooting is now to be had here, but at preposterous terms, I would say to those in search of suitable ground, try Belgium, and if you do not get suited, you will be hard to please.

To a man fond of the gun, a shooting with a good marsh, and near the shore, would give tolerable occupation for eight months out of twelve; and if that is not enough to satisfy him, he must be a glutton. I would recommend any intending hirers of shooting not to lose time, because already the Belgians are becoming aware of the value of their shootings for Britishers. Delaying may, therefore, enhance the terms. Let those who read take heed, then, and lay hold of time by the forelock—they will have no cause to repent that course.

CHAPTER XLIII.

UNEARTHING FOXES FOR THE BRITISH MARKET.

IN common with most sporting readers, I have frequently, during the hunting season, noticed in the papers advertisements offering foxes for sale.

Of course, in a thorough hunting country like the British Kingdom, there is nothing extraordinary in such offers being made, and the demand for foxes is so great, that almost every other country in Europe is made to bring its contingent, in order to satisfy the ever-persistent call "for more;" but as to where these foxes may come from, it would be hard, perhaps, except for one in the trade, to tell. However, this much I know for a fact, that *some* (and in no insignificant numbers either) come from the south of Belgium. I know it, because I have seen there once how they were caught, and as a fox-catching expedition has amused me, it may, perhaps, interest others also, and I will straightway proceed to relate it, just as it took place.

Last summer, then, having taken up my quarters for a shooting excursion in Luxemburg, I became acquainted with a fox-catcher, whose exact locality shall be nameless, as he does not wish it to be known; suffice it to say that the place where this man lives is very picturesque and thickly wooded; hence the presence there of numerous foxes.

Now, were I a fashionable novelist, I should straightway proceed, when describing my fox-catcher, to invest him with some unenviable physical peculiarities, as well as moral infirmities. Truth compels me to say, however, that he was as free from both as anyone could wish. He was a well-built fellow, about thirty years of age; he had good features, and exhibited good manners, so that, on the whole, he was the very antithesis to any preconceived idea one might have formed as to what a man engaged in such a peculiar trade ought to have been.

I got acquainted with him on the first morning our shooting began, when I was handed over to his care. He had been engaged to guide me over the ground on which we were entitled to shoot, to warn me against those fields and woods interspersed with our own over which we had no control; he was to carry my game, and to take me to a certain inn at luncheon time. He fulfilled his engagement to the letter—told me clearly where I could go, stopped me when we got dangerously near some neighbour's grounds, carried my game without stopping fifty times to wipe his forehead—as the generality of beaters will do—he only drank a thimbleful of cognac, and declined any more, and finally he brought me, insensibly, to the very door of the inn, in the very nick of time. So far so good. Whilst things were getting ship-shape for a *réconfortant*, we talked together—which we had not been able to do when in the fields—and it then came out that my man was a purveyor of foxes and other wild animals for the British market. I felt and evinced the utmost interest in his calling, and finally, as there is nothing like seeing with one's eyes how things take place, I agreed to accompany him on one of his excursions after foxes.

That, reader, is how it came to pass that one fine

morning, long before daybreak, I was on the road towards my quondam companion's house, the last in the village. When I got there, I found him quite ready and waiting for me. He took two spades, his brother slung four strong wicker baskets over his shoulders, then pocketed a lot of muzzles and some bits of cord that lay in a heap on the table, and we departed on our errand. The moon was just setting, and twilight began to appear. We walked on briskly along a winding-path through the woods for about half an hour, when my companions, simultaneously stopping, deliberately put out their pipes, begged of me to be as quiet as possible, then we left the path we had hitherto followed, and entered the covert. Daylight, in the meantime, had set in, and, indeed, it was lucky it had done so, for the wood was so cut about with ditches and holes, that I should have certainly broken my neck twenty times over, if I had not been enabled, by the increased light, to pick out my way.

Five or six minutes of pushing and crushing through briars and brambles, and my companions stop. The man with the spades looks carefully round about a fox's earth, he shakes his head doubtfully, then kneels down and probes the hole with one of the spades. His comrade, meanwhile, gets rid of his baskets and then joins him; they take off their coats, and then begin digging away, whilst, standing by on the tip-toe of expectation, I am curiously watching their operations.

Now the men talk, whilst their work proceeds.

"I don't think he is at home," says one.

"Maybe not, but it is hard to tell," replies the other; "there are so many tracks left that it is impossible to know what he has done. Hold on, now, that is enough."

They stop, and the last speaker, my former beater,

coolly rolls up his shirt-sleeve, and lying down at full length on the ground, he shoves his bare hand and arm, up to his shoulder, in the hole.

"I say, you will get bitten!" I spontaneously remonstrate.

"No fear," he replies laughingly.

"Why—do you always act thus?"

"Always."

"And that is how you take them?"

"Certainly."

"Then, by Jove, you are either more courageous or more imprudent than I am, for I should not like to try that dodge of yours."

"Bah!" he replied, negligently, "it is a matter of habit."

"Most likely," I retorted, dryly enough; "but I know it would take me a very long time to get accustomed to that."

However, so far, we had had no luck, for the man rose disgusted, saying, "Nothing here."

He then brushed away the earth that was adhering to his arm and hand, pulled down his shirt-sleeve, both men resumed their coats, the one taking up the spades, his brother the baskets and other paraphernalia, and we made another start.

"This time," said my ex-beater, "we are sure to have luck of some kind."

"Sure?" I asked, incredulously.

"Yes. We are now going to a vixen's earth, and to my knowledge she has several young ones; so that, if she should chance to be out, the young cubs, at any rate, are sure to be in."

"That is likely enough," chimed in the brother; "they are too young to go by themselves as yet."

"Have you ever seen young foxes, sir?" said my beater, addressing me.

"I have seen young foxes, certainly, but they were not very young. We hunt young foxes in my country, in order to enter young hounds and to blood them, though, very often, this alleged motive for cub-hunting is merely a shallow and superficial pretence for our hunting-men to enter the field a little sooner than they would otherwise do, so great is their enthusiastic greed for hunting. But this is a digression. To resume our subject, these young foxes that are thus hunted are, though young, yet able to take care of themselves, although they do not possess, as yet, either all the cunning or all the speed of their elders."

"Well, sir, those that I am going to show you must be now about the size of full-grown kittens, and very pretty animals they look, too, I can assure you."

"Then you have seen them?"

"Oh yes, half-a-dozen times."

"Why have you not caught them sooner, then?"

"Because I had received no orders, as yet, from London. But now it is all right, and as many as ever I can catch will be welcome."

Subsequently, I gathered from him that he received thirty shillings for every full-grown fox (dog or vixen), and fifteen shillings for every young fox able to take care of itself—*i.e.* thoroughly weaned from its mother. He said that he generally managed to send about two score of full-grown foxes and about as many young ones. Of course, he had to travel a good deal, in order to secure such a number, but all the keepers, for many miles round, were on the look-out on his behalf, and thus he was enabled to secure almost all the foxes that the province could boast of possessing. Of course, he invariably gave something as *pourboire* to the gamekeepers, for their trouble and kindness. This *something* averaged, together with expenses for travelling, &c., about five francs per head of fox. So that, on a rough calculation, forty full-grown foxes, at thirty shillings a head, and forty cubs, at fifteen shillings each, make a total amount of £90; out of which, deducting four shillings, incidental expenses, per head, it leaves a clear total of £74.

Now, considering that the whole business is carried out within one month, sometimes five weeks, never more than six weeks at the utmost, it seems to me that the calling is not, for such a man, without its attractions, monetarily speaking.

Meanwhile, as I had been foretold, we found the family, whose earth we were bent upon visiting, at home, and as the men said, *au grand complet*.

The man proceeded as he had done before, stripped his arm and investigated, with his bare hand, the contents of the earth.

"I have got the mother," he said; and he pulled her out, sure enough, by the nape of the neck. She behaved most violently, as might have been expected, but she was in expert hands. Quicker than I could describe it, a muzzle was clapped on her mouth, and secured to a strong and tight-fitting collar, her legs were tied together with a slender but strong cord, and she was deposited in one of the baskets, a helpless but savagely-growling bundle of bristling hair.

Next to her came her cubs. These were more summarily disposed of. They were not even muzzled, but merely placed, one after the other, in a strong basket, the lid of which was then safely secured. There were four of them, and prettier and more interesting-looking little animals it was never my lot to behold.

When this job was concluded, it was nearly 10 o'clock, so that altogether the affair had been swiftly expedited. However, my companions were not yet satisfied.

They knew, they said, another earth, and they meant trying it.

We went accordingly. We found the earth tenanted, and a fine, full-grown dog was pulled out of it. He, however, gave a deal of trouble. He snarled, gnashed his teeth, bristled all over, and rolled his eyes in a manner that boded no good to the man who held him, if he, by chance, could have used his teeth. However, he was at length safely muzzled, his legs were tied together, and, like his predecessor, he soon found himself the lonely tenant of a strong basket, wherein he continued his growling for some time, indeed until we reached my beater's cottage, when the baskets were shut up in a room.

Now to resume the business done, and its profits. Two full-grown foxes and four young ones represented to the men, in hard cash, the sum of £6; not bad, this, for a single morning's work.

The fox-catchers went out again the next day, and brought back three more foxes; the whole batch was then sent by rail to Ostend, from whence it was conveyed on board one of the steamers, which left for England on the same day.

YACHTING, SEA-FISHING,
AND
SEAFOWL-SHOOTING CRUISES.

YACHTING.

YACHTING.

CHAPTER XLIV.

OUR OPENING CRUISE.

A FRIEND of mine had bought a 4-ton yacht, with which he was so highly delighted that I firmly believe he meant to live on board the whole of his life. How long the fit lasted I know not, but a more contented man, for the time being, was not to be found anywhere in the United Kingdom. Howbeit, no sooner had the bargain been concluded, and the vessel changed hands, than I was asked by my enthusiastic Corinthian to pay him a visit on board, on his opening cruise, and I promised cheerfully, and faithfully kept my word. I will now proceed to give an authentic version of our adventures.

When I met Corinthian he accosted me in the following manner: "Look here, the Club are going, I hear, to have their first sail of the season on Saturday next. I don't see why I should not have mine on the same day, and I mean to; will you come with me?"

I rashly assented; but of this more by-and-by. On

that Saturday, then, I came to the Pier, and there I stepped into a very diminutive washing-tub, which my friend said was called a dingey. This nautical expression put a stop to my rising mirth. However, to tell the truth, I did not feel very secure, for when I was seated in the stern-sheets, as Corinthian said the hard board on which I sat was called, the water was within an inch or two of the boat's gunwale. However, I was "in for it," and I resigned myself to a ducking at least, if nothing more serious. Nothing of the kind happened, though, and beyond getting well splashed during our transit to the yacht, we got on well.

"There is my craft," said Corinthian. Then putting his hand to his mouth, " Yacht ahoy!" he shouted to a man who was on board, and who actually was looking at us about ten yards ahead.

"All right, sir," retorted the man; " I saw you coming; you need not have hailed. All the fellows on board the ships in harbour are looking out to see who is calling."

"Why did you hail at all?" I asked my friend; "did you not see that your man was looking at us all the time we were coming?"

"I had seen him well enough," said Corinthian, cheerfully, "but it is good form to call out."

Saying these words, we stepped on board, and whilst my friend was making the tub secure by means of a rope, which he explained to me was a "painter" (I should not have thought it), I became aware that his craft was very lively. Although at anchor, it was literally dancing and bobbing up and down, fit to give any fellow the lumbago. However, Corinthian and his crew (viz. the man before alluded to) were getting the yacht under weigh. Of course, ere long, I was in the way.

"I say," said Corinthian, "would you like to examine the cabin?"

I took the hint, and went (no, I crawled) into a black closet, the size of an Indian or American travelling-trunk, and there I sat down and looked about me. The rocking of the boat had increased, and it struck me, all of a sudden, that a breath of air would do me good, so I popped my head out. The yacht had slipped her moorings, and we were going towards a coal-wharf at a tremendous speed.

"I say!" I shouted in my alarm, "look out ahead. You will run the pier down next."

"Oh no," said the man, who had taken the tiller, "we are going to tack. There she goes!" saying which memorable words he put the rudder hard up, the yacht swung swiftly round, and the boom of the mainsail fetched me such a whack on the back of my head that my hat was sent flying overboard, and I was shot like a sack of coals into the blessed cabin.

"Never mind the hat!" I heard my friend shouting.

So I popped out again. "But," I remonstrated, "I must have my hat back; I can't go home without it. Moreover——"

I would, no doubt, have said a great deal more, but the man, who all the while had looked gravely ahead, said again suddenly, "Tack!" and the very identical boom came again—this time upon my mouth—and interrupted my sentence.

We had now fairly left the harbour, the wind was blowing terribly strong it seemed to me, and our vessel (!) slanted so awfully that the mainmast was nearly parallel to the sea, and the water bubbled up to the very top of the cabin. Of course, when the mast took that mighty uncomfortable position our bodies had necessarily to describe with it an angle of forty-five degrees, and if we had looked over the counter I am sure we ought to have been able to see the yacht's keel.

"Now we are comfortable and snug," said Corinthian, looking approvingly at his boat's well-trimmed sails.

"Oh, are we?" I said doubtfully.

"Of course we are; don't we spin along, eh?"

"We will spin under soon, I think," I said.

"Now I am going to get dinner ready. Come in and see how I proceed," he added.

He dived into the cabin, and, being drenched with sea spray, I gladly followed him. He raked up a microscopic stove with a poker about the size of a drawing-pencil, and then proceeded to light the fire; but no sooner had he applied the match than the wind blew all the smoke in, and we were literally smoked out.

"Come on deck," he said; "it will light well of its own accord."

I went and sat on deck, but then the chimney began to draw, and all the smoke came in my face, and I was fairly choked. I shifted again, but, what between the smoke and the boom, I had to keep pretty wide awake. I began to think that yachting, after all, under such circumstances, might not be so interesting as it looked *à priori*. Howbeit, the fire got lighted somehow, and Corinthian went down. First he made some coffee, and then he proceeded to cook a steak; but in the midst of the latter occupation, as I, stretched on a cushion, was watching him, the boat gave a sudden lurch. I tried to keep myself where I was, kicked over the coffee-pot, Corinthian fell on the top of me, and what between the hissing gravy on one leg and the boiling coffee over the other, without mentioning the incubus of my friend—easily ascertained by multiplying the fellow's dead weight by the square of the speed, and the latter must have been tremendous—I candidly confess that I wished I had never left the *plancher des vaches.*

When harmony was once more restored we found that all the coffee was spilt : we discovered, after a lengthened search, that the steak had been shot among the coals in a bunk, and that a flood of water had come through the stove-pipe and put the fire out. At this time a feeling of uneasiness again crept over me, and I went on deck "to look at the landscape." The tillerman was smoking some beastly tobacco, whose smoke no doubt did not agree with me, for I began, unaccountably, to feel sick. I wanted to tell the man to stop smoking. I looked at him, but I could not open my mouth, at least I was afraid to do so, somehow; so I held my tongue, but my thoughts were bitter.

My usual cheerfulness had completely deserted me. As the French say, " I saw everything in black." I became perfectly indifferent, and I remember perfectly well that I recklessly wished the yacht would sink, just for the sake of a change. But it did not sink, fortunately, no doubt. Things with me went on from bad to worse. Meanwhile, the wind had risen still more, and the captain and crew (?) thought that our best plan was "to shape our course" for harbour again. I heard this with pleasure, and wished to express my delight, but I could not trust myself to speak as yet, so I wisely kept my thoughts to myself. By-and-by we got back into the harbour, where, the water being smooth, I soon recovered my equanimity, and by the time we landed I felt a man again. At night I related to my friends how very rough the sea was, and how I had enjoyed myself, and they all thought I was a plucky sailor. One of them wrote to a friend all my daring adventures on that memorable day ! So is history written.

By-the-way, a few days after I met Corinthian again. He wanted me to go for a sail with him. I expressed my perfect readiness to accompany him, and to his evident delight I walked with him to the pier-stairs, where his dingey was fastened, but when there I remembered suddenly that I had an appointment for one o'clock, and so we parted, very reluctantly, at least apparently very much so on my part. But I promised him that some other day I would go—if he catch me again, that's all.

P.S.—It is now many long years since this memorable cruise took place, but I remember it quite vividly; and, no doubt, beginners in the art of yachting will find, in this chapter, their own feelings somewhat fairly depicted, although of course written somewhat in the light of a "squib."

CHAPTER XLV.

THE PLEASURES AND TRIBULATIONS OF AN ENTHUSIASTIC CORINTHIAN.

I HAD come up to reside in town, and wanted a yacht to knock about in, as the saying is.

Now there were plenty of yachts for sale, but all of them were very dear. However, as I had made up my mind to get afloat in my own *wessel*, I went through an immense deal of trouble, in inspecting a tremendous lot of craft, with praiseworthy perseverance. The journeys I took up and down the river, with and without friends, with and without yacht agents, you would not believe—there! so I will pass that over, and merely premise that, finally, one fine morning in May saw me, together with Mr. Batts (the well-known yacht dealer, buyer, and exchanger), in the train for that popular watering-place *Boatville*-on-the-Thames, where the aforesaid Mr. Batts " knew of a yacht that would suit me to a T," as he expressed it.

We had a very cheerful journey.

It is astonishing what an amount of animal spirits those agents seem to possess, and what an amount of free, jolly, and easy style they will bring along with them. Of course I paid all expenses, and it was understood that eventually I would come down for a handsome commission, in the event of a purchase; so it was no wonder that Mr. Batts seemed to be, and no doubt in reality was, in the best of spirits and on the best of terms with himself, with me, and with everyone else besides, as, after a jolly *déjeuner à la fourchette*, we were complacently smoking a cigar in a first-class carriage bound for the above-mentioned town.

"My dear sir," Batts was saying to me, between puffs, as we were steaming along, "she will suit you, and no mistake. The cabin is beautifully fitted out, and if ever you *should* happen to take ladies on board" (this with a wink), "why, they will find therein a perfect little drawing-room."

"——— Junction," shouted a guard.

"Here, my man," said Batts, poking his head out of the window; "I say, do you stop here any length of time? Eh? What? Ten minutes, eh? My dear sir" (turning to me), "we will just have time to drink a glass or two of sherry."

So saying, Batts got out and ordered the sherry, of which he took the lion's share, and for which I duly paid.

"There is nothing like keeping up one's vital energies," resumed Batts, as he lighted another cigar, and we got back into our train.

By-and-by we arrived at Boatville.

A watery-looking sort of individual, half sailor, half water-rat (*i.e.* unlicensed waterman), was waiting for us at the station; and this individual, who turned out to be the party in charge of the boat, was mighty obsequious towards Mr. Batts, and all but cautiously at freezing-point towards me. In fact, had Batts been the buyer, and I the agent, the man could not have acted his part better. Evidently Batts was all and everything; Batts *knew*, and I did not, and the man looked up to Mr. Batts. So far so good.

However, on the agent's hint, we first went to have a snack at one of the leading hotels, for which snack of course I duly paid again; but, somehow, I was getting tired of that paying business, and no wonder, I think. So when the agent hinted that we might end our snack by a bottle of champagne, I merely remarked dryly that I should like to see the yacht. He took the hint, for a wonder, and we went down to the water-side. There a waterman's wherry took us to the yacht, and we clambered on board. I overhauled the boat thoroughly—or rather I pretended I did, for I did not know quite so much about a yacht then as I do now—and finally, sick and tired of the business, I agreed to buy her.

Batts was all alacrity then, and wanted me to pay the money down there and then to him.

"There is no hurry," I remarked; "I can settle with the owner when we get ashore again."

Upon this Batts and the water-rat exchanged glances, and I felt convinced that the two had done a trick; but what was the good of making any unpleasant remarks? The boat was as good as any I had seen, and it did not matter to me if there had been any jobbing business in the transaction; so I did not appear surprised when Batts told me that the water-rat was the owner, but that he (Batts) was to receive the money, as there was some commercial transaction to be settled between them. I paid my money down, got my receipt, and, for fear of any mishap or misunderstanding, I took possession there and then, and engaged a man and a boy to work the boat with me. The same evening we set sail, and taking advantage of a fair wind and favourable tide we came up the river, and at 12 P.M. we were anchored off Erith.

As I had telegraphed to some friends in London before

leaving Boatville, I found two of them waiting for me at the hotel. We had a glorious supper, and, on the strength of the novelty of the thing, we agreed to go and sleep on board the yacht. We thought it would be awfully pleasant, and we prepared ourselves for a most entertaining night. However, what with the swell caused by the steamers that went up and down the river all night, so long as the tide allowed them, and the swerving of the boat as she strained on her cable in answer to the breeze, we did not have a very pleasant time of it. The grating of the chains, the creaking of the spars, the whistling of the wind through the rigging, and the rippling of the waves against the sides of the boat, were too audible to make sleep easy; and so it came to pass that not one of us had a wink for the whole night. Howbeit, we did not mind that. At 4 A.M. we were up and doing, much to my crew's displeasure. The man growled awfully on being called up, and said that he had not had his fill of sleep, whereas we had heard him snore ever since he had turned in. Howbeit, as he kept on grumbling, I told him, in plain language, that if he did not like it he might lump it; and if he preferred going back to his own sweet home (in the back slums of Boatville) he might do so, and that I would at once settle with him. I had no sooner proposed this than he went forward to pack up his clothes—viz. three stockings in half a handkerchief—and then asked me only £1 for his wages!

"Come," I said, "a pound is hardly enough, I should think. Could not you have managed to ask more than that?"

However, he said that he would do inexpressible things to his eyes first, and goodness only knows what he would do next, but he would not take a blessed penny less, so he said; but eventually I gave him five shillings, and when he got ashore he swore he would "county court" me. I need scarcely say that I have not heard of him from that day to this.

Meanwhile, my friends, in their shirt-sleeves, were pleasurably and profitably employed in frying a monstrous steak for our breakfast, and beyond getting three coffee-pots upset, one after the other, by the rolling of the boat, we got on without serious mishap.

After breakfast I went ashore and engaged another man. He, however, turned out afterwards to be an awful drunkard, and got "sacked" accordingly. Taken all in all, I had throughout the season the greatest trouble in keeping up a sober and efficient crew. How those who have large yachts manage it, I don't know; but getting my one man became to me a regular sickener, and finally we had to work the boat ourselves. The most wonderful part of the business, however, was that these men invariably came to me with excellent characters and testimonials! Now, for instance, one of them referred me to a certain gallant colonel with whom I happened to be acquainted. I wrote to the colonel, who in return duly stated that the man had been in his service on board his yacht, but that some alteration in his arrangements had necessitated the man's dismissal; whereas, as it turned out, the man had been discharged for having tried to steal a coil of rope. Now, what is the good of owners granting such evasive characters to men who do not deserve being trusted and employed? If owners dare not speak their minds, let them abstain altogether from giving any character at all to any doubtful individual who may have behaved badly in their service, rather than induce another owner to take him and run the risk of being also plundered. As things now stand, it is plain that gentlemen are totally at the mercy of their *employés*, for rarely, if ever, have I met with a gentleman who dared to write the truth about any bad servant of his. Such a course of action, however, is most unfair, not only to employers, but also to those servants who are really good and honest; for when an owner has had experience, he looks with distrust upon all new-comers in his service until these new-comers have *proved* themselves trustworthy. As it was, I could not find a suitable man to whom I could occasionally confide the yacht and its contents when my presence was required in town. I tried all sorts of men—sailors, watermen, water-rats; one and all looked upon their engagements as being a compact between us that they were to enjoy themselves to the utmost, eat and drink to repletion, get drunk, under pretence of making merry, on the slightest occasion and whenever opportunity offered, purloin all sorts of things, and pawn them or sell them for beer, &c. &c., *ad libitum*, and then say the things had gone overboard!

Finally, I hit upon the expedient of confiding my boat privately to a coastguard-officer, and I made a point of running the yacht to the coastguard-station every time I projected a journey to town. There the boat was safe. The officer took care that no harm should befall her, went on board and baled her out when it was needed, saw that no water-thief got on her to plunder her of her contents, and, altogether, I felt as safe as if I had been on board the yacht all the time. When I intended having a sail I used to send word to the officer, and everything was ready for us when we reached the place; the cushions had been aired, the boat-cleaned, the carpet beaten, the stove was lighted; we had but to get on board, fasten the dingey astern, hoist up sails, haul up anchor, and off we could go.

Well, we managed in that way for several seasons.

Then, I had to leave England, and some business that

was calling me abroad precluded my entertaining the notion of keeping the yacht any longer. I told all those I knew that my boat was for sale, but no one wanted a yacht. I then offered her to ship-carpenters, yacht-builders, calkers, &c. No, they did not want her either. Everyone of them found some fault in her. One said she was too deep; the other said she had not beam enough; another found fault with her sails; one did not like the cabin; and another objected to her rig. I then saw some watermen who used to take pleasure-parties on board their crafts for sails and picnics on the river, but they, in their turn, did not find her suitable for their calling; in fact, according to these people, she was neither good for fishing nor for pleasuring, and I began to feel very disgusted with the whole concern.

I then bethought myself of advertising her. I spent a couple of pounds and did not get a single *bonâ fide* answer. Plenty of fellows wrote. Some wanted a month's trial, others could not pay until the next season; and one actually wrote from abroad, telling me to send him the boat, and *if* she suited him, he *might* keep her, &c. &c.

My patience was exhausted, and I had almost made up my mind to keep the boat where she was, until my return to England, when I unexpectedly received from Mr. Batts the following note:

"MY DEAR SIR,—I hear that you wish to part with your little yacht. Why did you not let me know that before? I would have spared you a lot of trouble. You have but to send her to Mr. Waterrat at Boatville, and I will soon find a buyer for you.—Yours very sincerely,

"BATTS.

"P.S.—Kindly let me know your lowest price, and you

will hear from me within a fortnight. Of course, we will see the yacht will be quite safe; *but then you know we cannot be answerable for accidents*, barring which she will be as comfortable as in your own hands.

"BATTS."

"Well," I thought, "that Batts is not such a bad fellow after all; he comes very gallantly to my rescue, and I should not have thought that of him."

I at once ordered the yacht back to its old quarters, and wrote to Batts a note regularly overflowing with gratitude.

With my mind thus set at rest, I started on my journey for the Continent.

About a month later, I received a voluminous letter in Batts' well-known bold handwriting.

"Ah! here comes the inclosure," I thought; "the blessed yacht is sold at last!" And I opened the letter.

Yes, there were, truly, some inclosures—*i.e.* a long ship-carpenter's bill, including I can't tell you how many items, and coming altogether to a round sum of £43 17s. 6½d.

"What the deuce is this?" I wondered. However, there was no mistaking the thing; it was for me, there was no doubt about that.

"Dr. 'Snapshot' to Swindling Bob, ship carpenter at Boatville, for repairs done to his yacht, &c. &c.;" then came the details. I was getting more and more puzzled. I had never been at Boatville since I had bought the yacht. I had never had the honour of being acquainted with Mr. Swindling Bob, of the above-mentioned place; moreover, the slight repairs that I had had done to my yacht I had paid for as they were respectively concluded, so I was at a loss to make out the meaning of the bill and its contents.

However, Mr. Batts' note soon enlightened me. It ran thus:

"DEAR SIR,—Herewith I beg to enclose Mr. Bob's bill for repairs done to your yacht. She was, unfortunately, run down by a barge (*name unknown*) the day after your departure from England. Knowing how particular you are in having things in due order, I confided the job to my friend Mr. Swindling Bob, whose charges you will observe are most moderate, as he only charges 10*s.* 6*d.* per pound of real copper nails, whereas many jobbers in the trade would thrust upon you mere brass concerns at 15*s.* (and sometimes more) per pound.

"As Mr. Bob has undertaken the repairs at my earnest request, I have likewise undertaken to forward you his bill. If you could conveniently send me a cheque for him, per return, I should feel obliged, as I know Mr. Bob is in want of funds, and being a beginner, he cannot afford to give long credit.

"The boat now looks lovely, and I have had an offer for her yesterday. A man offered me £40 for her. If I were you I would accept those terms, as we might have to wait until next season to secure a buyer. My commission would be £5 on the sale. Believe me, &c.,

"BATTS."

Here was a go! £43 17*s.* 6½*d.* (bother the halfpenny!) to pay, and £40 to receive, deducting, however, £5 from the £40. I drew a cheque for £8 17*s.* 6*d.* (leaving out the halfpenny—"darn" the halfpenny!) and sent it to Batts *without* my compliments. And that is how I had to pay £8 odd to get rid of my yacht. *Avis aux amateurs.*

On my return to England, I accidentally fell in with

my ex-boat, and I made it a point to inspect her thoroughly. I could take my oath, any day, that no repairs of any kind whatsoever had been done to her. She was then in the hands of a young lawyer, who had bought her, like me, *through Mr. Batts' agency.* He had paid £150 for her!

From the latest accounts, Mr. Batts is a most prosperous man; and if he keeps on amassing money as he does, there is some talk, in influential circles, that he will be made a J.P., or be elected an alderman, before long. He will richly deserve this, and his future exalted position will conclusively prove that virtue is always rewarded!

SEA-FISHING

AND

SEAFOWL-SHOOTING EXCURSIONS.

SEA-FISHING
AND
SEAFOWL-SHOOTING EXCURSIONS.

(Being a continuation of the trips narrated in "Shooting and Fishing Trips.")

CHAPTER XLVI.

OLD SHOREHAM.

My papers on sea-fishing in *Bell's Life* brought me many applications from friends and acquaintances who wished to join me in some of my excursions. Of course, in every instance, when circumstances would admit of it, and our tastes were congenial, I agreed to the proposals with the greatest pleasure; but I have, sometimes, met with fellows who backed out of the undertaking before they were brought face to face with its matter-of-fact execution; or if they entered into it, and anything of a sea set on, got sick, wished they were dead, and swore they would not be caught at it again.

Now, all that sort of thing is very annoying to one, if not to both parties. In one case, however, the consideration of the expense and trouble he had, so far, been put to, induced my then unwilling companion to face the sea.

"Hang it!" said he; "I have not bought a brand-new

creel, and rigged out lines according to your directions, and come down here, eighty miles, for nothing. To sea we *do* go!"

And we went. That is the sort of spirit I like. But, in some cases, you will find most amusing scenes enacted, the moment a glimpse is caught of the sea. Well, I had just such a sort of companion (or rather companions) in my trip to Shoreham. We were four, and two of our intending amateurs, who, during the journey down to Brighton had treated us to their experience of sea-fishing, and the remarkable catches they had had thereat, began to feel restless and uneasy when we got near the town. The day, be it said, was lovely, but :

"I wonder," said one presently, "if the sea will be quiet. It was rather rough yesterday, I saw in the paper."

"Oh, bother it!" returned the second; "I hope it will be all right."

"You may make your mind easy," I said; "there is no wind to speak of, and we will have a jolly trip."

"But," remonstrated the first speaker, "I can't exactly see why we should sail to Shoreham. There is a railway line straight to it from Brighton, and it won't take us more than a few minutes by train to get there."

"True," I rejoined, "but the fact is, that at Brighton we shall find plenty of good craft to take us fishing, whereas at Shoreham we should most likely have to put up with a tub. In Brighton, too, we can get everything we want, from a good luncheon to first-rate bait; and a sail over the sea, on this lovely day, will be a most glorious treat."

To this they had nothing to say, and my fourth companion, with whom I had made many such trips before, looked at me and smiled grimly through the smoke of his cigar. The two other fellows, however, looked irrationally bright until the end of the journey, and we thought, after all, they meant coming. But it was not so. On reaching the shore they looked very wisely at the sky, then at the sea, and then they shook their heads.

"It does not look very inviting, does it?" said one to the other.

"No," was the answer; "the sea seems rising."

Now my friend is blessed with the shortest of tempers, and I am not over-patient either, so we exchanged a glance of something uncommonly like disgust, and I at once struck in:

"If you prefer going by road or rail, do so; you can get a boat at Shoreham and board us there, so as to have a little fishing with us, if you like."

They agreed to this, and with these words we parted, much to the amusement of our boatmen, and to the entertainment of the shore loafers, who did not side with our soft friends, as may readily be imagined. If the weather had been at all bad, it stands to reason that we should not ourselves have gone to sea, and, for the matter of that, no boatmen would have taken us; but it was a beautiful day, and this made our companions' refusal, after all their entreaties to come, all the more ridiculous.

Well, off we went, and they got back on the road, and presently we saw them get into a fly and make a start towards Shoreham.

"They will, perhaps, join us, after all, at Shoreham," I said.

"No fear of that," replied my friend; and the boatmen shook their heads and laughed.

"Them gentlemen has been scared," said the elder of the two; "they be afraid, they be, that is what they are!" And his companion entirely concurred with that opinion.

Meanwhile we were making way in fine style. We passed the West Pier, and hugged the shore against a mild N.E. wind, which took us in a truly pleasurable fashion to our fishing-ground. The journey itself was full of interest, for we were always so close to the shore as to render the use of a glass quite unnecessary. The first village — or rather town, for it is a "rising" watering-place—is Hove, about a mile from Brighton, and a very pretty place it seemed to be.

We anchored there for half an hour, and dropped two lines. In the first five minutes I got a whiting and a pouting, my friend catching a brill of about three pounds weight.

"We might get some fine sport here," said my companion.

"Yes, sir," replied the boatman, "it is quite as good for sport here as at Brighton."

"Then let us stop here," decisively argued my friend.

"Well, but, look here," I remonstrated, "what about our two companions, who are now on their way to Shoreham?"

"Oh, they be dashed!" he replied roughly; "why should we put ourselves out for two fellows who don't know their own minds?"

"All very well," I said, "but that is no reason why we should break our word. We said we would go to Shoreham, and to Shoreham we shall go."

I knew I had bad odds—3 to 1—against me, as the boatmen, but too willing to stop where we were, so as to save themselves any further trouble, were evidently siding with him. However, my friend gave in with a grunt.

Old Shoreham.

"All right," said he, "then let us go at once, for if we delay here much longer we shall not be able to tear ourselves away. I know there are some fine brill about here, and I am so fond of turbot!"

This he exclaimed so fervently, that both boatmen and I burst into a roar of laughter.

We wound up our lines, lit our cigars, and the boatmen set sail. We passed Cliftonville, Portslade, Southwick, and then the Kingston lighthouse was on our starboard side.

"Another mile," said the men, "and we shall be at Old Shoreham Harbour." We were in no hurry to get there, however, and we enjoyed our delicious sail to the utmost. Whenever we felt somewhat chilly, we took the oars, and a five minutes' good pull soon put us in a thorough glow, and a pull is always better than a "drop" at any time.

We arrived opposite the harbour at about two o'clock, so that we had fully two hours yet to the good, according to our men's arrangements. They declared that if we weighed anchor at four it would just give us decent time to get back to Brighton before night, provided the wind held as tolerably fair as it was then. Meanwhile we looked out for a boat likely to contain our two friends; but no likely boat was out. Then I saw a handkerchief being waved on shore; I levelled my Dollond at the spot, and saw our two fellows sitting on the shingle, and, to all appearance, settled there.

"They are not coming," said my companion; "I told you they would not."

"Very well, we can do without them," and we began fishing.

Whilst so engaged our conversation turned on fly-fishing, and I asked my friend if he had read an account of some fly-fishing for bass which had been published in *Bell's Life*, and which had been carried out at the entrance of the very harbour we stood at. Yes, he had. The sport, he said, must have been interesting; but its drawback was its great uncertainty, for, according to the writer's own account, he had been more than once to the harbour before he succeeded in meeting with fish. Such a style of doing things is only practicable when the angler resides at or near the place, and can afford to go and try repeatedly, until he meets with sport, and even then, it must be anything but encouraging to find that one has to go several times before hooking a fish worth putting into a creel. Now, hooking with hand-lines always answers, hence its popularity. There are, I warrant, a thousand hand-anglers to one rodman amongst sea-fishermen, and I therefore thought it rather questionable taste of the writer of the article to profess contempt for hand-line fishing, especially considering what miserable returns he had had on several occasions for his own efforts on his own hobby.

I for my part despise no man's way of enjoying himself. On the contrary, whenever I hear of any new dodge, or of any spot new to me where sport is to be had, I invariably endeavour to try it at the earliest opportunity, and I had accordingly noted the bass-fishing at Shoreham.

On the day in question, however, it was beyond possibility to try the pier-head, not only because our time was so short for hand-line fishing, but because we should not have been able to get back to Brighton before darkness had fairly set in. We therefore arranged to come on the morrow if possible, and, with this understanding, went on with our hooking; and such hooking I have rarely seen before. We got all sorts of fish, and remarkably nice ones in the lot, too. By good luck my companion (he who is so fond of brill) got one, a three-pounder, which tickled him immensely.

"Now," said he, emphatically, "I don't care a rap whether I catch another fish or not. Oh, you beauty!" he went on, addressing the fish, "you will be nice with proper sauce!"

And he smacked his lips in anticipation. Our boatmen were as pleased as could be, and one of them said to the other, *sotto voce*: " There's some pleasure in taking out men of that sort, John ; no grumbling, no bother; and ain't they pleased with the sport, too!"

Of course it is a treat for these men as well as for their fares when sport is to be had, for sport makes the fares very pleasant, jolly, and easy-going, whereas when there is but meagre sport one is continually wanting to shift to new quarters, and this entails no end of work for the boatmen.

As it was, I believe we could not possibly have fared better than we did where we were; and when I state that in our two hours over a score of nice fish were basketed, I think most of my readers will agree with me that there was no occasion on our part for grumbling.

Meanwhile our shore fellows sat gaping at us. At a quarter to four we began to get ready, but with my last throw I lost a line, and a good one, too, though it had once been mended. The fact was I was in a hurry, and had made of the two bits a coarse knot. In slipping the weight overboard the knot caught in a splinter over the gun'ale, and, snap went the line. I could almost have shed a tear, it was such a fine line, and so well hooked and baited! I hope nobody (I mean no fish) hooked himself to it, as it might prove a teaser to anyone to carry about in his mouth half a yard of whalebone, without mentioning two hooks and their guts, and fifteen yards or so of line.

Well, whilst our men were getting ready for a start we signalled our shore fellows that we intended going back. They waved their hats, and went up towards the town, whence we concluded that they preferred staying on *terra firma* to being picked up by us, and having to go back by sea.

"Of all queer fellows," quoth my friend, "these two are about the queerest I have seen. What was the good of their coming down at all if they did not mean to fish?"

"Begging your pardon, sir," said one of our boatmen, "for interfering in your conversation, but the two gentlemen as was on the shore were a-fishing."

"Oh, were they? How?" asked we.

"Why, I think with long lines. I saw them throwing something into the sea several times; I suppose it was their leads; and it looked uncommonly like lines they were holding."

We accordingly went back in expectation of hearing of some tremendous catches effected by our quondam companions.

The sail back was very fine, and when we arrived on the shingle our two truants were there to greet us on our landing. They did not care about bothering us, they said, and thought four would have been too many fishermen in the same boat to insure comfort and sufficient room to each, so they had determined to stop on shore, and try what they could do there.

"Well, and what have you caught?" we asked them in a breath.

"Nothing!"

When they saw our two creels-full they were slightly mad about it.

As we intended making a long day of it on the morrow —and to bring that about we meant starting early—we went to bed somewhere about 10 P.M. At 8 o'clock we breakfasted; at 8.45 our men appeared, and took charge of rods, lines, creels, and coats. We followed in their wake, and a judicious tack out of our street brought us on the shore just in the nick of time to see a brilliant cavalcade cantering about on the road towards Hove. At 9 o'clock exactly we were sliding over the shingle, and were launched. The wind had veered N.W., which was not exactly foul, but half-way towards it, so that we had to take some half-score of tacks before we could make the harbour at Shoreham. Well, once there, we agreed to try every dodge in order to secure a few samples of bass. My friend, who is a first-rate caster for trout or salmon, prided himself on having the first haul.

"But where shall we try first of all?" I asked him.

"Oh, here, from the boat," said he.

"Very well," I returned, "I am willing; but as two can't cast at once from the same boat—at least not very easily—I will sit out of your way whilst you try. Then, when you have had your swing, I will have mine."

Well, he cast his flies two or three times very scientifically, and an awful long way off; brought them in steadily, then jerkily, but no fish appeared.

"I don't think we are in the right spot," said he; but lo! he struck as he was yet speaking. "I have got one," he ejaculated, "and (winding-up) here he is! A coalfish, by good fortune?"

We commented thereon very extensively; and then I took my turn at the rod, but did no good. Then he tried again, with the same result. Then our two fellows tried, and our boatmen tried, and we all tried, and caught nothing.

"The tide is too slack," said one; "Or too low," said another; "The wind is too strong," suggested a third, "besides, the boat frightens away the fish!"

Happy thought! That is what it was. The boat was frightening away the fish.

Forthwith we landed at the pier-head, and at once tried what sport the spot would yield. I put on three flies. My friend had two. He tried the inside of the harbour, I tried the outside. He casts, and I cast, and we draw it in silently, and in great expectation, whilst our boatmen look on from a distance and smoke their pipes. Our two friends are sitting on the pier, smoking, and enjoying the sun and the fresh breeze. After half-a-dozen casts, and not a single bite, I put down my line, and proceeded to unjoint my rod.

"What is the row?" asks my comrade. "Give it up?"

"Yes, can't find a fish. Will wait for you."

He tried for a good hour, and got nothing. So he also put his line up and disjointed his rod.

"Let us go back," said he fervently, "to *nos amours*," and hailing our boatmen, "Come round here and pick us up," shouted he, "we can't catch a thing, we will go back where we were yesterday."

The boatmen laughed, and brought the boat round. We all re-embarked, and a five-minutes' sail brought us to the identical spot we had occupied the day before. Our wretched performance on the pier had made us eager for sport of some sort, and the advent of even a small pouting, as our first catch, was hailed with a perfect outburst of delight. Another pouting soon followed suit, then another, then a coalfish, then a dogfish, then a skate, a brill, then a codling, and another, and a third, until the sea began rising with the coming tide, and one of our comrades in sport declared that he should be sea-sick.

Old Shoreham.

Fortunately we were near shore, and as it was about luncheon-time, we got up our anchor, and ran into harbour, where the comparatively smooth water soon quieted so well our friend's feelings that he declared that he did not think he should have been sea-sick after all!

A good meal soon put him and us in trim once more, and at 1 o'clock we returned towards the boat for another turn at hooking. Some men who were fishing from the shore said that the harbour was good for eels, &c. We tried it, and caught flounders, dabs, plaice, and eels—about a score—all told, in an hour's time. Then we headed for the open sea. There, however, we found the sea getting bad, and our boatmen urged us to go in without loss of time. We naturally did not wish to get into a gale, and so it came to pass that at a little after 3 o'clock we were all safe and sound in the King's Road, Brighton, all the better for our trip. Our excursions to Shoreham proved conclusively that hand-line fishing just then was a regular A 1 sport there. As to rod-fishing, as we met with only one fish, I cannot speak very favourably. I daresay a dozen trials or so of the pier might bring a day's good luck to the fishermen, but the question then resolves into this: *Le jeu en vaut-il la chandelle?* That is the point at issue, and if my opinion be asked I will say try both, and stick to the one that gives you the best fun.

CHAPTER XLVII.

FROM BRIGHTON TO WORTHING.

I HAD noticed, during my previous excursion, that when we had landed at Shoreham there appeared to be on either side of the harbour—Kingston way or Lancing side—vast mud flats and waste lands, where, in all probability, many birds were to be found if diligently sought after. I had made a note of this; and as I intended going for a sea-fishing trip from Brighton to Littlehampton (weather permitting), I made arrangements with an American friend at Brighton to accompany me. As he arranged to bring the boat to me as far as Shoreham, I had an opportunity for a walk on the shore with my gun and Rover, to have a little wildfowl-shooting. This was highly satisfactory to all parties, but the only thing we now needed was suitable weather. What with rain and strong winds, big tides, and so forth, it looked long odds on our having to postpone our trip *aux calendes grecques.*

However, I went down to Brighton, and at once paid a visit to my friend, where all preliminaries were arranged. I intended starting the next morning very early, come what might in respect of the weather.

Shoreham harbour is said to be only six miles from Brighton; but making full allowance for deviations from

From Brighton to Worthing. 89

the straight road, I reckoned it close upon nine miles, which I calculated on covering by 11 o'clock or noon. Weather suiting, the boat was to be at Shoreham about that time, it being then my intention to embark and go to Littlehampton. This was agreed to.

Well, things took place just as we had anticipated, and I started at 7 A.M. from Brighton; but wishing to save my legs a good deal of unnecessary tramping, I took the train and booked myself and dog to Portslade. Anyhow, that was a good three-miles' tramp saved, as I knew there were no birds to be had between that place and Brighton.

Portslade reached in a quarter of an hour, I wended my way to the shore. I found two or three ships (colliers, I think) at anchor there, but very few signs of birds could I as yet discover. There were plenty of seagulls about, however, and the weather being very rough these were "tossed about considerable," as my Yankee friend subsequently expressed it. Now, whenever seagulls appear in large numbers, and seem very lively, one may take it for granted that other sea-birds are equally abundant; but then these pitch into all sorts of nooks and corners for shelter, and it is a work of patience to find them. Beyond Portslade the coast is bare, and consists of a shingly beach backed up by waste lands of a marshy character, with some creeks here and there, and muddy flats along the harbours, where sea-birds would be sure to settle for a rest after their exertions. Well, I passed the coastguard-station at Portslade, and then perceived a small boat under reefed mainsail and foresail heading for Shoreham harbour. At first I thought it might be my friend's, but a moment's glance satisfied me that it could not be; for, first of all, the sails were of the brown and patchy order, whilst our boat had a neat set of sails, as white as a seagull's wings. It was a fisherman's boat, and from the manner in which she was tossed about I surmised that we should not go fishing that day. Past Southwick I had my first shot at a redshank. While walking on along the beach, and peeping occasionally into the hollow behind the belt of sands which protects the harbour, I saw suddenly the bird stalking into the shallow water near some mud flat. "Welcome to our shores, little stranger," I fervently ejaculated, and with that I flushed, and floored the long-legged individual. Thought I, on examining the bird, if I had, for instance, legs in the same proportion to my body as you, I would stand on some ten or eleven feet legs, and my feet would be provided with toes varying in length from two to three feet or more, which would certainly prove extremely useful for wading over the flats. It would do away with mud shoes then, and no mistake; but at first, men of that "rig" would probably look uncommonly queer, and rather too conspicuous. Having indulged in such wild fancies, and regretting that I had no one with me to whom I could impart the sense of my thoughts, I put the bird in the bag and reloaded. The wind abated somewhat towards half-past 9, and I then began to have some fun, as birds commenced showing themselves in abundance, particularly along the mud flats in the harbour at Kingston. I picked up there half-a-dozen birds in a quarter of an hour; and by going alternately to the harbour and then to the sea, I managed to keep the gun going until I arrived at the wooden piers that mark the entrance to Kingston and Shoreham harbours. These two places of refuge are very narrow, but are, I believe, sufficiently protected by the belt of sands which separates them from the sea. There were lots of small boats, both afloat and aground, in the harbour, and several men appeared to be spearing or laying pots for eels in the creeks. By that time the boat I had seen out was in, and the fish on their way to the station. I inquired about the sport in that line, and was told that it paid pretty well just then, and that fish were very fairly abundant, so that the laying of long lines was sure to be repaid pretty handsomely. My informant—an elderly, weather-beaten, sailor-looking man—told me that hand-line fishing was getting well-nigh impossible, for the time being, on the south coast, on account of the rough gales that had lately been sweeping over the Channel; but whenever the wind moderated several boats generally put off, and besides laying long lines they try hand-line as well, whilst their long lines offered their allurements to the fish. Brills, he added, were numerous, and uncommonly fine fish some of them turned out. According to his account one of the best spots for them was opposite Worthing, where several times the Shoreham boats had caught splendid specimens.

Whilst conversing with the old salt, I observed that several companies of black ducks appeared to be flying past the wooden jetties in no inconsiderable numbers. Now the jetties were quite deserted, and the tide going down, so I thought I might get perhaps a crack or two at the fowl if I hid somewhere behind the timbers. Of course such shots are rare, because the birds are so very shy; but when no one else is about to disturb the spot, they sometimes venture into taking a short cut over the jetties. Thought I, a couple of barrels loaded with No. 4 shot, and well directed, may bring down a cripple or two, or kill one outright; so I got the old boy to ferry me over.

Before I reached the piers there was a flock passing. Just my luck! for had I taken up my position five minutes earlier it would have been sudden death to a couple or more of the "darkies." I made all the haste I could, keeping the dog well at heel, and reached the piles right enough. I chose a comparatively dry spot, and stopped there, looking out westward through the chinks for any birds that might choose to come. Whilst thus engaged a shadow popped suddenly over my head, and I was just on the point of pulling when I bethought myself it was a crow. How the deuce he came there I cannot tell; I never heard him or saw him coming, and he may thank his stars that I did not choose to pull the trigger. However, when he discovered my gun and I in ambush, he was still more startled than I, and seemed to cry "Coack! What a start you gave me!" and, as fast as he could, made good his escape.

My dog had at first been disturbed by the appearance of this dark gentleman, but eventually he recovered and looked about, then stood looking heavenwards. I knew what that meant, and popped down, opening my eyes wide. Up they come in Indian file, making a whirring noise as they sail—five black ducks. They cross the harbour, and appear likely to pass between it and the place where I am waiting. But when about half-way their leader seems to be struck by the idea that it might be imprudent to do so, and he wheels back to sea, with the line of his followers perfectly unbroken. Well, they pass at something like a hundred yards from me. I cannot resist the temptation, and my ardour gets the better of my judgment. I know that it would be almost odds of a million to one that I could possibly hit one severely enough to get him, but shooters are proverbially sanguine.

"One single pellet may do the job," I think inwardly, as I aim six feet ahead and two feet above the leader, and pull.

To my utter astonishment the *third* bird is evidently much hurt at my proceedings. I thereupon select him as my next point of aim, and send him, privately, the second barrel. He, however, manages to keep on sail, and goes off to sea by himself, when I have the satisfaction of seeing him settle on the waves some distance from the shore. The others are nowhere to be seen by that time, and I reload with gloomy thoughts—"Why did not the blessed bird fall here?"

Meanwhile, what with my being ferried over, my talk with the old man, and my watching at the piers, time had flown on very rapidly; and I thought all at once that a roast fowl, with suitable accompaniments, would be just the thing I should have liked to have seen just then before me.

I went back to the shore, crossed over again, went to an hotel, and ordered a sound luncheon; but while eating a well-deserved fowl, I caught a glimpse of a gunner passing before the windows, and he turned out to be my friend.

"I guess," said he, when he stalked in, "that you are having a fine 'go' at this bird."

"Help me to demolish him?" I asked.

"Don't mind," he said, and we sat and played *des mâchoires* in almost silence for a good half-hour.

Our meal finished, I mentioned my morning's work. This done, a move was made, and we crossed over the long bridge, and then found ourselves on a road seemingly running parallel to the shore. On the right were some flats which the low tide in the harbour had laid bare; on the left were some waste lands extending from a sort of sea-wall to the sea, and over that bit we went. It was about 3 o'clock then; and as we wanted to be back for the 5.10 train we had no time to lose. Well, on we marched towards Lancing, and on the way we met with tolerably good fun, especially when evening drew near, but my companion did not seem much entertained, and complained of the birds being small. I told him the season was early yet, and there had been no frosts worth mentioning.

Whilst we were discussing thus, on our return journey to Shoreham, the dog evinced, quite suddenly, a very lively interest in a trail he picked up in the rank grass by the first bridge.

"A hare, for a thousand!" I called out, and I went after the dog.

It was lucky I had done so, for within one hundred yards of the bridge, out of a tuft of grass, Rover sprang puss, and being near at hand, I relieved the game from all further anxiety by tumbling her.

"That's worth shooting at," said my long friend, holding up the hare by her hind legs.

"If I had missed it, and you had not seen it," I said to him, "I daresay you would have thought I had dreamt there was such a thing as a hare hereabouts."

"Waal, I don't say I should not," he replied deliberately.

Yankees are perfectly irrepressible.

At the station we found ourselves in company with three more shooters, none of whom appeared overloaded with birds, so that it was rather impudence than sympathy which prompted my Yankee companion to inquire of one "if he had sent on his game by special train?" The addressed party vouchsafed no reply, however, and we took our seats laughing, I am afraid.

The weather had turned quite mild in the evening, and when we dined at Brighton we agreed to an early start by boat if the weather remained fine, which it fortunately did.

And thus it came to pass that about 10 A.M. on the

following day we were passing Shoreham harbour with a quiet south wind that wafted us along gloriously. Yankee Doodle was there in his element. He had put his long legs out of the way on the thwarts, laid himself down at the bottom of the boat, and told me no end of awful crammers, until my head swam, about what he had done in the boating line in his own country. Anyhow it was amusing, and the boatmen were awfully tickled at having such a good yarner on board, and they drew him out capitally, and he seemed to like it too.

At 11 o'clock we had passed Lancing, a small place, and were nearing Worthing. When I heard one of our men mentioning the name of the latter, I bethought myself of what I had heard the day before at Shoreham respecting it, and told our men that we would just try there. As all on board were agreeable, it was suggested to take down mast and sail, take to the oars, and lay a long line, or else we could anchor and try hooking.

"Look here, friend," said the Yankee, "it will be infernally cold holding wet lines such a day as this. I vote we get a long line out, and see what it will bring forth. If it catches a good many fish, we will set the whole three lines going, and be content with that. Will that do?"

"Beautifully," I said; "just as you like."

And we accordingly got up and took down the mast and sails, whilst the men prepared the line-buoys and anchors. I had told them that we wanted to go to Littlehampton, if possible; but when we agreed to try Worthing, it altered our plans altogether, as far as Littlehampton was concerned, for we could not possibly manage the two places. It took us half an hour sinking our first line, and by the time that one was down, we did not know what to do with ourselves until it would be time for us to take it up. I said that the best plan would be, while we were about it, to lay the three lines.

"Whilst we get the two others baited, buoyed, and anchored safely, it will be time to lift up the first, and when the first is in, and its fish sorted, it will be about time to look after the two others. So I vote that we put down the lot."

As soon proposed as soon carried out; and we all set to work. Yankee thought it rather nasty work to bait the line, but "in for a cent, in for a dollar," said he, "so here goes!"

And so saying, he threw off his overcoat and coat, turned up his shirt-sleeves, and set about the second line with a skill and expedition that betokened no inconsiderable experience on his part in the long-line fishing way.

"Bless you," exclaimed he, "in *my* country we set lines with hooks the size of my head, and we catch gurnards the length of my leg, and cods the length of my body!"

"Now," I said, "considering that you are fully six feet two or three inches, I protest emphatically against your statistics; there must be something wrong somewhere."

But he heeded me not, and asserted things much more wonderful still.

"Large congers, sir, in your country?" asked one of the men.

"Aye, I believe you there! Why, we got one once so large, we could not get him on board."

"What did you do with it?"

"Cut the line; let the brute go!"

"Are you sure it was a conger, sir?"

"Quite sure; why?"

"Because it might have been a sea-sarpint," the man

added slyly, with a wink at my address; "there are plenty of 'em in your country, sir."

The boatman scored there, I think, for Yankee Doodle laughed, opened his mouth, and scratched the tip of his nose with a thoughtful air, but replied nothing.

He soon finished his line, however, and we set it. Then the men did theirs, and we laid it down also.

This done, it was 2 o'clock, and a more hungry lot than we were then could hardly have been matched. The worst of it was we could not go anywhere for refreshments, and all we had on board was a bottle of sherry, which did not go very far among four. You see we had intended going to Littlehampton, and stopping where we were had put us out of our reckoning altogether.

"The only plan I can see," said our senior boatman, "is to wait until the three lines is took up, when it will be time to make tracks back to Brighton; here is my best respects to you, gentlemen!" and saying these words, which took us all by surprise, as he had pronounced the latter part of this speech in just the same tone as its beginning, he threw back his head, and "spliced the mainbrace" with a half-pint glass of dry sherry, which must have done his heart good. The glass emptied, he made a show as if of throwing away the dregs, and passed it to Bill, with the remark that "that was the best as we could do, as far as *he* could see."

"His grammar is not of the best, but his sense is not to be overlooked or despised," remarked my friend. "Let us do as he says. Only I hope I won't die of starvation before we land, that's all!"

We then rowed back to the first line, and began hauling it up. We got a rare lot of gurnards on, several fine brill, an immense plaice, half-a-dozen skate, a codling, and several smaller fish. Yankee thereupon showed his experience in unhooking our fish, and, by himself, he went almost as fast as the three of us put together, seasoning his work, all the while, with such tales as he thought would edify us.

When the three lines were got in, it was 3 o'clock, and time to go. We rigged on the mast once more, hoisted the sail, clapped on the big foresail and jib, and away we went, as merry as could be, in spite of our hunger.

My companion wanted to light a fire to cook a fish or two, but we had no firewood and no stove, and he had to give up his wild fancy.

We got back to Brighton somewhere about 5 o'clock, with some seventy fish of all sizes, and I need not say that we were glad we had spent such a pleasurable day, and were also mighty pleased at being once more on *terra firmâ*, and able to procure anything we wanted in the way of drinks and edibles.

I then arranged for a trip to Littlehampton the following week, if all went well, and Yankee Doodle booked himself to come with me on that expedition.

CHAPTER XLVIII.

LITTLEHAMPTON.

THE wish I had expressed that I should be blessed with fine weather for my next trip was fulfilled, to my great gratification. The sun shone brightly, although the air was rather cold, and not a breath of wind rippled the sea. According to agreement, I telegraphed to my Yankee friend at Brighton that I was coming, and found him on my arrival waiting for me at the station. Even then the weather was very fine, and everything promised us a lovely morrow. My friend had brought his gun and traps with him, so we straightway booked ourselves for Ford Junction. This he could not understand. I explained that the tide was just going to turn, so that we should arrive at Ford in time for a stroll and a "shoot" along the river Arun.

"And where does that river run to?" said he.

"Well, where do all rivers run to?" I replied.

"True," he said; "to the sea, of course. But I mean, to what place will it take us?"

"To Littlehampton, whose harbour is formed by the mouth of the river."

"Well, and when we reach Littlehampton, what shall we do?"

"Why, then the tide will be half down, the sand and mud will be bare, and we will keep on our 'shoot' along the shore. We shall see plenty of birds; they always watch for a receding tide to come down for a feed. Will that do?"

"Your programme," said he, "suits me to a T. Let us make tracks; but first let us liquor up. Waiting here in this smoky station would make a Good Templar drink."

We had a liquor up and took the train. We landed at Ford, with very few more passengers, but there were three other shooters among them.

"That looks well," quoth Doodle; "for if these fellows, who evidently live about here, come down this way, it shows pretty conclusively that there must be birds about."

I signed to him to come along quickly, and we went over the bridge and down by the river-side at once.

"The early bird gets the worm," I explained, "and we had better go ahead, or else these men will get the benefit of the river."

"Truly," said he, "this is another edition of 'The Battle of Life.' Even in shooting, one nowadays must fight one's own way. That is all through this little island of yours being so small, you know. In the U-nited States . . . ."

He was probably going to say a good deal about the said U-nited States, but I cut him short by remarking that there was quite as much competition there as on this side of the water; and, a sandpiper getting up from the bank, I shot it, and that put a stop to any further discussion.

Meanwhile the three men with guns had stopped at the station, and booked themselves to Littlehampton, thinking, probably, that they would "do" us in the long run by getting first to the shore. But I knew better, and

Yankee laughed heartily when I told him how "sold" they would eventually be.

"Why," I said, "this blessed train will not start for another three-quarters of an hour, perhaps. This is a local line, and waits for two or three London and Portsmouth trains to come up; so if we get on as fast as we can we shall be on the shore long before those three shooters turn up."

"What a lark!" he said, "and the best of the fun is they think they are going to serve us out."

Well, we went on, but found only two or three oxbirds. My companion rattled away at fieldfares and starlings, and we also got a shot at a flock of lapwings, bagging two. Then we arrived at Littlehampton, and took a fly to the shore, about a quarter of a mile, just when the Ford train was turning up at the station.

We found the tide running out very strong, and nearly spent, so we put our best feet foremost, and started towards Rustington. The shore there is very flat, and consists of sand and mud, mixed. In that mud there are plenty of worms, and birds invariably come there to feed on them. We had only an hour or so of daylight to spare, and therefore it behoved us to do the best we could in that time. Well, when we were about a quarter of a mile away, on turning round we perceived the three shooters standing at the harbour and looking our way. Probably they were disgusted at our having outdone them. Such is life.

We had divided the shore between us, and as I did not object to getting wet, I had taken charge of the mud and sands near the sea. I had first a rattling double shot in a flock of ring-plovers, flooring eight. Doodle, not to be behindhand, blazed away at them also (though they were virtually out of range), and, to our mutual astonishment, his first barrel brought one down. We then had another quarter-of-an-hour's walk without seeing anything, then we came upon four curlews. We tried to stalk them, but they went their way. Next some flocks of lapwings came over from the fields, but they would not settle, and kept out of range. As for small waders, we saw a good many, and bagged half a dozen before dark, when we held a council of war.

"Where are we now?" asked my companion.

"About a mile and a half from Angmering station. Shall we go there, and book ourselves to Littlehampton? That would take us a couple of hours to do by the celebrated 'local,' you know; or shall we walk back to Littlehampton? We are only a couple of miles from it, and on our way back we may fall in with a duck or two."

We adopted the latter plan and went back. It was dusk then, and if any flighting were to take place we were bound to see some of it. Moreover, the waders had increased to an alarming extent, and we kept popping at them very merrily, filling up the bag most creditably. We saw several "files" of ducks, and my friend fired at one, but much too high. And so we came back to the town, where we had agreed to remain for the night, so as to be ready for the morning's sport.

During the evening we went and arranged with a man to take us out to sea, and to get bait if possible. We had a long confab with him as to the best spots where we could go with a prospect of enjoying ourselves.

"Near Littlehampton," he said, "there is not much to be done. In the harbour, or from the jetty, one may catch a few flounders, eels, and so forth; but outside there is but little to be got unless we go to the Kingston Rocks."

I thought he alluded to Kingston near Shoreham, and told him I did not wish to go there for two reasons, one of which was that it was too far, and the second that I had been there lately. He explained that Kingston near Shoreham is called Kingston-by-Sea, but that the Kingston he alluded to was about four miles from Littlehampton eastward, and the Kingston Rocks were about a mile and a quarter from the shore. Altogether six miles would cover the whole distance.

"And is it a good place?" we inquired.

"Yes," he said, "very fair; plenty of brill there, and crabs, and lobsters, and rockfish."

That would do nicely, so far. Where else could we go? Well, there were the Kingmere Rocks, very fine for lobsters. They were about ten miles away in the Channel, but perhaps the lobster-men would not care much about our going there, as they consider it their own ground.

"As far as that goes," remarked my companion, "we are not going to ask their leave. So if we can manage it we will go there."

This being settled, we went to bed, and early in the morning set off, taking our guns, in case birds came in our way whilst fishing.

The sun was rising in lordly style, and it was a beautiful morning altogether, but, oh, so cold! We at first turned our coat-collars up to our ears, and muffled our legs in our ulsters; but as we could still feel the sharp morning air I stripped off the said ulster and took an oar. Doodle did the same, and we soon were in a glow. But what slow progress one makes at sea when there is no wind to help one along! We crawled, and crawled, and crawled— rowed, rowed, and rowed—and still were in sight of the harbour.

"At this rate, when do you think we shall reach the Kingston Rocks?" I asked our pilot.

"Oh," he said, "we are near them now; it does not look like it, sir, but we are now fully four miles from the harbour."

We were then passing Preston, and Kingston loomed in the distance. Another half-hour, and "There we are, gentlemen," said our boatman.

We then shipped our oars, resumed great-coats, and proceeded to rig on our tackle. The work of rowing had warmed us finely, and when I suggested that hand-line fishing would prove a rather cold and damp sort of sport, Doodle scorned the idea, and bravely went in for it, but half an hour afterwards he was blowing on his fingers and flapping his "wings" violently on his sides to establish a better circulation.

Our bait consisted of a few mackerel and some lugs. I had also brought two spinners, a spoon and a minnow, and meant to try them on our journey to the Kingmere Rocks, though I had no great hopes of doing much good with them.

Whilst at the Kingston Rocks, fishing with our deep lines, we had quite a laughable event to cheer us in our sport. It seems that from some formation of the rocks over which we stood it occasionally happened that our tackle got into some holes totally inaccessible to the fish. Thence an amusing series of scenes was enacted with us in this wise: I would for a time get all the bites and Doodle none. Then, through the boat sheering off he would, I suppose, get his bait into a fine open spot, and have all the bites, whilst mine would then be in a hole, and I got none. Thus it happened in turns that only one of us caught fish. I remember having experienced just such a treat at Dalkey Island on one occasion, when we were four fishing from a boat, two on either side, when, according as the boat shifted, the starboard or port side fishers would have all the fun.

We stopped fishing at 11 A.M., a rather early hour, but the fact was the keen air of the sea, combined with our early rising, had sharpened our appetites, and we could hold out no longer. Doodle had been since 10 o'clock bothering me about our luncheon-basket, reverting with such gusto to the provisions it contained that my mouth watered, and I could not keep away from it any longer.

To begin with, we cleared our seats of bait, etc., as being no very appetising sight when fellows mean to have a try at their luncheon. This done, I solemnly opened the hamper, and handed its contents to Doodle, who placed them in respectable order astern ; the bottles below, and the eatables on the seat. We then set to, and our boatman, nothing loath, was pleased to accept such delicacies as we thought but fit and proper we should offer him.

Have you ever, reader, had a lunch on the sea on a brilliant autumn day? No. Well, then, let me inform you that you eat twice as much as in summer time ; and since we in this world live to eat (if we are to believe certain philosophers), and the sea is such an excellent appetite invigorator, one cannot do better than go there in cold weather. At any rate, we did wonderfully well, and were astonished when we had done to see how little we had left.

Luncheon discussed, it was 12 o'clock, and the tide was just on the turn.

"If we get up her anchor now," quoth our man, "we shall have a fair tide to go over to the Kingmere Rocks, and could leave there for harbour at the next flow."

Whilst preparing to get under weigh I observed a diver at no great distance from the boat, and it evidently took us for ordinary fishermen, and never thought of guns. I quietly picked up Doodle's duck-gun, which was loaded and at half-cock on the seat; I cocked it, "unbeknownst" to anybody, and if ever any bird and any fellows were astonished that bird and my companions were. The boom startled Doodle nearly overboard, and the boatman for a moment seemed dumfoundered.

"Haul away!" I said, "and let us pull. There is the bird, perfectly dead."

And so it was. This was not, by a long way, the first diver it has been my luck to kill outright at the first shot; and I will tell you how I manage it, for it is a wrinkle worth knowing. Problem to be solved : Given a tolerably smooth sea, a diver within sixty yards, a good duck-gun loaded with something better than dust-shot or bullets, and a fellow who can aim passably straight, how is he to proceed in order to bag the said diver? If you aim at the bird, and he sees the flash, he will be down, and out of harm's way long before the shot reaches him. But if you aim quietly, and wait for pulling the trigger until the bird turns his head away from you, there are good odds that you will bag him. The explanation lies in a nutshell, and I will give it to the best of my ability. The fact is, sound does not travel faster than shot propelled by good powder, and therefore before the bird can hear the explosion, the lead has reached him. If, consequently, you bide your time, and only fire when the bird cannot see the flash, you are pretty safe to have him, all other conditions being reasonable. If, however, by any chance the bird can see the flash, down he will go like lightning, and you will probably have a tedious and long chase after him. This, then, is the explanation. Light being so quick in travelling that it is instantaneous for a short distance, and sound on the contrary, travelling by slow coach, if you take care that the bird can only depend on the latter, it will eventually become yours. Q. E. D.

To return to our muttons—*i.e.*—fish, we went to the Kingmere block of rocks, filled with enthusiasm. We reached the rocks in an hour's half sail and half row, and our first catch there was a monster gurnard, which came up with a mouth as wide open as a blatant democrat's when he "holds forth" against those landlords who stupidly and unfeelingly decline giving up what they have had so much trouble to acquire, for the benefit of vagabonds and idlers who care only for loafing.

Well, the said gurnard was a beauty, but he was mighty awkward to handle. He had such a hard head, so full of sharp points and corners, that holding him in the hand was out of the question. We rolled a table-napkin round his gurnardship, and then we had a good look for the hook, which he had managed to swallow to an extraordinary depth. This being the case, we looked around to see if no members of the Society for the Prevention of Cruelty to Animals were near, in a lobster-pot boat close at hand, and satisfied that the two men at work therein were not disguised officials, but honest *bonâ fide* toilers of the sea, we resorted to an operation; and Yankee Doodle, who performed it, declared that, like the tooth-extracting surgeon, he had done the deed, *sans peine et sans douleur!* "Joining," exclaimed he, "mercy to science, I have succeeded in removing the foreign substance, and there it is!" holding it up at arm's length. The lobster-men, who regarded him with astonishment, had caught so far half a score of lobsters, and some of them were very fine fellows. Unfortunately, the poor men had been kept away from their work a good while, on account of the bad weather they had experienced, so that theirs had been a rather precarious calling, but now that the weather seemed to have settled in some degree, they were hard at work, trying to make up for lost time. It must, in truth, be very awkward to have to rely on the state of the weather for one's living, but then, as the men said, "good and bad, put together, ain't quite unbearable." And they are quite right. Confidence in one's pursuit, and good sense in a sufficient dose to take the rough and the smooth as they choose to come, are the proper ingredients wherewith to carry on any manly calling.

The men left us to go to the north belt of rocks, and we carried on our hooking with but little interruption until past 2, when we really began to feel benumbed, in spite of our warm overcoats. Yankee Doodle was the first to remark on the state of affairs.

"I could not, at this moment," said he, "take my oath that I possess the usual number of toes; and, as for my nose, it is lucky I can see it, for, otherwise, I should think it was gone."

"Well," I returned, "it is red enough to be very hot instead of cold; but look here, old fellow, if you are tired of this, let us be off by all means."

Off we went accordingly, and began warming ourselves with a row for a good half-hour. Then we relinquished the oars to our worthy boatman, and sorted our fish, packing up only half a dozen of the best, and leaving the others for the man. We did not forget the diver either. We had caught about thirty fair fish, amongst which we had two handsome brill, several fine gurnard, and two or three very good whiting. The remainder were smaller. Still, enough is as good as a feast, even in sea-fishing; and a whole day at it, with little if any interruption, will satisfy the most ardent hooker, simply because the fun palls on one, through having nothing else to fall back upon and vary it with. At the same time, in an open boat, what could we do else? Nothing. Had there been any birds about we should have gone in chase, but the diver was the only big bird we had seen.

Of course, if we had been in a decked boat—in a yacht, for instance—matters would have been considerably modified, and we could have resorted to the usual dodges inherent to yachting, such as trawling, taking a cruise to some spot, going below for a game at cards, for a feed, for a glass, for a pipe, for a sleep, or for a read; but in a small open boat all these are well-nigh impossible luxuries.

Well, when we had got everything in order I tumbled on my spoon and phantom minnow, and the thought then struck us to try them whilst we were going back towards Littlehampton harbour. We each got a line, and were soon at it.

After five minutes of this sport I volunteered the original remark that I had not had a bite. Doodle said the fish were "scarce," beyond all doubt, and the boatman shaking his head grimly, we put off whiffing and resumed our seats. Winding up our lines, however, brought them in contact, and we had our work cut out to disentangle them. We arrived at dusk at Littlehampton, just when the lighthouse began to shed its light, and thus ended our adventures. A more favourable day no man could have, and we enjoyed to the utmost the glorious sun, the bright green sea, the keen, bracing air, and the entertaining sport of hooking.

CHAPTER XLIX.

BOGNOR, MIDDLETON, AND BARN ROCKS.

THE aspect of the sea-shore at Bognor is rather more depressing than cheerful, owing to the numerous tops of black stakes that crop up all over the sands, making them resemble, to some extent, an old and neglected burial-ground. These stakes are, I suppose, the local break-sands, and therefore are very useful in their way; the pity is that they are otherwise an eyesore and a nuisance. How, for instance, can one enjoy a walk there? It is almost impossible, at least as regards the east side of the shore, for the wooden impediments crop up there every few yards. This being the case, I should very much like to know on what authority certain guide-books recommend the place as having "a good beach." I don't call that a good beach by any manner of means, and for cheerfulness it can be put on a par with that at Seaford. Nevertheless, Bognor boasts of a good sea-frontage, of pure air, and of a delightful situation—at least so says one guide-book.

As regards the purity of the air, nobody can doubt that, and I would back Bognor against any town, almost, as regards health; but, bless me! we want something more besides pure air to make life enjoyable. It is all very well for a dozen old maids or so to go for walks along that fine sea-frontage, and have their fill of that pure air; but to other beings, with more vital energy than the aforementioned old maids, the pure air palls at last, when there is nothing more to be had; and for fun, therefore, I would back Littlehampton to lick Bognor into fits—at least in seafowl-shooting, if not in air and in sea-fishing. Besides, to some people the salt marshes (even when they do not shoot over them) are perfectly unobjectionable, and I believe those who are said to have died early through having lived near marshy lands have died because they thought they could not live there. Imagination goes a long way in such matters. Those Bognor old maids will live to Methuselah's age, simply through believing that they ought to do so, on account of the pure air, and they would die in a week at Shoreham if they thought the mud flats would hurt them. As for myself, a week at Bognor would kill me with *ennui*, for there is absolutely nothing to be done there barring very fair sea-fishing. As regards the latter, it ought to be still better than I found it, considering that rocks abound in the neighbourhood. On the west are the Barn Rocks, about two miles from Bognor; opposite Bognor itself, and about a mile out on the right side of the pier, are the Bognor Rocks; and on the east, some two-and-a-half miles, half-way between Bognor and Middleton, are what are called the Middleton Reefs, or the Middleton Ledge. Now, with such a variety of spots the sport ought to be unexceptionably good, but it was only very fair, and that was all.

From the pier itself (a very long one, with an insecure appearance, owing probably to its length and the apparent slenderness of its iron piles) there is not much to be done, and, in fact, I was astonished at the meagre sport to be had there. The best parts of that pier, I take it, are the stairs at the head, from whence one may cast in all directions; but for some reason or other best known to themselves, the large fish won't come there. I went there on my arrival with a line or two and bait, found a young fellow trying his best, and entered into conversation with him. He had caught about half-a-dozen whiting, small ones, and complained of being bothered by the boatmen and fishermen, who were continually drawing to or leaving the stairs in their craft.

"I wish the beggars luck," said he, "but I also wish them anywhere but here. When I chance to hit upon a nice spot up comes one of the lumberly boats, and I have to haul up as quick as possible, and sometimes lose a line as well, in spite of having made all haste."

"Well, but," I remarked, "why don't you fish higher up, towards shore? The fishermen would not come in your way there."

"No," he said, "they would not. But then I should have to contend against the eddies round the piles; and, besides, there are no fish there."

This last reason was quite sufficient in itself to explain his unwillingness to remove, and was on a par with that given by the authorities of a small seaport for not firing salutes on the arrival of a royal personage. They gave about ninety excuses for not doing so, and concluded by saying they had no cannon, which in itself, methinks, was a sufficient reason why they could not fire any.

Well, having cheered the pier-angler in his pursuit, and satisfied myself, after waiting a quarter of an hour to see what he would catch, that his chances of making a nice creel that day were decidedly remote, I entered into a bargaining match with a surly fisherman, who was going out to lay crab and lobster pots. He thought at first I was chaffing him when I asked him about going with him, hence his surliness.

"Fish!" he exclaimed, in answer to my inquiries, "yes, there be plenty of fish where I be going, but I must first put down my pots. When that is done I will anchor the boat in a nice place, and I daresay you will catch as many fish as you like then, if so it be that you really mean coming."

"Of course I do," I returned, and went down and stepped into his roomy boat. "What made you think I was only having a bit of fun with you?"

"Oh!" he said, "that be easily explained. Whenever there be any promenaders on the pier they be always bothering us fishermen with questions as to fish, where to go, how many they would catch; what we would charge them for an hour, for two hours, for three hours; and could they have it a little cheaper if they went the whole afternoon, or maybe the whole day? And then, when they have kept us waiting, and talking, and giving them all the information we can, and offering to take them at the most reasonable of terms, they say they will think about it, and we never see them again about the matter. So I thought you were one of that stamp, and I was not going to be humbugged again, not if I knew it."

Well, now, there is some truth in that accusation against visitors to the sea-side. Some fellows dress like awful swells, and talk "tall" to suit their clothes, but they never spend a farthing beyond their cheap lodgings and meals, and are always making a grand fuss with the boatmen and fishermen of the place, just as if these people were inferior beings, who ought to feel highly complimented and immensely gratified at the condescension of his highness the City clerk, who lowers himself so far as to bring himself on a level with them. It is really laughable. But the time is past when a fisherman was a poor devil, literally starving on his earnings, for many a boatman and fisherman nowadays makes as good a living as most men of, supposed to be, higher stations in life than they, and a patronising air is to such men highly offensive. Besides, to them, more, perhaps, than to anyone else, time is money, because as the tides wait for no man, they do not wait for them, and they must make the best of everyone of them, if they wish to get on. Therefore, fiddling about, and inquiring from them just when their work ought to be taken in hand, is a silly proceeding, and that is why many fishermen look at first with distrust on any inquirer who wishes to try sea-fishing. Nine out of ten of such inquirers have no thought whatsoever of trying it. They talk to the fishermen because it looks *de bon ton*, and they like caps to be touched to them; but precious little real business is transacted out of many of these pertinacious inquirers. And that is not as it should be.

Well, the weather being quiet, though very cold, there were a good many boats out, laying and lifting up their pots, so that we were quite a little fleet together. There were also two or three pleasure-boats (sailing-boats) from Littlehampton, and of these one came to an anchor near the south point of the rocks. They then brought down their sails and began fishing. I had to remain idle in our boat until the pots on board were down. This was effected very quickly, with the help of another man on whom my boatman called for assistance. I was wondering within myself how he would have managed it otherwise, and asked him if I should help him. I did not mind, and would have liked it, in fact, for it was beastly cold and silly work to be sitting there doing nothing.

Bognor, Middleton, and Barn Rocks.

"If you like I will row," I said to the man, "and you may put your concerns overboard."

"Thank you, sir," said he; "if so it be that you are cold, you and I will each take an oar and row; but I see several friends of mine yonder, and I will ask one of them to come in here and lend a hand."

Out, then, of another boat our new companion turned up. When called he waved his hand, and when his lot were out they rowed to us, and he came into our craft.

Our job done, we came to an anchor, and I produced my bait. I lent a line to one of the men, and he chose to bait with some crabs he had in his boat. We then lighted our pipes, tucked up our coat-collars, and set to work in earnest.

The first thing that struck me was the shallowness of the water. I never had more than three or four fathoms of line out, hence our not catching many monsters. Very large fish, as a rule, keep somewhat farther out to sea, and like deeper water than that. Nevertheless, we caught some decent fish, but not so many as I should have been led to suppose by the conformation of the ground. I had fully made up my mind to make such a monster creel that my own basket would have been insufficient to take home my catches, so I had brought a net-bag or two in order to make sure of having sufficient accommodation for them. But I only caught eight passable fish, and I need not add that, had they chosen to do so, they could have danced the Lancers within my creel, and have then had room and to spare.

When we had been some hour and a half thus engaged, we found the tide rising fast and night getting nigh, so we had to pack up and be off.

I arranged with my man to go on the morrow to the

Barn Rocks, and, if possible, to the Middleton Ledge as well, and then we parted. He could not understand why I wanted to try those two places, since, as he averred, the Bognor Rocks were by far the best, both in extent and in position.

"You can do very well there," he said before we parted, "and be near the town. If I were you I would stick to those rocks."

But every man knows his business best, and I wanted to see what the other spots were like, and had therefore fully made up my mind to go there.

We had landed at dusk, and when I made my way through the town I heard in the direction of Aldwick several shots fired consecutively, at ducks, I presumed, as it was flight time. The lands towards Aldwick are rather flat, and I daresay some of the inland pools are pretty fair in hard weather, but of course they are in private hands. I had observed also during the day many flocks of lapwings in the cultivated fields and over the waste lands, so that those who have the right to sport thereabouts may do tolerably well occasionally. I saw three or four shooters subsequently; they were together, and appeared anything but highly elated, from whence I concluded that their sport had, like mine, been of a rather meagre description.

The next day turned out as fine as could be wished, but very cold, and a little snow began falling. Naturally I did not get up very early, so that when my friend of the Littlehampton and Shoreham trips turned up he found me in bed.

"Waal!" he exclaimed, "had I known this, I guess I would not have hurried so much. As it is, I came without my breakfast."

"So much the better," I rejoined, jumping out of bed,

Bognor, Middleton, and Barn Rocks. 117

"I hate having a meal by myself; now you will keep me company."

We went downstairs and found the place thoroughly dull-looking. There was no one about in the street, the shop-doors were all closed, and the shopkeepers, probably, cozy in their back parlours. Bognor is one of those out-of-the-way places where the good old-fashioned system of doing no business when the weather is bad is still stuck to, and a very good plan it is too. So that whenever it rains, hails, or snows, everybody makes up his mind to make himself comfortable, as there is not the slightest shadow of a probability that anyone would dream of coming to bother them about purchases or gossip. The consequence is that Bognor, in nasty weather, is as quiet as a Quaker meeting; and as the Bognor folk fear wet as much as they would the black gentleman himself, there is not, consequently, a soul to be seen, then, in the streets.

Our breakfast was, notwithstanding these outward damping signs, of a rather jolly character, owing to the superabundance of our animal spirits.

"We must have *le diable au corps*," irreverently quoth Doodle, who was going to join me, "to think of going to sea in such infernally cold weather. True, we are not obliged to, and probably that is why we do not mind it; but I know, for a positive fact, that were a law just now passed compelling me to go fishing in such weather, I would say the law was a swindle, and that it was a blank shame to send a Christian out in such times; there! Such is human nature."

Having delivered himself thus, Doodle attired himself in so many great-coats and mufflers that when he had done he looked twice his original size, and his back being turned when I came in with the things, I did not recognise his contour in the least, for, instead of a lean and long individual, which he naturally is, there now was before my astonished eyes a man of portly dimensions and apparently quite respectable weight!

We went towards the pier and saw our men waiting.

"Cold weather, gentlemen," said one of them. "We thought you would not come. Step in, sir, on the seat. Right you are. Let go, John;" and we were off.

A lovely sea, but a dirty sky; not stormy, but leaden-hued, and very low, laden evidently with snow. We got a few flakes whilst on our way to the Middleton Ledge, which we reached in something less than an hour, and a precious cold look-out we had when we reached it. Still we had not come so far for nothing, and accordingly we prepared our lines. My friend had been whiffing part of the way, but had not had a bite.

"If hooking is as successful as whiffing," said he, as he wound up his first line, and got the second one ready, "our stay here, methinks, will be short-lived; what do you say?"

Of course I quite assented, and we began. We caught under a dozen fish in an hour, and not two alike, except three whitings; the others were a regular mixture.

But what a difference there is in the feeling of a line according to the sort of fish that is hooked. The whiting hang on, dead-like; then, as you begin hauling, they dart here and there rather suddenly, but that is all—they soon tire. The codling pulls all the way, but does not go quickly about it. He seems taking it cool, as though the fact that he was caught had not yet reached his intellect. Flounders flounder about "considerable," and no mistake, as do most flat-fish; but for obstinacy and unruliness, commend me to a good-sized skate! It comes up just as readily as a large slate would if it pertinaciously *would* keep parallel to the bottom of the sea, and possessed, withal, a screw of one-horse power, more or less, at its tail. Dab! slap! whish! it goes; and so vicious it does look, too, when you finally get it in and proceed to get your hook out of her skateship. They have, however, a very good point, viz. they don't keep you in suspense. A skate that means feeding does feed; and when it means feeding on your bait, you very soon know it, for it goes at it like a bull at a gate, and then shakes the line like a thousand *diables*. Those fishermen who are not accustomed to the pulls of skates are generally very much deceived when they catch one, for one is always likely to make out, at a rough calculation, that the as yet unseen fish must somehow weigh at least four times as much as it actually does when brought to boat. On the other hand, when the skate, whilst being hauled up, suddenly turns up sideways, its body acts as a thin wedge in the water, and you would almost think you had lost your fish, were it not for a certain undefinable something, a sort of quiver, along the line that indicates something on yet, although you can hardly then feel its weight. Finally, the fish abruptly resumes a flat position, and wriggles and dabs about quite unexpectedly, and roughly enough to try your tackle if the fish be large and the line old, or is made of inferior stuff.

Well, I should think that the Middleton Ledge, in nice warm weather, would be a very likely place for visitors to try a little sea-fishing during the bathing season. Of course, in winter the shore does not look half so nice by any means as it does in summer time; but one can very well picture to one's mind how it appears during the fine season, when visitors are on the beach and on the bank, and when the fields are in all the glory of their summer grass and flowers. Yes, it must be a rather pretty spot. It was decidedly gloomy when we were there, simply because the season was against it, and a few flakes of snow falling around you on the sea does not improve one's point of view, or make things look more cheerful by any means.

We tripped our anchor at 1 o'clock, and went back to Bognor for luncheon. Calling at the town did not take us out of our way, as the place we wished to reach during the afternoon was on the other side of it, and about the same distance from it as the Middleton Ledge.

At half-past 2 we re-embarked and went over the rocks where I had fished the previous day. In fact, I think the Barn Rocks are but a continuation of the Bognor Rocks, and are probably connected with them by a long belt of low reef. We found half-a-dozen boats about, but all were professionals. We were the only amateurs afloat, and no wonder.

I intended coming back to town by the 5-something P.M. train, and we had, therefore, but a very short time to try our new ground in. One hour and a half, at the utmost, is never much at any time, and that was all we could spare if I wished to make sure of not losing my train. We began close to shore, and I caught a conger, Doodle secured a whiting, a pouting, and a gurnard, and we removed west, where we found the fish quite on the feed. It always happens so. It is generally when you cannot stop that catches are likely to be frequent. We hooked every moment almost, and soon filled a basket of pouting and whiting, together with a few gurnards and an odd conger and brill. We were all of us exceedingly hard at work. The two men cut and otherwise prepared the bait, and got each dose ready. Moreover, they helped us to unhook and rebait, so as to save time, and we went on like steam.

Meanwhile the evening breeze sprang up, and some more snow fell. I suggested, then, the advisability of getting up our moorings and going.

"If a heavy fall of snow should come down and intercept the light of the lighthouse," I said, "we should not be able to make our way quickly ashore, and I must not be later there than 5 o'clock. I therefore think we had better go. The wind is rising too, and, worse luck, getting foul, and we will have our work cut out as it is to reach the pier in time."

So it was. A nasty land-breeze had blown our bows right up towards shore and our stern to sea, and it was plain that, under the circumstances, ours would be a long and tedious pull against both wind and tide. The men, however, are accustomed to that sort of thing, and never put themselves out, which is quite correct when you have nothing better to do; but when one is anxious to be ashore in time, for some particular purpose, it is annoying to see your men taking things cool. Ours did at first, but they soon warmed to their work, then we joined in, and soon made good way. It was not then much more than 3.45 P.M., and as we had only a mile and a half to row in order to reach our destination, I calculated that there was no occasion, after all, to worry ourselves about getting ashore in time; and as the men declared that they had seen an amateur, a few days before, catching fish on that very ground with a spinner, I made up my mind to try a little whiffing; but it was so very cold, that handling the wet lines had been, throughout, anything but enjoyable, and now regulating the sinker on my whiffing-line taxed my powers of endurance severely. At last I got a sinker that suited, as it neither put the line too low nor too high, and I cast it over the stern. To my astonishment, I had scarcely let out twenty yards or so, and was just feeling how the line stood, when it caught. I thought it had gone too deep, and was hooked in some weeds or rocks.

"Hold on!" I called out to the men, whilst I let out more line. "Back water now!" and they did so, when I began taking up the line again. "Confound it," I said, "it is a new spinner, and I have had too much bother to put it on to lose it now; we will back carefully, so as to disentangle it. If it breaks I won't spin again, for fitting a new spinner would freeze my fingers off."

But, in the midst of my talking, the line suddenly got taut, and the welcome tug sent a thrill through me. "It is a fish, by Jove!" I called out triumphantly; and I would not then have changed places with the Prince of Wales, though I had frequently, during the previous fortnight, wished I were in his shoes, just to enjoy the sports he was having in India. Well, I hauled in my prize—a stunningly-fine gurnard, about two pounds weight. Doodle was wild with excitement.

"Let me have a try," said he; "that is grand fun!"

He tried, and we caught, all told, three more nice fish—one pollack and two gurnards. Meanwhile, the fun of the thing had diverted everybody's attention from the ultimate object of our row; that is usually the case when sport is concerned, but we still managed to land in good time for my train.

The shooting in the fields was still going on, as it had been the day before, but it must have been at thrushes and fieldfares, or some such small fry, as we could not see any flighting taking place anywhere about the horizon.

Thus ended our trip. We got, my friend and I, into the

train as far as Barnham Junction. There we parted. I took the next London Bridge train, which happened to travel *via* Horsham, whilst my companion had to wait for a Brighton train. On the journey back I fell in with a sporting clergyman, who happened to be alone in the compartment I chose, and we went in so heartily about shooting, fishing, coursing, and hunting, that when we arrived at London Bridge we had not packed up our rugs, &c., thinking we were only about half-way yet! Such is the love of sport in sportsmen.

My next trip was on the Blackwater, in Essex. The owner of the *Fairy* had asked me to join him again in a three days' excursion, yachting, shooting, and sea-fishing; of course I accepted, and of course I will let my readers know in the next chapter what luck befell us in our trip. Till then, *Au revoir*, friendly reader, and *portez vous bien*.

CHAPTER L.

THE BLACKWATER (ESSEX).

OWING to the severity of the weather I found it impossible, on my trip to the Blackwater with the owner of the *Fairy*, even to attempt a little sea-fishing. The weather was bitterly cold, and had driven all the fish worth catching to deeper water. The week before a few good catches of whiting had been made on the Colne and at the mouth of the Blackwater; but the weather was by far more open then, and I was informed by Barnes, the captain, that a good many large whiting had been taken there with the hook. The sprat fishery is still carried on as usual, and we saw two or three sprat smacks at work opposite St. Peter's-on-the-Walls; and as one of the said smacks eventually crowded all sail and headed towards Heybridge, we concluded that the catches had been good, and that this smack was the "carrier to market." There were, besides, a few trawlers out; but there was, in truth, but very little doing. The sea was moderately rough at times, with occasional splendid outbursts, which sent our gunwale under water and knocked our furniture about; but of all this more anon.

First of all, we began badly, owing to some misunderstanding. The owner had telegraphed to Barnes, from my instructions, to take the *Fairy* round to Heybridge basin, near Maldon, and to send the lad to meet us at the railway station, as we were sure to have a tidy load of luggage, besides our guns.

Well, worthy Barnes found, on his arrival at Heybridge, that the yacht would have to sit on the mud; and not liking it, he ran her into the Heybridge lock, where he remained until we turned up. This we did at about 6 P.M., and found the lad Isaiah (what a fine name for a sailor!) waiting for us. It being very dark, and snow half a foot or more thick on the ground, we sought a conveyance to take us and our traps to Heybridge. We then drove to the "Blue Boar," and, after dining, were driven to our destination. Judge, then, of my astonishment when I found the yacht lying against the quay! Here was a pickle! The tide would not be high till 5 A.M., and as it would not then be safe to take the yacht out of the lock in the darkness, she was positively "locked up" there until the following tide in the afternoon. This was an awful "sell" to us.

But as it was of no use to grumble, I ventured to suggest that, if the dingey were available, we would take it and go down the river with it until such time as the yacht could be got out. With this understanding we retired to bed. When we awoke in the morning we found a tremendous fog on the river. Nothing daunted, however, we went on; but it was rather dreary work at first, as the fog completely surrounded us, and shut the shores from our view altogether.

We went down as far as the Osea Island, and there went ashore for a tramp; our feet being perfectly benumbed with cold and our beards covered with icicles. When we had walked as far as the shingle would allow us, and had got somewhat warmer and more comfortable, we re-embarked and went over to beat the long creek that goes to Mundon. There we found plenty of curlews, greenshanks, and redshanks, besides many different species of sandpipers, and altogether we bagged some ten or twelve birds.

The sun then had dispelled the fog, but dark clouds had collected astern, and a heavy fall of snow began. This was the straw that broke the camel's back. As we could not see to shoot, our presence in the small boat had absolutely no *raison d'être*, and we turned her head back towards Heybridge, where we arrived at about 2 P.M., very glad to find a good fire and a warm cabin. After luncheon and several pipes, the lock-keeper came with the welcome information that he could let us through, and that tedious process began. In something like twenty minutes we were off. There was no wind to speak of, so Isaiah had to tow the boat along, and Barnes lent him a hand with a sweep. When, however, we rounded the point off the Northex Island a slight breeze sprang up, and down the river we went. Now the channel being rather narrow and the marsh under water, it behoved us to be careful where we went, if we did not wish her to be stuck; but as there were several barges and ships about, both sailing and at anchor in the roads, we took counsel from their bearings and managed to get as far as Goldhanger Creek, near which we anchored for the night.

I woke up in the night, went on deck, found the sky clear, the river very black, and the wind on the roar. Went back shivering to my berth, and did not wake up until 7 A.M., when I heard Barnes about, and we set sail. Just as we were starting Isa signalled two ducks ahead. I got a long single-barrelled 6-bore gun that was on board, and with some trouble loaded it, as it is a muzzle-loader, and I did not know what were its proper allowances of powder and shot.

At last, when all was ship-shape, a blessed punter turned up, and began working to the birds! When he was about sixty yards from them he pulled trigger and killed one, the second getting off, I believe, unscathed. The trick was nevertheless very well done, and it looked a pretty picture in the early morning to see the man lying in his white punt, paddling quietly to the birds, sighting the gun, and finally letting go its contents. When he had picked up his bird he went to the lee-shore, and ran his punt aground to reload his swivel. By that time we were fairly under weigh and flying down the river.

Of course there might have been a few straggling birds about; but as we knew there were flocks in the Main, we despised such small fry in the hope of meeting with the hosts, and contented ourselves with shooting at a diver and a grebe. Thus we went on, passing Rolles and the creek east of it, when I sighted the first company. My sight has always been of the keenest, and I can detect birds half a mile off on the sea. No sooner had I announced the welcome news than we took our stations.

Mr. B. went in and stood in the fore-hatchway, and I stuck in the cockpit with the long gun, and my new 12-bore gun at hand for the cripples. This weapon is on the modified choke-bore principle (Messrs. Tolley, of Birmingham, are the makers), and I am perfectly satisfied with its performance. It shoots rather close, and I like it, as it drives very hard. The Schultze cartridges answer admirably. Their recoil is far less than that of ordinary powder, and I think they carry shot far quicker than black powder. In fact, it is almost instantaneous—pull, and the bird is dead. Whereas with black powder you can almost take off your eye from the barrel when you have pulled, and then see where your shot is going. I therefore think that the Schultze is, in every way, preferable to the last, and have, ever since, used it exclusively. I was told before starting by Captain B. (brother to the owner of the *Fairy*) that the Schultze cartridges, two or three years ago, were rather weak. I do not know if such was the case then, as this was the first time I had given them a trial; but one thing is certain, the cartridges supplied to me were superior to any I had yet used, and I think it but fair to state this in the common interest of sportsmen.

With a fair wind taking us onwards I called out the proper directions to Barnes, who was at the tiller, according to the way the birds chose to swim away from us, as they invariably do when they see a boat crowding on them.

" Port, Barnes!"

" Port it is, sir!" he answered.

" Steady!" I whispered.

" Steady it is!"

Then, as we were getting too near the birds to speak at all, I signalled the helmsman with my hand, and up we came with them. When we were about a hundred yards from them they began to "smell a rat," and crowded together. At ninety yards the leaders rose, and the company followed suit, and I sent the contents of the 6-bore after them. Mr. B. fired both barrels in the thick, but they all went their way, though one or two " hanged fire" considerably. Better luck next time.

Ten minutes elapsed without anything of importance' happening, although we were kept all the while on the *qui vive* by single birds and small companies on the wing, some of them passing across our bows within a hundred and twenty yards.

Finally I saw, a long way ahead, a lot of black heads and necks dancing on the waves.

"Another company ahead!" I sang out.

"Whereabouts?" asked Barnes.

"Starboard."

"Will that do, sir?" said he, after luffing a point or two.

"Finely," I replied; "now you are right in a line with them; keep her a little farther to leeward—that's it!"

We again took up the guns, and were once more frustrated, the company rising before we could get within range.

Then a heavy fall of snow began, and we had to get all the ammunition for shelter on the table in the cabin, out of the way of dampness. Moreover, it came down so thickly, it was so cold, and the wind blew so cuttingly, that we had to put on extra coats and rig on rugs around us. Still, as it is just in such snow-storms that one is most likely to overreach the birds, I kept watching, and we soon had a crack at a company. They were about fifteen all told, and we were then taking a long tack from West Mersea to the Buxey when I first spied them. This time I went forward with the long gun, and when they rose I was fortunate enough to hit one and disable it—a fine mallard. He fell and tried to get away, but could not. As, however, he would not let us pick him up we gave him a barrel or two out of the 12-bores, and he dived desperately, only to come up belly upwards.

Then Isa jumped into the dingey and went to pick him up.

Thus we kept going the best part of the day, firing a score of shots and getting five birds. The fact of the matter was, we wanted large guns for that sort of work, and the muzzle-loader we had did not answer as well as it should have done, perhaps because we did not know what loads would suit it. Besides, it was so long in the barrel as to make it awkward to fire with the motion of the boat jerking one about. Had we had two or three 4-bores like the one I use for such work in winter-time we should have bagged, I am certain, forty ducks, for I have rarely seen such a number of birds on the Main. There were swans, black geese, divers innumerable, teal, widgeon, wild duck, &c. &c., in perfect shoals. The puntsmen were all out, and several punt smacks were at them also, with their heavy swivels rigged in the bows. Altogether a better time to kill wildfowl there had not been for the last ten years, I should say. The shores were positively lined on the flats with fowl, and if the men, better armed than we were, did not get home with heavy loads they must be far worse hands than I take them to be. Had we had a swivel-gun rigged forward, we could have bagged a hundred birds.

The best spots were: first, between Shingle Point and Sales Point; secondly, between West Mersea and Sales Point; and, thirdly, anywhere in the main, *i.e.* along Sales Point, St. Peter's-on-the-Walls, Eashall, Sandbeach, the St. Peter Sands, and the Dengie flats.

The bother was that we could not get near enough to the shore, as the tide only covers the flats to the height of several feet. Of course, that is where the largest flocks remained, and the yacht could not go there; she draws too much water for that sort of work. I have rarely enjoyed myself more, and though Mr. B. declared that the weather would try the constitution of a white bear, I rather enjoyed it than otherwise. Smooth sailing is too tame for me, and I soon get tired of it; but when a good wind is blowing then there is some fun, and I never mind the cold. In fact, there is hardly anything more exhilarating than such a cruise in a sailing yacht. I dislike steam-vessels (at least for pleasure) for many reasons: first, you can't shoot with them, and you can't fish with them. They rarely, if ever, sail well, if they can sail at all, and it is a great nuisance to have to wait, in an emergency, until "the steam is up." It is alleged by the partisans of steam that in a gale or a half-gale they can at any rate try to hold their own, and perhaps will get ahead somewhat. But this is also the case with a sailing yacht. A sound boat of that description will stand a most terrific turn at knocking about, and will literally fly in a half-gale. In a gale, with half the reefs in, she can go as fast as most steam concerns. Some people entertain a hazy notion that a steam-launch would be just the thing to knock about with and try to overreach wildfowl. Those who tried the experiment I warrant altered their minds. The idea that a steam-boat is the best thing that can be devised for shooting wildfowl is a most erroneous one. The smoke and the noise are quite sufficient of themselves to drive the flocks away, and killing any birds worth having is almost an impossibility, except in the case of cripples, or in overhead flights. A sailing yacht, say a 10 or a 12 tonner, is just the sort of thing for the purpose. A 6-tonner is still better in one way, viz. it draws less water, but it is worse in the other, inasmuch as it has very little accommodation for the sportsmen; whereas a well-built 12-tonner, with a plan properly laid down, ought to accommodate, pretty comfortably, two shooters and two sailors, fore and aft. In such a boat it is a pleasure to be out, and I can conceive no greater treat to a man than being either at the hatchway, in the fo'c'sle, or in the cockpit, on the look-out for the birds. The buffeting of the wind, the sharp sea air, the occasional spray in the face, lend to the pursuit a perfect enchantment. At least, " them is my principles, to which I sticks,'· But, then, I am an acknowledged enthusiast in these matters; so much so, that on our return from Blackwater, the owner of the *Fairy*, relating to our fellow-travellers in the train our experiences of the fun, described me as being perfectly sport-mad.

The snow came down in blinding sheets, but we stuck to our work like leeches, and enjoyed it amazingly. We had a rather rough time of it, but then one must take the rough with the smooth, and wildfowl-shooters are always ready to do that, when there is sport to be obtained.

At 2 P.M. we sailed to the Colne Point, turned her head to the wind, and all went below for luncheon. Whilst thus engaged another blinding fall of snow came down. In fact, the weather throughout was first-rate for wildfowl-shooting.

As for fishing, I cannot add anything to what I have stated at the beginning of this chapter. The mullet had gone, the whiting had gone, and barring sprat-netting and trawling for plaice, dabs, and soles, there was no fishing worth mentioning. In ordinary weather there are some very fine spots about the Blackwater, and in years gone by I have done very well indeed there with the mullet.

Some of my readers are, perhaps, not aware that mullet are rarely, if ever, caught within the jaw, most of them being positively hooked outside. The hooks for mullet are square, not rounded as ordinary hooks, and the fish rarely gobble up the bait. They come and fuss about it, nibbling at it, and so forth, so that hooking mullet is positively an art. You must have a sensitive hand, and the moment a nibble or two takes place, up you go sharply; the right-angled hook twists round and catches the mullet under the chin, if I may so express myself. Some men on the Blackwater are very expert hands at the business.

To conclude then this chapter, and to make a *résumé* of

what sport we had on the Blackwater, I may say that, although sea-fishing was next door to *nil*, wildfowl-shooting was seldom, if ever, better there. Those of my readers who have a tendency that way will do well in due season to book themselves to Maldon, in Essex, travel from thence either by path or by road to Heybridge basin, and thence make a bargain with one of the numerous resident puntsmen, of whom there are perhaps thirty. I need not add that the very warmest of clothing must be taken, and a wide thick rug strapped round the legs will prove a real comforter.

Some of the puntsmen own smacks. In fact, several puntsmen generally go into partnership, and use a smack as a common place of refuge during the night. As a rule these smacks, though small, are cosy and warm, and their cabins in severe weather prove an inestimable boon. An intending wildfowling amateur will therefore do well to make such arrangements as will ensure him such comfort when he has brought his day's sport to an end.

CHAPTER LI.

BEACHY HEAD.

THE weather had given us during the previous week or ten days a sample of each of its moods in turn. We had a severe frost for a couple of days. Then a thaw began, but did not quite run its course; then we had fogs, some rain, a little more snow, an hour or two of frost again, then some sunshine and warmth. I was on the look-out for genial atmosphere in order to undertake another trip on the sea, and it was with pleasure that I discovered one evening that a warm overcoat had become, owing to the sudden change, rather *de trop*.

"Now," I thought, "if it is as mild in the morning, off I go. But where shall I go?"

I thought of several places, and finally gave up the attempt until I could at home consult a reliable map, whereon I had written notes as to the sort of sport to be met with at various parts.

On my return home I spread on the table the aforementioned map, which there is always a great charm in consulting. As each well-known name catches my eyes, there come back to me the very aspect of the place and its incidents of sport. Thus, when I began westward, and my eyes dropped on Chichester harbour, I had only to

Beachy Head.

close them mentally, and was once more on the shore of the harbour; snow was falling, and covered the shore and fields; many fieldfares were passing overhead, and I shot once more the teal and the widgeon which I shot there last year. No sooner had I skipped over West Wittering, passed Selsea Bill, and arrived at the Barn Rocks, than Doodle, with his long legs, crossed my mind, and the incidents of our fun at Bognor were rehearsed again. Thus it went on for Littlehampton, the Kingston and the Kingsmere Rocks, Worthing and its Brill Rocks, Shoreham, with its muddy flats and long narrow harbour beginning at Kingston. Then I saw Brighton in bold letters, and with them arose the promenade, the piers, and the aquarium. Then the fishing opposite Black Rock was recalled, and that at Newhaven commented upon. Seaford, the "rising town," grew before my memory, and up to its signal-house I felt at home. Past that, however, until arriving at St. Leonards, was a blank, at least as regards this year's doings; but several notes, taken two or three seasons ago, were there, and I looked them over to refresh my memory. Opposite Beachy Head were pencilled these few significant words, "Jolly lot of fish about here;" over the Royal Sovereign Shoals, "Nice spot this;" and some eight miles farther out to sea I had booked, "Twelve fathoms of water, and large whiting." I sought to recall what I had done there, and had a dim recollection of having come home with a boatful of fish; so I exclaimed mentally: "This is the spot for me. To Beachy Head to-morrow morning I go."

With this resolve I began packing up lines and etceteras, and sent a telegram to my "American cousin" at Brighton, explaining to him what I meant doing, and asking him to join me. I got no answer to it, but on the train arriving at Lewes the next morning, I saw Doodle waiting for me, and ogling a pretty young lady.

Once more under weigh, we arranged our plans. Quoth Doodle:

"I don't know if you are aware of it, my fine fellow, but this line does not run to Beachy Head, and though I consulted sundry railway maps, I could find no trace of any line going there."

"I know that well," I returned. "Make yourself easy; we shall land at Newhaven in half-an-hour's time, and there we will hire a boat and boatmen to take us wherever we want to go."

"How far is Beachy Head then from Newhaven?" he asked.

"About twelve miles; we can do it in three hours or less if the wind be fair."

I explained to him that I had been lately to Newhaven, and that I knew a man there who would get what we wanted in the way of bait if he were in the harbour, and sober.

Soon after we arrived at Newhaven harbour, and forthwith went to the hotel where I had stopped before, and sent for the boatman. The messenger came back after an unconscionably long time, and said neither the man nor his boat was to be found. Here was a pickle!

"Is there no other boatman to be had, then?" we inquired. The boy was stupid, and "did not know." Riled, we took up our things and went to judge for ourselves the state of affairs.

The weather was very fine and mild, which explained to some extent the absence of the men. Of course, after the rough gales lately experienced, they were glad of a fine day to try a little harvest of the sea.

Whilst we were standing by one of the Continental steamers, wondering what we should do, an open sailing-boat entered the harbour. In it were two boatmen and a gentleman. The latter had a large gun between his knees, and several birds, ducks, and divers were on the stern-sheets.

" That is just the sort of boat we should like," quoth my friend. " I wonder if the fellow who has hired it would let us have it for a consideration ; I will ask him."

So he hailed the men, and when they drew up we entered into conversation with their hirer. As chance would have it, it turned out that we knew him, and the bargain was soon struck.

" The men," said our new friend, " are, I daresay, somewhat tired ; but half-a-crown ahead will go a long way to smooth that over, and if they get some refreshments aboard we will start immediately."

The men at first did not seem to relish the job, but "the power of gold," as the song hath it, "is perfectly untold," and it soon won them over; and after procuring edibles and drinks, with a cheery hoist they got up sail, and away we went.

A more lovely, quiet day no one need wish for, and it was quite a contrast to the weather during my trip on the Blackwater. Well, we passed Seaford and its cliffs, Crickmere Haven, and soon were opposite the Beachy Head lighthouse. We had no bait, be it remembered, but our new friend and his men having intimated that, as several boats were out, we should experience no difficulty in procuring bait from them, we had left Newhaven without bothering ourselves any further about the affair, although I had my misgivings on the point, for I know professional fishermen pretty well by this time, and they are, as a rule, as fickle as pretty women. If they are in a jolly mood, they will part with their last mackerel or herring-bait to oblige you ; if they are surly, they do not even condescend to reply to your queries, but grumble away to themselves, and ask you whether you take them for double-blanked fools, &c., and then sheer off without listening to anything you may offer them. I have met with such, and we did on that day. The first man we met had a bucket quite full, and Doodle, putting on his most winning manner, addressed him as follows : " I say, could you oblige us with a mackerel or two, or a squid ?" putting his hand in his waistcoat-pocket at the same time.

But the gruff reply came, " Can't spare any," pronounced in a surly and sepulchral voice, sounding as though it came from a coal-cellar. The manner of the man was so repulsive that we at once went on.

The next boat had a man and a lad in it, and they were quarrelling as we drew near.

" If ye don't do as ye're told, ye'll get your head well punched, and so I tell ye !" the man was shouting.

Nothing daunted, one of our men hailed them. " Got any bait to spare, governor?" asked he.

" No, got none."

At last we came upon a lonely man who was baiting a long line, and he, with a broad grin, replied to our inquiries that if we paid him well for it he would sell us all the remainder of his bait, which consisted of three mackerel not very fresh and an old squid quite stale.

" I will let you have the lot for half-a-crown," he said. We could not help ourselves, and were glad to avail ourselves of the bargain (?), such as it was.

We anchored just opposite the lighthouse, and when the sails were brought down, and everything made ship-shape, we began. The mild weather had evidently brought back most of the "finny denizens of the deep," as poets have it, for we had a rare deal of hauling in for the first half-hour or so.

Whilst we were fishing, our Brighton friend enlivened us with news from the queen of watering-places. He, himself, did not care much for fishing; shooting was his hobby, and he had been doing pretty well with his gun on the shore from Brighton to Shoreham during the late hard weather. He told us that the fowl came down in abundance along the coast, and some day in the week a large swan, weighing above 20 lb., had been shot on the sands at Cliftonville, half a mile from the Brighton pier, by a Brighton gentleman, who, like himself, was perambulating the shore.

Meanwhile we were having such a deal of fun with our catches that our new friend was tempted to try, and I lent him a line, showed him how to bait it, and no sooner had he caught a fish than he took a thorough liking for the sport, and confessed that he had never thought it would have proved so amusing. There are many more like him.

When we had been about an hour so pleasurably engaged, the biting turned very slack, and we got up our leads and agreed to remove a little farther. Meanwhile, though our bodies were quite warm and comfortable, our feet had got very cold, as is usually the case when one is fishing from a boat without a cabin and without a fire. I felt my extremities were perfectly benumbed. Our American friend suggested that taking off our boots and socks, plunging our feet in the sea, and rubbing them violently afterwards would soon re-establish the circulation. I daresay it would, but we did not fancy trying it on, and were content with stamping our feet until the men had brought up our moorings. I then took a sweep, and a quarter-of-an-hour's pull soon brought me into a state of pleasurable warmth and comfort. We then got into a somewhat deeper part, where we found that some six or seven fathoms was the average depth, whereas where we had previously been fishing four or five fathoms had been the utmost. My friend wished to see what could be got there, but I opined that, as the day was drawing to an end, it would, perhaps, be as well for us to go at once over the deepest parts, if we could possibly get to them, as probably the best fish would be there. We saw several boats, probably from Hastings, at anchor, somewhere by the Royal Sovereign shoals, but they were fully six or seven miles away from us. The wind was fair, however, and had our men thought fit to venture so far, even at that late hour, we would have gone, so great was our enthusiasm; but there was no gainsaying the wisdom of the advice tendered us by our head man.

"It is now 3 o'clock," said he, "and it will soon be dark; in fact we could not possibly reach those fishing-boats before it was dark, and supposing you fished there for an hour, we should have a twenty-mile sail before us before we could reach Newhaven harbour."

It was agreed, therefore, *nem. con.*, that after a quarter-of-an-hour's try we should go back, which we did.

We had about threescore of fish, after returning many to the sea, and when we had all sail set, and our head boatman at the tiller, with the boat's head fairly turned homeward, we congregated amidships, and took to yarning, whilst we smoked pipes innumerable and emptied several glasses of wine, of which our men very gladly accepted their part. Beachy Head light was in full bloom astern, and the lights of Newhaven were fairly discernible miles ahead on our starboard. Then the moon rose. We drank a glass each in her honour, and I trust it did her good.

In the midst of our libations a conger which was loose somewhere in the boat got into the luncheon-basket, and played the very deuce with the things. We had a lively hunt after it, and after several unsuccessful attempts the man collared it, and in his own words, he "did for it."

We arrived at Newhaven harbour rather late, and were all heartily glad when we landed. We had a good supper, and our friend, wishing to be with us on the morrow, proposed that he should drive over to Brighton, and come back again at once, so as to be ready to start with us in the morning.

"How far are we, then, from Brighton by road?" I asked him.

"Ten miles," he said; "and the boss's mare can do that easily, I should think, in an hour."

"Then," I said, "I will go with you."

Eventually we all went, and came back at about 2 A.M.

At 8 o'clock one of our men called for us, took up our things, and we went. He had taken care to provide plenty of bait, and we had every promise of making a fine day of it; the only thing which we could not get, but which would have been very welcome, was a foot-warmer or two. We, however, borrowed three rugs, and got on better than on the previous day. We sailed straight away with a nice land breeze, but had to get out farther to sea when we passed the high cliffs at Seaford and Beachy Head, as these stopped the motive power from reaching our sails almost altogether. Off Beachy Head we did a little whiffing with a small spoon, and had a bit of fun. Doodle called out to ease the boat, as he had a fish on. The men eased her by bringing her head to the wind, and one of them actually took the oars to back water, whilst Doodle played his fish scientifically. But it was only a seaweed, and when the rower perceived it, his face was "a study." Well, we tried the spoon, and then rigged on a spinning minnow, as we had heard that mackerel had appeared; but we never got a bite. I think the water is hardly deep enough there for the fish to venture so near the shore, hence our want of success. We were then about half-way to the shoals, and, disgusted with whiffing, I was putting away the line, and reinstating the minnow in my bag, when I saw, about half a mile ahead, two or three, and then half a dozen or more, small heads and long necks, bobbing up and down on the sea.

"Ducks ahead!" I said to my companions, and thereupon a great commotion took place amongst us. Our Brighton friend took up his gun, a double 8-bore, breech-loading of course, and popped in two cartridges, No. 2 shot. Our men, my friend, and I meanwhile kept our eyes on the birds, and it was forthwith agreed to adopt a plan of action.

"He who is going to fire the big gun must go in the bows," I said, "and all the others must hide themselves the best way they can, whilst the steersman sits at the bottom of the craft, and shows as little of himself as possible."

The shooter went forward, taking with him his gun and his bag of cartridges, and he squatted there, so that only his eyes and the top of his head were discernible under the foresail. The second boatman crouched by his side, plying him with advice, and then I saw that the said boatman had taken out, from under the seats, a long single-barrelled gun, and meant to use it too. The American regretted deeply that he had not brought his gun, so I lent him my double Tolley, 12-bore central-fire, and he was happy.

We were about three hundred yards from the birds when all our arrangements were completed, and beyond the occasional creaking of the spars, the flapping of the jib, and the flip-flop of the wavelets as they broke against our bows, everything was supremely quiet, and as I sat watching my companions, I experienced a feeling of unalloyed pleasure. I daresay they themselves were very contented; and when for a lark I crept to Doodle, and whispered in his ear to give me back my gun, his look expressed such unutterable contempt and suppressed anger that I could not help laughing. Satisfied that I was only joking, he resumed his watch, and I went back to my place. Two hundred yards, then fifty yards less, then a gust of wind blows the boat's starboard thwarts nearly under, and we spin another fifty yards with the speed of an arrow just let loose. As we get nearer still I see all our shooters' backs straining, their right elbows get up, they are evidently clutching their guns, and mean early business. I enjoy the treat as much as if I were one of them, and when we get to within eighty yards of the fourteen birds I am quite as enthusiastic as any. The steersman was well versed in the art, and he brought the boat very nicely just ahead of the birds. Another gust of wind, and when the boat rises, the birds, we perceive, are also on the rise.

Boom! boom! from the double 8-bore! Boom! from the waterman's gun; and bang! bang! from the Tolley 12-bore. Five birds are dead, two are wounded, and amongst the seven that are going away, two, at least, seem awkward in their gait, and one hangs certainly one of its red paddles in unmistakable sign of distress.

Doodle reloads quickly, and as the boat sails amidst the dead and two wounded he kills one of the latter outright, and sends the other barrel to the address of the second. This one, however, was wide awake, and, at the report of the first barrel, he sprang up his stern, and when the load destined for him was fired he was down under water.

"All right," says the steersman, "we will have him. Look out on this side, sir; he is sure to turn up about here."

Meanwhile our Brighton friend has also reloaded, and the two are watching for the bird, whilst the first boatman is desperately reloading his long muzzle-loader, and puts into it any amount of powder, as he is not looking at what he is doing. However, the gun is a strong one, and will stand a good deal, so I said nothing.

"There he is!" shouts the man; and boom! from the 8-bore lays the duck flat where it has just risen.

Now begins the picking up—always a pleasurable job that.

When they had done I observed that one of the birds that had escaped had settled on the sea, some four hundred yards away, and I pointed it out to them, but they couldn't hit on the spot, and did not see it. So I told the steersman where to go, and when we got two hundred yards nearer everybody saw the bird. He was full of life as yet, and I cautioned my friends well on the point.

"Fire as soon as he means going," I stated emphatically; "if not, he will lead us a deuce of a dance;" and we got nearer and nearer to him.

Well, they waited until he offered to rise, but he would not or could not.

Beachy Head.

"Shoot him where he is, sir," then the boatman said, "otherwise he will dive."

The words were scarcely out of his mouth than the bird did dive, and disappeared for a couple of minutes, and when he turned up he was at least a hundred yards astern. A shot from the 8-bore sent him under water once more, and we tacked about. Then he reappeared on our port bow, and a shot from the Tolley laid it dead, much to our boatman's astonishment, for the range was over fifty yards, and he did not think that the 12-bore gun could kill there.

We were about two miles from the shoals, and seeing no more birds, we sailed there, and anchored for a fishing-match in about eight fathoms.

We only caught half-a-dozen fish in half an hour, so went farther on, until we found ten fathoms. Then we were near, or over, a shingle bank, and the whiting abounded. At 1 o'clock we had luncheon, duly baptised our birds and our fish, and got very merry altogether. At 2 o'clock, not wishing to be quite so late as on the previous evening, we agreed that it was time to make tracks for the harbour, and a rattling breeze springing up, we set sail, and had a fine spin to Beachy Head, when the wind altered somewhat, and at half-past 6 we were at the mouth of the harbour. Then we had to take to our sweeps, and a good pull, a strong pull, and a pull together soon brought us to our landing-place.

This concluded my trip. I took the last train to town, and my two companions, not wishing to bother about travelling by rail, very wisely ordered the trap we had used the day before and drove back to their respective quarters in Brighton. It began to rain the moment we parted, so

Sea-Fishing and Seafowl-Shooting Excursions.

Our trip to Beachy Head was concluded not a moment too soon, and, when parting, we congratulated ourselves on having been so very lucky in the choice of days for our excursion over the sea.

CHAPTER LII.

THE NORTHERN WATERING-PLACES OF KENT.

ACCORDING to the wisdom of self-elected soothsayers, the winter was to be a very cold one indeed. This news quite exhilarated me. I saw, in prospective, flights of fowl coming down on our shores from the North, and (in my dreams) I brought down hundreds of them. But our worthy soothsayers are soothsaying humbugs, I think. In fact, when I undertook my trip round the coast of Kent the weather was quite mild, and all our extra coats had been brought in vain. When this takes place on board a small yacht, where, at the best of times, there is but little room to spare, it is enough to make a fellow kick all weather almanacks into the firewood locker. Although the weather was mild during our trip, I must acknowledge that it was, on the whole, supremely nasty; not too windy by any means, except one evening; but rain and fogs, then fogs and rain, for a change, I presume. When once started, we were not to be turned back by a trifle, though, and we accordingly went as far as the South Foreland, in spite of many drawbacks. The object of the trip was to see what winter sport was to be had at those Kent watering-places which I had already visited, and thus make a *résumé*, in one chapter, of their fishing and shooting capabilities.

We started from Gravesend at about 10 A.M., and, before going farther, let me state that there is but little to be done there in fishing, and nothing at all in shooting. Nevertheless, you will always see plenty of men trying to hook a fish or to pot a bird, but both are mighty scarce, unless one considers an eel or two, about twelve inches long and the thickness of one's small finger, a prize sufficiently important to warrant dangling one's legs over a wharf for twelve hours, more or less, in a drenching rain. Yet that is what some men may be seen doing, any unlikely day you like to choose, along the shores of old Father Thames, from Northfleet to the Ship and Lobster.

But if you wish to see a man worthy of having a statue erected on his behalf, for untiring perseverance, contemplate a Gravesend shooter—worthy soul!—who, with his gun and a boy to carry his game, and a retriever or two to pick up the dead and wounded, sallies forth before daybreak, and beats a number of leaden-coloured ditches, in the hope of finding a snipe. When the man and boy and dog have been at it ten hours, and have walked, in zigzags, some thirty miles or so, they come home very tired, but very happy, with one miserable starling *pour tout potage*.

But what surprises me is this: instead of wasting their time in beating about those sheep-marshes, where nothing can be expected, why do not the men go straight to Northfleet marshes, either by train or on foot? It is only some three or four miles at the utmost; and there they would be sure, at any rate, to bag a good many oxbirds, sandpipers, and, when the weather is hard, curlews, &c.

They might also cross the river with the ferry, land at Tilbury, and shoot along the shore on either side, either westward, which would take them past Grays, Purfleet, &c., where there are always birds to be found; or if they went

The Northern Watering-Places of Kent. 149

eastwards, they would meet with still better sport, as the ground is open, very marshy, and totally unfrequented.

The next best part would be at Shorn Marshes, some three or four miles west of Gravesend, and on the same side of the river. There the whole of the marsh comprised between the river and the sea-wall is free to everybody, and with a little cold wind and moderate luck, a good bag can be made there with sea-birds.

As regards fishing in the Thames, at or near Gravesend, I have already given a hint as to what one may expect to catch on an average. The favourite spots for that sort of thing appeared to me to be from Rosherville pier, or from the stone wharves near that pier, from any of the town wharves and town piers, and finally, from the river-bank, near the Ship and Lobster public-house.

There is at Gravesend, as everybody knows, a shrimping fleet, and during the season it is good fun to go for an excursion in one of the little smacks, for a shrimping trip; but should you ever wish to do so, be sure to put on the very worst clothing you can find, and choose well your company before you start. The same may be said if you venture with a trawler. It stands to reason that, should the skipper and crew turn out to be a drunken or filthy lot, your trip would be anything but a treat. There are in Gravesend, besides the professional fishermen; very many boatmen, who own both rowing and sailing craft, nets, &c., and they, as a general rule, are very well-behaved indeed. They will take you out for a mixed expedition, for twelve or fifteen shillings a day, including two men as crew, and when they like they show you sport. With them you may trawl or shoot down the river, or you may land at the marshes and beat them, and get, on the whole, good fun for your money.

During our sail past the Lower Hope Reach, we saw several of these craft, with gentlemen busily engaged shooting along the shores, and one of the boats got well within range of a flock of sandpipers, when its occupants must have floored over twoscore of the birds, judging from the time it took to pick them all up. Past the Hope Point there extends a great mud-bank, right down to the Little Nore; and those of my readers who are not practically acquainted with the part, will do well to bear in mind that at high tide, and on the turn, they must keep at least a mile from the shore proper, or else they will be liable to be stuck. With a rising tide one may run that risk comfortably, if there be not much of a wind, because, in the next few minutes the flood will lift you up and clear your craft; but on the ebb, if you do get stuck, the chances are a thousand to one that you will have to remain there until the next flood. At the same time, however uncalled for these mud-banks must appear to the essentially sailing men, to the shooters they ought to be very welcome sights, because they attract birds in immense numbers. The difficulty is how to get at them. They generally feed out of range from a yacht, and the mud is so soft in some parts as to be unsafe, even with mud pattens. I confess I have never ventured on these flats, and never saw anyone walking them; therefore I would not advise anybody to try them. But, with a good retrieving-dog, a punt drawing but very little water, and a hard-driving, large-bore gun, I have done there very well indeed occasionally. During our trip I had only one crack there, and it was at curlews. There were about thirty of them feeding somewhere opposite St. Mary's Bay, and my friend, the owner of the little yacht, smacking his lips, wondered if any of them could be had for supper.

"Well, there is nothing like trying," I remarked, and

We called the lad to the tiller, whilst we launched the punt, a very small one, just fit for that sort of river-work, but one in which I should not care to face the sea at Poole or on the Southampton Water. When we had launched her, I got in, and kept her steady on the port side, whilst my friend went below and brought up my double 12-bore and his single 4-bore. He handed me his cartridge-bag, remarking that the cartridges were all loaded very strong in powder, and the shot was No. 1 or No. 2, he did not exactly remember which.

"They would do nicely," I returned. "Now, where is your poodle?"

The poodle was asleep in the fo'c'sle, but he soon jumped aft on his name being called, and joined me at once.

"Will he keep very quiet?" I inquired.

"Perfectly," said his master. "Down, Dash!" Dash went down on his belly at once.

By that time we had sailed pretty well as near the birds as the yacht could go, viz. four hundred yards. The tide was flowing, and the flats were about half-covered already.

"I will let the tide drive me to the birds," I said; "meanwhile take a tack across, and pick me up on your return. I could not row back to you against the tide."

"All right!" he said, and I shoved her off so as not to bang against the dingey astern.

For the first two hundred yards I rowed away over the flats with a will. Then I took it quietly, and when I got within a hundred and fifty yards of the birds I lay low, and paddled as noiselessly as could be, the dog meanwhile behaving very well, never moving a muscle; but his eyes told a whole tale. When I had been paddling four or five minutes I reconnoitred, and perceived that ninety yards, at the utmost, was the distance I stood at from some of the birds; but I saw, also, that the flock had divided. The bulk—some score—had gone towards land, over a creek fifty yards farther, and only nine or ten were at their old place. Of these, three had separated from the remainder, and fed five or six yards away from them. I took up the big gun, and placed it quietly over the bows. The tide lifted the punt, and pushed it two or three yards nearer, then two or three more; finally, I got within seventy yards, when, from some—to me—unaccountable motive the birds got up. I fired and killed four, wounding another. Overboard flew the dog, and the water was so shallow that he actually waded to the birds. He saw the wounded one running, and, of course, it attracted his attention first. So he brought him to hand to begin with, and afterwards went for the others. The yacht then was coming back; she was hove to, and we eventually got aboard with the birds.

It was then 2 o'clock, and we had luncheon. Whilst enjoying that meal the lad called out that some ducks were coming ahead. We popped out, but found that the birds were flying at least half a mile off, crossing our bows. We watched their course until they had disappeared somewhere about Leigh, and then resumed our repast.

At four o'clock we began setting our sailing lights for the night, and with a fair wind kept on our course until we reached the Nore Sand. We then ran into the Little Nore, and dropped anchor in mid-channel, in order to try the fishing. We were about a mile N.W. from the Sheerness lighthouse, and, by all accounts, the place was as good as I had been told it was.

First of all, the lad went towards shore to get some bait whilst we were having dinner, and when he came back from the fishing-smacks, it turned out that the first he had ventured to call upon had been willing to sell him bait. After dinner, by the light of our riding light and an extra large ship-lamp placed on the cabin-top, we tried hooking. In an hour's time we had about two dozen of decent fish. My friend had left his line over, and had gone to look for his tobacco below, when his tackle, through the sheering of the boat, fouled mine. At first I thought I had on a fish or a crab of importance, and was accordingly disappointed when I found out what had happened. However, I said nothing, but quickly disentangled the lines, then called the lad quietly. I had seen, forward, several red herrings hanging up in the fo'c'sle for his own private use, so I whispered him to bring up one quickly. I then signed to him to hook it on my friend's bottom hook, and when he had done so I let go the line, just as my friend was coming out of the cabin puffing very contentedly at his newly-lighted pipe.

"Any sport?" asked he.

"Not since you went below."

"Ah!" he said, "I may have been luckier than you. I had better get my line up and see if I have got anything."

The boy ran off at once, and dived into his hatchway, only keeping his head out to hear the rest. Up came the line, then, with the remark that it was very light.

"Nothing on the first hook," said my friend, "but, by Jove! what a rum fish on the last!" The boy then disappeared, stuffing his handkerchief in his mouth. My friend's astonishment soon made room for mirth, and we had a good laugh over the incident. Whilst thus enjoying ourselves, draining a glass and smoking our pipes very contentedly, rain began to fall, slowly but thickly, and it almost completely obliterated the lighthouse from our view.

"We had better stay where we are for the night," said

my friend, when we had taken refuge in the cabin, "for this rain will probably last till daybreak."

At 9 o'clock we felt tired, had supper, and retired to rest, nobody keeping watch but the dog.

Now, concerning the shooting capabilities of Sheerness, very few words will suffice, as I have already explained what we did in the way of fishing. The wildfowl-shooting at Sheerness may be carried on either on the shore of the Thames or of the Medway. The shores of the Isle of Grain, those of the Isle of Sheppey, and all the creeks in the Medway are fairly good in their way. In suitable weather there are few better spots within easy distance of town, and as one can go down by train either to Queenborough or Sheerness, and enjoy there the cream of the fun, I wonder that many more do not patronise the place. I have always done well there. Any man with a good gun, ready to put up with smooth and rough, would spend a week there very pleasurably. A boat, of course, will be a *sine quâ non*, as well as a boatman who will act as guide, for the shores are always shallow where they ought not to be, and *vice versâ*, so that a certain knowledge of the neighbourhood is absolutely necessary.

To return to our trip. At 8 A.M. we made a start, with a fair N.E. wind, a quiet sea, and no tide to speak of. There was a 40-odd-ton schooner at anchor close to us, and by the show of punts lashed on her deck we judged her to be Flushing-bound, as, indeed, she turned out to be. My friend has never done any wildfowling in Holland, but I have, and still retain a most lively recollection of it.

"Now," inquired my companion, as we sailed astern of the wildfowling schooner, "how many birds do you think those on board could bag in a good day's work?"

"You mean day and night, I suppose?" I replied. "Well, it all depends on the state of the weather, wind, tide, and spot. The first time I went there, my four companions and I, besides the crew—three men and a boy—bagged in one night one hundred and twenty birds."

"Do you know," he remarked, "I have often thought I would like to sail over myself in this boat, and try my hand at the fun."

This made me laugh; and I explained to him that in ordinary weather small craft of the size of his own would tolerably hold their own, but when rough weather sets in it is rather awkward to be cramped in a small cabin and jerked about without comfort.

Whilst thus discoursing, we had several shots, amongst which was one at a grebe, which I bagged, and another at a diver, which I missed. We then arrived at Warden Point (that is to say, opposite to it, but about two miles away from it), and on our starboard, eight miles ahead, was Whitstable, whose shipping we could, as yet, but very dimly discern.

There is but little sea-fishing to be had at Whitstable, so we agreed not to stop there; but, to make up for it, we got the trawl out for an hour or so, and found, on getting it up, a goodly array of the usual mixture of goodies and nondescripts. We then sailed as straight as could be to Herne Bay. Then we went about a mile towards Bishopstow, and there dropped anchor over the rocks. It was nearly 2 P.M., and we got our tackle out at once, and did very well indeed. Pouting and whiting were in majority, of course, over such ground. At 3 o'clock we got up sail, and a spanking breeze springing up, we clapped on all sail we could make, and covered the distance to Margate before it was quite 5 P.M.

In the morning we had a little fishing, but it was poor in the extreme—only a few flatfish the size of a dollar.

Early we left, but the wind was quite foul for the way we wanted to go. I therefore struck out a new line of thought.

"We heard last night," I said, "a good deal about the *Deutschland* steamer going aground on the Kentish Knock. Let us go and have a look at her. We have read much about the absence of pluck in the shoremen, inasmuch that they did not go to the rescue, from men who probably know nothing about the sea or the east coast either. Now, I flatter myself that I know a little of the last ; and if the ship went aground where I fancy she did, it would have been a sheer impossibility for anyone to have gone to the rescue of her passengers, even if her signals could have been seen."

We flew on our new course with a fine southerly breeze, doing seven knots an hour easily. We got the binnacle on deck, a chart of the coast, and, with these indispensables, got on in first-rate style, the boat spinning along gloriously. We went thus for a good hour, building all sorts of *châteaux en Espagne* as to the probable appearance of the wreck and the cause of the mishap. This, by-the-way, seems to me to be quite out of the common—viz. for a ship—a steamer too—bound for the Straits of Dover, to wander about some thirty miles along the east coast of England, without the captain or officers perceiving the mistake. It is simply an astounding affair, if the compasses were right.

When we had been an hour going the wind fell, rain fell, and our spirits fell in common with the rest as we stood there, rolling helplessly to and fro, in mid-Channel, seemingly with no way whatever on. But it was not to be so bad as that, for within half an hour the wind came S.W., then turned W. The latter suited us both ways; but as it was a toss-up whether it would keep up from that direction, we thought it best to resume our first course with the now fair wind, such as there was of it, and that was little, for it took us two full hours to come back over the ground we had covered in one just before, and the rain had made everything very damp with us.

We voted a short stay at Ramsgate to make up for it, and to get the papers.

On our way thither we saw several times flocks on the sea, but too far out of our course to warrant a chase. We saluted such birds as came near us; but only one, a widgeon, was bagged. We anchored off the harbour, but only sent the lad ashore for news. He brought us several papers, and we set sail directly he got aboard, never stopping until we were off Deal, where we came to an anchor for the night.

There were, as usual, plenty of weather-bound vessels about, and when we went ashore to get bait we learned that several large yachts had been going down in charge of Flushing pilots for the duck season, and a man who had just returned from piloting a schooner told us that the flocks were, along the Dutch coast, in thick shoals, from whence it may be readily inferred that the English shooters took a tolerable share of the spoils with their superior guns and powder. Dutch powder is not remarkably strong, and the greatest present one can make to a Dutch shooter is a canister of real English stuff, if you can smuggle it to him. Of course, with the yachts no one can interfere (once we had over 200 lb. of best gunpowder on board), so the wildfowling yachts are generally courted by the natives, for the sake of a couple of canisters or so, in return for good advice, and so on.

In the morning we began fishing, and I could not tell how many fish we caught. Several other boats came out too, and seemed quite *au fait* as to what sport to expect, and where to get it. Therefore, any tripper in search of a good station for winter sea-fishing will do well to book himself to Deal. Either opposite the town, or by Walmer Castle, there are plenty of places for that sort of thing.

Those who like to take a gun with them I do not advise to try anything better than the north side of the shore, where they will find, from the town to the mouth of the river Stour, fully nine miles of very fair shore to walk over, and plenty of birds.

Ramsgate sea-fishing consists mostly of flatfish. Plenty of hooking and trawling may be there indulged in, and a good deal of shooting in hard weather over the South Flats.

As for the sands, there is not much to shoot on them at any time.

Margate has a little fishing, and very little shooting, if any.

Broadstairs has far better fishing, but its shooting is almost *nil*, except under exceptionably favourable circumstances.

Herne Bay is about on a par with Broadstairs.

Whitstable has poor fishing, but many sea-birds are to be found some six miles from it, near the Faversham Creek, and on the Swale, behind the Isle of Sheppey.

Of Sheerness, Queenborough, the Medway, and Gravesend I have already given details. Suffice it to say that the northern watering-places of Kent, though they do not all boast of good sport, have several very nice spots where a shooter and sea-angler may thoroughly enjoy himself. Where shooting is the principal object in view, I would recommend a stay at Queenborough or Sheerness, the former for choice. If both fishing and shooting were desirable, then Deal would be the place.

CHAPTER LIII.

THE SOUTH-EAST COAST.

THE weather was still too mild, to my liking, and a little seasonable sharp frost would have been most welcome to shooters. As things were, one had to undergo the most awful tramping if he wished to bag anything; because the mild weather and late floods kept moisture and water a little everywhere, and snipe and woodcocks consequently pitch in the most un-snipy and un-woodcocky spots. Indeed the prospect for shooters was none too brilliant. Partridges were mighty few and far between, grouse done with, pheasants had been considerably thinned, rabbits were still teeming; but one gets tired of shooting rabbits. Therefore the enthusiastic gunner looks to woodcock, snipe, and wildfowl to fill up the chinks; but, thanks to open weather, none of these were to be had in sufficient numbers to warrant a regular campaign.

On the other hand, sea-fishing looked up wonderfully. Cold weather drives the fish away into the deep channels, but mild weather allows them to come pretty near shore; and as winter is the season, almost *par excellence*, for sea-fish, the creels that have been made were simply monstrous.

The sport is gaining ground every day, because it is a *bonâ fide*, honest, and invigorating sport, where the fun

The South-East Coast.

never flags and the incidents constantly vary. I, for one, cannot conceive anything more thoroughly entertaining than a trip on the sea, where sea-fishing and wildfowl-shooting may alternately be enjoyed.

To begin my story, I must mention that my friend had remained cruising about near Deal, where I joined him for my trip round the south-east coast. We slept there one night, and, well provided with bait, started at about 8 o'clock the next morning. The yacht had been anchored in the roads, so as to let her have the benefit of the wind from whichever quarter it might blow; but during the night several other craft, amongst which were some large ships, crowded about us, and when we got up anchor it required all our attention to make our way out without running into anybody. When clear we found ourselves opposite Walmer Castle, with the South Goodwin lightvessel ahead on our port side. The wind was fair and moderately stiff. At one time we thought it would eventually come on to blow, as the sea behind us looked occasionally uncommonly ruffled; but by 10 o'clock the day settled quiet, though not bright, and we took our turns at the tiller every two hours. We passed Kingsdown, then the lightship, and then St. Margaret's Bay, with its lighthouses at the South Foreland. We had then a spin of four miles without any incident beyond shooting at two or three passing birds, and then ran into Dover, where I wanted to get some hooks. I obtained a goodly collection from an old fisherman, and we had our first winter fishing near Dover, off the Shakespeare Cliff.

It is "all rocks" there, and therefore good fun may be relied on. I hooked from the dingey, which was more comfortable than from the yacht, as far as angling was concerned. The yacht's deck is so high that one cannot sit on it without running the risk of being shot overboard like a bad sack of coals, whenever the boat gives a plunge or a lurch when swerving on her anchor. I tried from the cockpit also, and then sitting on the cabin-top, but I continually caught my hooks in the gear, and wasted more time in clearing them than in hooking fish. At last I took my seat in the dingey, and, with all my tackle about me, my bait spread on the fore-seat, my knife at hand, my box of hooks handy, together with a tidy roll of new line to mend mine in case of accidents, I felt, with an occasional glass of sherry and a pipe, as happy as could be. My friend leaned over the stern, and we conversed all the while. We baited our hooks, and soon were hard at work. I worked two lines at a time, and had my hands full for a while, as I had to keep going from one to the other. For the first time I adopted the bell system, of which a friend had spoken to me in very high terms. This consists simply of a slender piece of wood, which can be held by screws over the gunwale; on the top of that piece of wood is a mule-bell, firmly fixed with a piece of twine. Now, when your line is overboard, and you feel that your weight is well down, give the line a fathom or two for "play;" then give a turn or two, or a hitch of the line, round the end of the piece of wood, and there you are, quite ready. You may then go to the other line and attend to it in comfort. The moment a fish bites at the first line, drlin! drlin! drlin! goes the bell, and you know what is up. An ordinary bell will not answer, for it keeps a fellow running all the time for nothing, ringing, as it does, with the slightest sudden motion of the boat. The mule-bell (which consists of a hollow brass sphere, with an iron ball loose in it) never produces any actual ringing but when the slender piece of wood which holds it is suddenly jerked about by a fish that has just hooked itself, and tries to get loose. Well, I tried that dodge, and whether it is because it is new, or because it is really good, we became quite enthusiastic about it.

"Look out!" my friend would say, for instance; "the port stick is on the move. Now for a ring!"

Then drlin! drlin! drlin! the bell would go, and I would get the line up and proceed to unhook the fish. Of course the system is not perfect. When the hooks catch in some peculiar species of long weeds you might almost swear that a fish is ringing; and when they catch in a rock the line is rather apt to be strained, and if not relieved I daresay it would snap; but such accidents would only happen when a man has many lines to attend to. When he has only two or three he can always detect pretty well what is up, and ease his lines accordingly when necessary. Moreover, it will be found that if the line be simply rolled four or five times round the blade of wood it will offer enough resistance to induce the ringing of the bell when the line is pulled; but if a great strain is put on the line will run without breaking. This system of employing bells to detect when fish are "on" is far from new in fresh-water angling; but I had never before seen it used in sea-fishing, and can recommend it when more than one line is put overboard. Crabs, however, rarely shake the line and ring the bell; when they do, I suppose some other crab or fish is approaching whilst they are holding on to the bait, and they try to bolt with it; but even when they do it takes a good crab to ring, because the blade of wood requires a good deal of pressure to make it jump. If, therefore, a piece of whalebone were substituted for wood, the ringing would be made tolerably easy; but then probably the boat itself would cause the bell to ring at any one of its motions. Of course I always held one of the lines; for I contend that nine-tenths of the fun of sea-fishing consists in feeling the fish taking the bait and hook, just as nine-tenths of the fun of shooting consists in looking for game. Some sea-anglers use iron winches screwed on the gunwales of their boats, to save them the trouble of hauling in their lines, but they thereby deprive themselves of all the enjoyment of angling. What would a trout-angler think of a contrivance that would relieve him from the trouble of bringing his trout to land? Iron winches are all very well for professional fishermen, with whom numbers and expedition are desirable; but the man who goes out sea-fishing for the fun of the thing must be foolish to be saddled with a lot of things professedly invented to help him in his pursuit, but which really cheat him of what he is looking for—*i.e.* fun. Beginners are always beguiled into that sort of thing, and the stock of fishing apparatus which they are induced at first to invest in is quite astounding. A couple of pounds judiciously invested ought to rig out a man for any amount of sea-hooking. But ten times that amount is hardly enough for some, and of the lot purchased only a very small percentage comes into real use. In some future paper I will give a detailed list of what I consider amply necessary for hooking round the coast of England, and I warrant my practical estimate will not reach above £2. For the present I will confine myself to our trip.

We caught a hamperful of fish off Shakespeare Cliff, Hay Cliff, and Abbot's Cliff, and, towards dusk, got up sail and went back to Dover, only four miles off, where we took shelter for the night.

The next morning was damp, and there was hardly any wind when we went away. We were two good hours reaching Folkestone, and met with very fair success again between the harbour and the point. We only stopped an hour, and sailed past Sandgate, where several boats were out. Shorncliffe was very quiet, so was Hythe. We passed the forts, so as to give the firing a good berth, if any was to take place, and crawled along the Dymchurch stone wall until we reached Romney Bay. This is tolerably good for fishing, but the sand-banks are a nuisance, to which we had to give good attention.

At 2 o'clock we were within two or three miles of Dungeness, where we found over twelve fathoms of water, and very nice sport with the whiting. But the tide ran "a caution," and we had to increase our bottom-weights to an alarming extent. Nothing daunted, however, we kept our lines going until dusk, when a lot of birds began to appear, and I got aboard the yacht, and took the guns out of the cabin, ready for action, whilst the lad got into the dingey, cleared my lines, &c., and undertook to wind them up and bring them in. The whole of our neighbourhood, for five or six miles either way, east, north, or west, was made up of marshes, hence the presence of so many birds. The Romney Marshes to the north-east, the Dunge Marsh to the east, the peat-bogs along the shore, and the Walling Marsh to the west, offered them good feeding-ground, and we made up our minds to get a duck or two for next day's dinner.

To effect this we sailed right opposite the peat-grounds, and anchored there. I got a crack into a company of seven, and brought down two quite dead and another wounded. My friend went after that one in the dingey, and he had no sooner bagged it than I crippled another; then an immense flock of sea-birds flew within range, and I fired the long 4-bore gun into the file, when I floored over thirty birds of small size, so that we had birds at almost every meal during our stay on board. My friend hid in the dingey, and fired at some black ducks, bagging one.

Then it was too dark for further operations, so he rowed back against a strong tide, and was almost exhausted when he reached the yacht.

"I could not have rowed another hundred yards to save my life," he said, wiping the perspiration from his forehead and neck; but the sight of all our spoils soon reconciled him with the hardships he had endured, and he would have gone again in chase had it been light enough to do so.

Well, we looked at the barometer very carefully; and as it gave no indications of weather likely to disturb us, we thought we would stop where we were until daylight.

"If it comes on to blow badly, we will run into Rye harbour," I remarked; "it is but four or five miles away. It is an awkward harbour to make, except at high tide; but at any rate we will sail towards Rye to-morrow, and, if you like, will land with the small boat and beat over the marsh. I don't think we shall do much there, as the weather is so mild; but we may find a teal or two, or a stray duck."

This was agreed to, and we then devoted all our attention to feeding.

After dinner we prepared our ammunition, read two or three papers, then had supper, and went to bed.

In the morning we set sail, and went to anchor just at the mouth of Rye old harbour, when we tried to land, but found the tide running out so strong that it was impossible to row up to the shingle or the wall. In fact, the water rushed out with the speed and volume of a stream let loose through a sluice. We therefore gave up the attempt, and allowed the tide to drift us back to the yacht. A mist fell just when we were setting sail once more, so sou'-westers and oilskins were at once at a premium. We sailed across

The South-East Coast. 167

Rye Bay, and went fishing at the Boulder Bank, some five miles from Hastings. There we got only a few small fish, but then the water was comparatively shallower than where we had fished before.

We stopped but a short time, and went to Hastings and St. Leonards, where I knew a good deal of fun was to be had. I accordingly got into the dingey as soon as the weather cleared up, and rigged out the bells and their wooden supports. I had scarcely let down the first line and hitched it on to its signalling apparatus, when ring went the bell, with a persistency that foretold a conger uneasy in his mind. I relieved his congership, and let the hooks down again, but before I had quite done with the other line two whiting were on the old one again. Seeing that matters were so urgent, I called to my friend to come into the dingey with me and have his share of the fun. Congers were very fair, and extremely voracious. We lost two lines through either very large ones hooking themselves and overpowering the tackle, or through ordinary ones getting in the same predicament, but insinuating themselves under rocks, and resolutely declining to be pulled out. The breaking of a line is always a queer experience. The steady pull of one's hand, the tautening of the line, the strain on the fish, its giving way a little, and then holding on again, finally the pull that is to decide the question, and the tear that ends the affair, are all eminently curious experiences, both to the beginner and to the old hand.

When congers are on it is no good slackening the line, and allowing free play to it, on the off-chance that the conger will eventually allow himself to be brought up, for in nine cases out of ten he does nothing of the sort, and it is a perfect waste of time to let a line lie thus idle. Either break it and mend it, or else get your fish. We caught a very large ray on a piece of mussel, and were glad to let it go again. It looked so horrible as it was being brought in that, without hesitation, its presence was voted as *de trop* in our boat. The ray gone, we had a dogfish, and as "It never rains but it pours," we caught three more in succession. There must have been a squad of them about.

We killed them all before turning them adrift, and went to try the Boxhill reefs. These reefs are three miles from St. Leonards, and about a mile, more or less, from the shore. A lot of whiting were waiting for us to catch them, and for the first time during that trip we got a solitary codling some eighteen inches long, and weighing probably 3 lb.

We remained at sea until dark, in the hope of seeing some birds about at dusk, but were disappointed, as not a single one turned up.

At 4.30 P.M. we were back at Hastings, where, in accordance with instructions we had given during the day, a man came to us in his boat and put us ashore.

At 6 o'clock I wended my way to the station, booking myself to London Bridge, whilst my friend was on his way back to the yacht. If the weather I had experienced was rather disheartening to a wildfowl-shooter, it was just the reverse to a sea-fisherman. The sea was tolerably smooth, the fish were numerous, acutely on the feed, and in the primest condition. Therefore, if sport be sought after, as the showman has it, "Now is your time, ladies and gentlemen," for in truth I never experienced better sport than during that trip of mine round the south-east coast.

CHAPTER LIV.

PORTSMOUTH.

A FRIEND, who resides in Portsmouth, had written me word that some nice sport was to be had with gun and line in his neighbourhood. I was glad to avail myself of the suggestion, and I duly landed at the Portsmouth Railway Station, with gun and creel, in the course of the week.

Now, although I had been in Portsmouth a score of times, I was unacquainted with its streets and sights, simply because I always went there in yachts during the summer season, when all the attractions were concentrated near the shore of the sea. I am not singular in my indifference to shore affairs. I know a fellow who went several years running for cruises in the Mediterranean, and never thoroughly visited any of the stations there, so that it does certainly seem queer, when you ask him what he thinks of Naples and Gibraltar, to receive for answer, "'Pon my word, I don't know; they look pretty from harbour; picturesque, very, and all that sort of thing; but I never went for a perambulation through the streets." Well, I must confess to some such soft impeachment myself. Still, though I never had the curiosity to inspect old Portsmouth, I knew a lovely bit of a mud-bank some little distance off, where mostly a good bag could be made of birds and of lugs, and to that bank I hinted to my friend we should have to pay a visit.

"As regard lugs," said he, "I have spoken to the man I usually sail with, and he will provide everything necessary in the way of natural bait. We will go and see him after luncheon, and you will be able then to give him a hint as to the places where you wish to go."

This we did. At the door of a public-house stood an elderly, short, stout man, as broad as he was high, clothed in sea-boots, dark blue breeches, very wide, a guernsey down to his hips, and an old brown overcoat, with collar turned up over his woollen comforter.

"That is my skipper," said my friend, as he came towards us, with his arms elbow-deep in his pockets.

"My son is on the look-out for bait, gentlemen," he began, "and I told him to get a rare stock if he can; and as the lad likes fishing he will take good care to have plenty of it."

Thereupon we walked into the parlour, and I drew from my pocket a chart of our neighbourhood, pointing out to the old man the spots which I fancied most in the gun line. He knew all the spots, but under different names, as usual. What a queer thing it is that fishermen and smacksmen always will alter the names set down officially for the different points and bays. For instance, that bit of mud-bank just mentioned was called by him Gull Point, and its creek Gull Creek. Why? Because when the tide turns early in the morning a rapid stream is somehow produced round that point, and a lot of seagulls are wont to congregate there.

"Are there any other birds but seagulls?" I inquired.

"Ah! I believe you," he exclaimed. "Why, during that last snowy weather we had I went there myself, with my son, and," with a knowing wink, he went on in a stage whisper, "with our guns, of course ; you understand, and the birds we got! lor' bless ye! we filled the stern-sheets with them birds."

"Well, but are there any more? It used to be a very good spot, that I know right well."

"As for now, of course there may be a few, and there mayn't, but I daresay we could pick up two or three."

"Very well, then, we will go there the first thing in the morning, and will fish on our return."

We agreed that 7 o'clock would be quite early enough, and after treating the old man to a glass of whisky with a drop of water in it, we went home. Portsmouth, in winter time, is not a lively place. I found it dreary, and after two or three visits to the principal sights, I was glad when evening came, and turned in.

At 6 A.M., whilst dreaming that a codling had hooked me, and wanted to smother me under water, I was awakened by a thundering row at my door, and found that my head was under the bedclothes, hence my uncomfortable dream. I lighted a candle and dressed, shivering. Went downstairs, and found a roaring fire lighted and a glorious breakfast served. Enjoyed both, and at 7 A.M. punctually arrived the old man and his son, a man as old as myself, so that the expression " lad," applied to him by his father failed to give an idea of his years. The son shouldered everything he could, and carried the rest in his arms, whilst the old man imperturbably looked on, with his hands still elbow-deep in his breeches-pockets, only taking one hand out to grasp another glass of water, &c.

It was not a very inviting morning. There was a slight mist falling, and that did not improve the naturally lugubrious aspect of the shore. Two or three men were loitering about, and they lent us a hand out. There was but little wind, so we clapped on all sail and tried to make the most of it. Meanwhile we got a couple of rugs at the bottom of the boat, and my friend and I spread them to windward, and then sat there, somewhat sheltered from the cold breeze and mist. We all lighted our pipes, and the son, Frank, went forward to trim the boat, which would have been too heavily loaded astern to be even on her keel had he remained with us. He sat by the foresail, and whilst puffing at his cutty I told him to keep a look-out, and to let us know if any birds turned up. They had not, as yet, seen any mackerel, the old man told us; but when the shoals came, it was very good fun catching them. A London gentleman, a customer of his, caught one year (but later in the season) some six or seven dozen, with a spinner and flies, in the course of a morning. Some other gentlemen in the summer months go also for mackerel with spinners, and some bait with lugs, and have very good sport. There are, besides, a few bass about the forts at Spithead, but no one seems to go in regularly for them. As for pollack and whiting, they are very abundant; whiting all the year round, pollack only in summer and autumn. Hakes were then to be taken, but there is not much fun in catching them, as they are awkward customers to deal with, and not particularly handsome to look at.

I inquired about the sea-fishing to be had at the Isle of Wight, and learning that lots of anglers were daily at work there, I concluded there must be fine sport to be had, and I decided upon going there soon. Our old boatman mentioned that he had seen several gentlemen landing at Portsmouth from the Isle of Wight steamers with tremendous baskets of fish.

"One of them, an officer belonging to the barracks,"

said he, "had a large hamper, a yard high, quite full up to the brim; his creel—more like a baby's cradle than anything else I can call to mind—was crammed too, and he had left about as many fish on the other side of the water."

At 8 o'clock we had sailed some four miles, and, barring a good many seagulls, no birds had made their appearance, but as we kept on for the Point we fell in with several early companies of widgeons and coots. The latter are most careful birds, and understand the policy of keeping a safe look-out and of remaining out of range of any gun but the 81-ton Infant. We sailed to leeward of them, and that would not do. We then sailed to windward, and that would not do. We then tried sailing right in the midst of them, keeping well out of sight as far as we could, but they would not allow us to get near enough for a crack at them. On our port side there loomed, a mile or two away, another shore. "Hayling!" called out the old man. We understood hailing at first, and turned up our noses towards the sky, and as it was bright then, we looked at the old boy, then at each other, at though we meant to imply that he must be "tight."

"Hayling Island," he then repeated, with a nod towards the shore.

"Oh ah!" we said; "of course it is the Hayling Island. Well, we will just turn round here if possible; that is where the creek is."

We accordingly went in, and as the place is not safe for large vessels to sail either in or near, we felt certain that unless some shooters had been there before us we should find some birds safely sheltered therein.

We therefore began to shift our seats, and to get the guns ready forward. In the midst of our preparations, bang went Frank's old musket.

"Missed! dang it!" exclaimed he.

We look up. A fine mallard is sailing by, but now out of range.

"I never saw him," said the young fellow, apologetically, "till he got nearly over us, or would have called you. I thought the best I could do was to fire at it myself, and kill it if I could."

We soon reached the creek, and he took his mud-shoes and went ashore. Presently Frank fired; we took the guns and looked up. A number of birds—curlews, redshanks, and sandpipers—came down towards us, seemingly taking us for fishermen. Four barrels floored three birds—two curlews and a redshank. Thereupon a file of ducks rose from another creek, and they sailed past us towards Hayling, but quite out of range. That was rather mortifying, but it could not be helped. One of our curlews died a double death, if I may so express myself. He was shot and he was drowned. My friend had hit him hard with both barrels, but the bird kept going, when, suddenly, down he came on the water, and there he kept bobbing his head up and down. But his long bill was too heavy for him in his disabled state; it dipped into the water, and actually drew his nostrils under; so that I am afraid if a jury sat on his remains, the doctor's *post-mortem* examination would have revealed that he had come by his death through a couple of shot wounds in his body, and his nose then getting under the water, asphyxia had intervened.

My next shot was at a grebe.

"There is a bird just dived," said the old man, "on our starboard. If you look out, it will come up directly. There it is!"

The grebe was then about sixty yards off.

"Just you see," I said to my friend, "how far the shot

will carry. I am loaded with Schultze powder. Are you ready?"

"Go on!" he said.

I fired. The grebe never moved. It was lying quite dead on the water.

"That was a good shot," he said; "but your shot went so close together! It seemed not to scatter more than two feet at the distance. That is a good performance for both gun and cartridge."

And so it was.

In the meantime Frank had not been idle, for we heard him fire several times, and when he came back he had two birds, a curlew and an oystercatcher.

We then sailed a little higher up, and indulged in some free shooting at any birds that came by. Then at 12 o'clock we came to a full stop, turned the boat's head back towards Spithead, and whilst the men were rowing us out we had luncheon.

At 1 o'clock we once more set sail. The old man told us that he was going to take us to a rare whiting and gurnard spot, where, if we did not fill our creels, it would be very wonderful indeed. We got our tackle ready, and at 2 P.M. were hard at work baiting whilst the men were mooring the boat. The sea was not smooth, neither was it rough. It was just the sort of day to spend comfortably at sea-fishing, and we enjoyed our outing amazingly. As soon as things were ship-shape the two men went forward to have their luncheon, and then Frank joined us. The old man did not care for it, lighted a pipe, and laid down for'ard, but he was not long left quiet.

"Here, father!" Frank called out presently. "Hi! I say, father!" Then he administered, rather undutifully I must say, a kick under the fore-seat.

"Now, then, what's up?" inquired the old man, gruffly.

"Why, get ready the hamper, that is what is up; I have got two fish on."

And all the while he was hauling in his twenty-fathom line, which was vibrating under the dashes of his catch. "Here they are!" And he got a whiting, 2 lb. weight, and a small pouting in. Frank rebaited expeditiously, and then it was time for his father to pay attention to my needs, for I had a gurnard weighing pretty nearly 4 lb., and measuring two feet in length. My friend and Frank then simultaneously got up excitedly, and called out to get the net ready. Here was a go! I got up, and secured the gaff in case it were needed. The old boy collared the landing-net and looked out for squalls, when it turned out that they both had but small fish on.

"Now, look here, Frank, my lad," the old man remarked, "draw it mild, will ye! What is the good of causing such a flurry for nothing?"

And he, disgusted, threw the net in its place, whilst I replaced the gaff, swearing inwardly that they would not catch me at it again.

Presently my friend said he was sure that time he had a monster. I laughed in my sleeve, and indulged in a wink to the skipper, who returned it with a shrug of his shoulders and a look of pity towards the clouds. But, by Jove! it was no false alarm this time, and we nearly caused the loss of the fish—a monster codling, some 15 lb. weight.

"If you don't come," expostulated my friend, "I shall be quite unable to land him;" and as I chanced to look over the gunwale, and then caught sight of a green back a yard or so, more or less, long, I said nothing, but let go my line, jumped on the gaff, and told my friend shortly to bring him up. He came, and I caught him well under the gills. This was the great prize of the day. It was a wonder he had not smashed the line merely with his weight.

The next catch was still more sensational. I observed Frank holding his line very thoughtfully, and with his head slightly turned towards it, just as if he could hear what was going on (many fishermen assume that position occasionally, of course unknown to themselves, when much excited or expectant), and then he hauled in quickly with a look of disappointment.

"I thought," he exclaimed, as he brought up the end of his line without any hooks or weights attached, "I felt the beggar having a tug. All right! We will see this time. Will you kindly lend me a conger-hook?"

I passed him a strong hook with gimp sewed with wire, and he baited it in ominous silence. Presently he fixed on a lead, and down went the line.

"I have got him this time," he said. "Father, be you ready?"

"Ay, ay," said the old man, and an enormous dogfish made his appearance with two hooks and a yard of line sticking out of his jaws, and one inside. As for the lead, it was nowhere to be seen.

The dogfish removed, sport began to be very lively once more. Gurnards began to take the upper hooks, the whiting, pouting, and a few coalfish took the bottom ones, and, between them, they made the fun grow fast and furious.

Unfortunately, it was getting late, the tide was rising fast and strong, and the wind being against it, our cockleshell began to tumble in the most unpleasant manner, jerking us here and there and everywhere; first from the port side to starboard, then back again; then a heave would come, sending us all nearly heels over head from stern to bows, and, at the next heave, it would upset two or three of us from bows to stern. I was nearly shot overboard in one of those mad jumps of our craft; my friend sat neatly in the hamper, on the top of our fish, and if he had remained there a minute longer our dogfish, who was there clacking his teeth together, would probably have given him a gentle reminder that the weight of his body was there rather *de trop*.

Neither were the boatmen exempt from our predicament. Serious thoughts began to cross our minds that getting up her anchor and setting sail would, no doubt, steady her, and give us some relief, but the fascination of sport was so great, that we actually remained until dark, and the great vessels at anchor at Spithead had run up their riding-lights to the masthead for the night. We lost innumerable lines from large fish taking our baits. In fact, we got quite crippled in the way of hooks, and shifted with small ones. At last it was so dark that I could not mend my line. I struck a fusee, and looked at my watch.

"Do you know," I asked my friend, "what is the time?"

"No; no idea," said he.

"Well, it is nearly 5 o'clock."

"Five, eh? And we have a good two hours' sail to get back home. I vote we go now."

No sooner said than done, and we packed up and headed due west for Portsmouth.

A queer evening it was too, with its overcast clouds, its small quarter-moon, now and then hidden from our sight under a flitting shadow, and the heavy black waves breaking angrily around us. The wind had risen considerably, and we crowded to windward, to make her more stiff to the breeze, whilst all her canvas was on her, and she sped along like a live thing. At 7 o'clock we stood on the Hard, rather glad, after all, to find ourselves there safe and sound, and able to stretch our legs a bit after our twelve hours' riding on the deep green sea. We emptied the bottle before parting, as "it brings ill-luck to leave any dregs about"—at least so the old man told us, and we took his word for granted. Then, "Same time to-morrow morning, gentlemen?" asked Frank.

"Yes, same time," answered we. "Bring the fish, &c., when you call in the morning; it is not worth your while going down all that way to-night."

"All right, sir. Good evening, gentlemen."

"Good evening to you," we replied, and parted.

The next morning turned out fine.

When we were fairly under weigh I explained to the old man that, if possible, I wanted to be back in time for the 3 o'clock train in the afternoon, and he promised that we should manage that comfortably.

We went this time to a station nearer home than that of the previous day, and anchored in twenty-five fathoms of water, with a good firm bottom, where our moorings gripped directly. Our catches were again excellent, and the hamper was filled to overflowing ere we said, "Hold! enough!"

At 12 o'clock we were on our way back, and we landed at as near 2 o'clock as could be, in comfortable time for my preparations for departure.

"I hope, sir," said the old man when we went, "that we shall have the pleasure of taking you to the Isle of Wight when you do go?"

"Of course you shall," I answered, and we parted on the very best of terms.

CHAPTER LV.

SEAHAM HARBOUR AND BAY.

I WAS interceding with a military acquaintance for leave for his son to accompany me on one of my trips, but my gallant friend was obdurate.

"Not until he has passed his exam.," he said decisively; "these are serious times for him, and I should not like him to be disturbed, do you see?"

"I understand your argument," I remarked; "but allow me to observe that Frank has been very hard at work of late, and that a little change would do him good. He will get silly at last. Not that an army examination is a very hard thing to pass, but still, cramming one's head with all sorts of things makes a fellow rather dull in the end."

He admitted that there was some truth in what I was arguing, but was nervous as to the result, and so we came to a compromise, in which the result of the examination was largely concerned.

"If you get on well," he said to Frank, "we will all go to my brother's, and then you can have your trip on the sea."

Frank, accordingly, "wired" into his books more than ever, and passed with flying colours. In consequence thereof, one fine morning all three of us were in the train for the north, and a very dull journey we had of it too. Frank's uncle lives in the neighbourhood of Seaham, and the only way of getting there was by dismounting at a certain station, whose name now escapes me, and thence driving through Houghton-le-Spring to Seaham. This part of the journey was no joke for the mare, as the roads were hard-frozen and very slippery. However, the coachman had got her " roughed " at the blacksmith's, and we got on tolerably well, reaching the house of our entertainer at about 6.30 P.M. The country from the station to Seaham is not particularly pretty, and the district being a coaly one the dust settles a little everywhere, and a good deal in the neighbourhood of the pits.

After dinner, we discussed our plans of action for the morrow. We agreed to make it a shooting day along the seashore, there being, according to the keeper's account, lots of curlews about, in the cliffs and over the rocks, at low tide. Meanwhile, whilst Frank and I undertook that part of the affair, his father would get a boat ready for us for the following day, so as to have some sea-fishing also.

At daybreak the keeper woke us up; the weather was fine and bitterly cold—all the better for the success of our undertaking. Filled, then, with enthusiasm, Frank and your humble servant drove with the keeper to the shore, where we no sooner arrived, than we heard many curlews calling almost on all sides. Seaham was not quite awake yet; but already its gunners were out, or at least some of them, for whilst we were putting our best feet foremost to reach the sands, we heard several shots fired consecutively, and saw a bird or two being knocked over. The fact of the matter was simply this: owing to the frost, the fields and meadows were all hard, and the only place where the birds could find something to feed on, was in the cliffs, where little threads of water always run and keep the ground moist; and on the seashore proper, when the receding tide left the sands soft and easily investigated by the hungry birds. We saw thousands of larks in the course of the day, and the seafowl—at least shore-birds—were also very numerous.

The keeper, with his double duck-gun, walked at the top of the cliffs, whilst we two divided the shore between us. Frank walked near the land, and I kept near the sea. Between us three and the keeper's strong retrieving spaniel, some birds were bound to come into the bag, and some did.

The keeper opened the ball by firing both barrels towards the fields. Of course we could not see what he had been shooting at; but as he disappeared, and we heard him calling to the dog, "Fetch 'em, lad!" we conjectured rightly that he had brought some to grass. They turned out to be lapwings, and he had shot three with his two barrels. I was looking at him and waiting until he was ready, when I heard the *frou-frou* of many wings on my right side. I turned hastily, instinctively shouldered the gun as I did so, and let drive right and left into a flock of sandpipers. The keeper sent Sam, the dog, down, and he no sooner spied the wounded birds fluttering in the sea, than he went at them, in spite of the breakers, and brought them up one after the other very sensibly. There were seven of them. I fastened their heads together with a bit of string, so as to make a lump of the lot, and gave them to the dog. He did not know what to do with them, and when his master whistled to him he went, but without the birds. However, the keeper no sooner had him by his side than he sent him back with the order to "Fetch 'em, lad," and he came down at a gallop, took up the lot, and went up with them like a shot. There is nothing like patience and perseverance in such matters.

A little farther on the keeper signed to us to proceed steadily. I stopped, being in the open, but he and Frank kept going. Suddenly they came upon their birds—three curlews, feeding on the side of the cliff at a pool. The keeper fired and did not hit. Frank fired and missed with his first barrel, but his second told on an old curlew, with a beak the length of my gun-barrel, more or less. The said long-nosed bird, though winged, had kept the use of his long stilts, and he began a rare run, both of us backing him in a breath against the dog to reach a pool first, which he did; but his exertions had told on him, and Sam nabbed him and brought him back very proudly, whilst the curlew at the very top of his voice was shouting ten thousand murders! This being the first curlew Frank had ever bagged, we agreed that the proper thing for us to do, under the circumstances, was to celebrate the event with the usual baptism. Sawyer (the keeper) came down with the flask, and I wished Frank many happy returns of the event in a bumper of sherry.

"But," said he, "I read somewhere that killing seven curlews is all a man can do in a lifetime. Have you ever shot a lot of them in one single day?"

"Yes, I shot fourteen once in two hours, in a couple of meadows on the south coast, during the hard winter of 1870. The frost was so hard that only one brook was running, and they would stick to it in spite of my firing. They rose, of course, at every report, but after sitting down for awhile inland, they would come again to the brook, when I would stalk them again. I could have shot more, but being alone, and loaded already with my fourteen birds, I gave it up."

Thus conversing we were making way, and when we reached the belt of rocks, the tide being on the ebb and half-spent, we agreed that hiding in the rocks would not be a bad plan, and at once chose holes facing the cliffs, on the top of which Sawyer squatted, and agreed to sign to us when anything should turn up. I got a very nice rock, standing about five feet six inches from the sand on both sides of me. On the top I disposed two or three bundles of grass, through which I could keep a look-out, and having made myself comfortable, and ascertained by a glance that no birds were as yet near, I called out to Frank.

"Yes," he said.

"Are you all right?"

"All right," he replied.

And now began the watching.

Soon after we had ensconced ourselves, a flock of gray plovers flew our way, but they settled on seaweeds some hundred yards from our guns. Thereupon Frank left his hiding-place and came towards me, taking advantage of the rocks in the way, so as not to let the birds see him.

"Let us drive at them," he said in a whisper.

"No, no," I said. "They will attract more birds if we let them alone."

And the words were scarcely out of my mouth when Sawyer telegraphed to us from his "exalted" position. I peeped through the grass and bobbed down again at once.

"There are two curlews now," I said to Frank.

"Where?" said he, with sparkling eyes.

"Near the plovers."

"Let me look; so there are!" Then he looked again, and declared that the whole lot were stalking about, but coming our way.

Just then, however, someone fired a shot towards Seaham, and the birds got up. The plovers went out to sea, and the curlews passed between us and the cliff. We fired our four barrels, and the keeper his two, but we only got one bird.

Now, after all this firing, it was likely enough that a little time would elapse before any more birds would come near us, so I volunteered to go over the rocks and see if I could see any shots there.

When I reached the extreme edge I saw several birds on the sea, but quite beyond reach. There were two or three companies about, and I made a note of it for the morrow.

When I came back we sat on stones and began our lunch, but we were kept continually on the *qui vive* by passing birds. Our sandwiches gone, and the bottle of sherry emptied, we stepped forward once more. Sawyer climbed back to the top, as before, and in so doing he flushed a snipe from the soft mossy ground, and being unable to steady himself, he let it go. We did not expect it either, so that when the man called out in a stentorian voice, "Mark snipe!" we did not fire at it until it was nearly a hundred yards from us. Of course we did not get it.

Sawyer no sooner reached his post than he sent the spaniel to beat the intervening softs, but we did not see any more snipe, although plenty of other birds were flushed.

We turned back at about 2 P.M., and arrived at Seaham at 4 o'clock, thoroughly "done for the day."

On reaching home, we heard what preparations had been made for our next day's trip on the sea. A hamper of provisions was ready in the hall, and the boat would be waiting for us at 8 A.M.

"What about bait?" I inquired.

This, it appeared, had been overlooked altogether.

We then sent into the town to get some mackerel, fresh if possible; and the man coming back, after a good search, with half-a-dozen, we were content.

The boat placed at our service was a large, roomy, open sailing-boat, no decked boat being available; and the two men who were to take us out knew the coast thoroughly well.

After dinner we commenced preparing lines, guns, and cartridges. Sawyer came to help us in this, and he took the opportunity of mentioning that he should not be able to accompany us on the morrow, as his "stummick" would not let him. .

Next morning the weather was much milder than it had been on the previous day. We started somewhat late, and got on board with traps and baggage, and went away amid the cheers of half-a-dozen urchins who had been watching the work of embarkation. Frank had brought his double gun and his uncle's single duck-gun, and I had my double Tolley central-fire 10-bore.

Presently Frank stood up to load his uncle's 6-foot ducking-iron, but owing to the boat's motion, and to the breeze, and his uncomfortable position, half the powder was dropped in, and the other half out of the barrel. That is the worst of long muzzle-loaders, you can't get at them; and if it had been raining, I doubt very much whether we could have loaded the weapon at all. Howbeit, I helped my young friend by holding him tight by the waist, and he resumed the loading process. Then ramming the loads home was another queer job. When the ramrod was placed at the muzzle, the whole lot almost reached the top of our mast. We managed at last to feed the gaping muzzle, and looked out greedily for something on which to try it.

"I see a bird," said Frank, pointing in his enthusiasm to a log bobbing about with the tide.

"That is not a bird," I said.

"Bet you it is," he replied, and he was going to fire the 6-foot gun into it, when the men asseverated that it was a log, just in time to save a load of powder and shot and the nuisance of reloading.

Thus discomfited, Frank made up his mind to find something else, and I was as anxious as he. Men are, after all, but great children, and the four of us were as anxious to see what the big gun would do, as the artillery officers at Woolwich are when the 81-ton Infant is going to be fired. At last, we saw three widgeons on our starboard, a quarter of a mile off.

"You come over here, sir," said one of the men to Frank, making room for him forward, "and if you put the barrel over the gunwale you will be able to fire quite comfortably."

"Don't fire until they rise," I told him; but he did not act to the letter of my advice, for when we were at least a hundred yards from the birds the man began to whisper all sorts of nonsense to him.

"You are within range now, mister; get ready. Fire away, sir, fire away, or they will go!"

Of course the man was well-meaning, but no gun could have floored swimming-birds under such circumstances except by a fluke. Whereas, when they rise, even spent shots may break their wings, or hit them in the head and settle them. At an unheard-of range Frank fired, and had the mortification of seeing the three birds going off apparently perfectly unscathed. I blew the man up, and told him to give no more advice until asked for it, and then remonstrated *sotto voce* with Frank.

We were then opposite the first ledge of cliffs, and several divers turned up. We would have fired at them had we not perceived ducks some way off, flying. We watched them until they settled, and then went in chase.

The first lot we came to consisted of fifteen birds. We drew up to them capitally, and Frank waited very patiently, but just when they rose I think the boat lurched, and the verdict in consequence was only one—a splendid mallard. He had had a shot through the head, and one had broken his wing. Whilst we were reloading the long gun, another company turned up. Frank wanted me to try for them this time, but as I knew that, in his heart of hearts, he would feel much obliged to me if I would let him fire, I professed that I did not care much, and would be glad to see him do it. So he went forward again, and this time did the affair beautifully, getting three birds—two dead ones and a cripple.

After that we saw nothing near us, so we went to a nice place and anchored for some fishing.

It was just 12 o'clock when we began. The men told us we had been lucky, so far as concerned our birds.

"The artillerymen," they said, "fire cannon occasionally, for practice, from Seaham into the sea, at a barrel or something of that sort; and of course, when they do so, there is but little chance for shooters."

I was surprised that there appeared to be nobody fond of sea-fishing about Seaham. Ours was the only small boat on the sea, although there were plenty of sailing vessels and steamers moving up and down and along the coast. Frank is very fond of sea-fishing. The previous year we had had a little bit of it together at Kingstown, and he was then very proficient in the art, but now he has become quite an artist.

"I have got two on," he began, and brought up a whiting (the everlasting whiting are everywhere, seemingly) and a conger-eel some yard long. " That is not a bad one, is it ?" he added, on perceiving the latter, which came on the bottom-hook.

" No, 'tain't a bad one, sir," said one of the men, " but you will get better ones here. It is a good place for them."

I had one about half the size of Frank's, and he was jokingly affecting that all large fish would patronise him and ignore me, when with my next throw I caught a monster weighing fully 10 lb. This reversed the tables at once; but presently Frank got one almost exactly the size of mine. They seemed to be very fond of mackerel in that spot, and it was lucky, for that was the only bait we had been enabled to procure.

In the midst of our fun one of the men called our attention very quietly to four birds that were dancing about on the waves behind us, some two hundred yards away.

"They are ducks," I said, "let us get our anchor up and go in chase."

I then explained to the men what we were to do. The wind would drift us right on to the birds, so they had only to get up our moorings, and then we would squat in the boat and trust to chance.

When we had been drifting some five minutes I took off my hat and peeped over. The birds had seen the boat drifting on them, and not liking it they had swum away, and were now fully two hundred yards on our port side, and were paddling away from us. I got up and signed to the men to put up the mast and sails. They did so, and we sailed towards the birds, and eventually fired at them when they rose, at an awful range, and hit one; but he kept on flying for two hundred yards, and then settled on the sea, whilst the others disappeared. We went for the cripple, but he got up again, and kept us half an hour at that game. At last a lucky shot turned him on his back, and we got him. We were then at least three miles from the shore, and in ten or twelve fathoms of water. We took up our lines, and for two hours stuck by them devotedly. We caught a variety of fish—codlings, whiting, coalfish, a brill, two skate, and a lot of small fry not worth mentioning. The weather kept very mild and inclined to a thaw, but when the afternoon was somewhat advanced we began to feel chilly, in spite of our rugs and overcoats. At 4 o'clock we cried " Enough!" and up went the mast, up went the sail, and we returned merrily to the harbour.

CHAPTER LVI

OFF THE SHIPWASH.

I HAVE rarely spent a more thoroughly enjoyable day than I did during that of my trip to Harwich.

I went there overnight. The morning broke clear and bright, but not cold, and old Joe had got his boat ready for me, and punctually at 8 o'clock we made a start with lines, my double 12-bore central-fire gun, and his muzzle-loading, flint-converted, antiquated, single-barrel.

"She is not," said he, apologetically—when I glanced at the spliced stock and wire-fastened barrel of the old weapon—"she is not a wery nice gun to look at; but she is a rare good 'un to kill."

"Well," I rejoined, "we will soon see about her power; but do you think she is safe?"

"Safe!" he exclaimed, "do you think I would let you or anyone else fire off that gun, if I did not think she was safe? Why! lor' bless ye! she will stand anything! you can put in her all you like, and never mind the mendings about the stock and etceteras."

"Well, then," I said, " I will load it."

When I tried to put the cap on the nipple, I found that the half-cock did *not* half-cock; in other words, the nut was worn out, and the hammer had to be put up at full-cock with a jerk. I thought to myself, "Had I known the state of the old piece when Joe wrote me that he had a good single gun, I would have brought another with me;" but it was now too late to alter things, and when once started I detest turning back.

A great many birds were about on both rivers; but as the Stour is always disturbed by the railway trains which run along its south shore, we thought the Orwell would suit us better for the little time we had to spare for wildfowl-shooting.

We saw four birds opposite the Point, and went to them, but they got up beyond range, and we went back towards the shore. The tide was just turning. It had been high tide at about 7.30 or 8 o'clock, and as soon as the mud-banks began to appear, multitudes of birds came to the river to feed. The ducks, widgeon, and teal appeared uncommonly wild, and would not settle. Nevertheless, my first shot brought one down—a teal. We were rowing up a small creek in the hope of finding a nice flock of redshanks, which we could hear whistling, when the old man suddenly stopped rowing, and I, who was in front of him on the first seat, turned back to see what had caused him to "strike" so suddenly.

"Look out, sir!" said he, in a whisper. I took up the long gun, and then saw the teal coming up from the Orwell at great speed, and straight to us. I waited until he got within good range above our heads and fired. The bird collapsed like a concertina. He shut his wings, dropped his head and feet, and came down with a rare flop on the water.

"Number one!" called out the old man triumphantly, as he backed water to pick it up. It was a lovely bird, in first-rate condition. I tried to reload, but the shot I had fired had set all the denizens of the creek on the move, and I had to fire half-a-dozen shots from my breechloader ere I had quite done loading the single. My shots were both successful and unsuccessful, but two of these were very pleasant of their kind. One was at a curlew a very long way off, and though he kept going, both Joe and I remarked that the shot had well covered the bird, and we kept our eyes on him as long as we could, but lost sight of him. The second double shot was at two shanks, and floored both. When we had picked them up we went farther ahead, intending to go as far as the water would be deep enough for our craft, and keeping well in mind that the tide was ebbing fast. On reaching the next bend of the creek we found a much smaller one, branching off on the right, and one opposite branching to the left.

"Joe," I said, "land me on the starboard shore; there is a bird about two hundred and fifty yards away on the mud, quite close to the bottom of the creek. I can stalk him there, but there is not enough water for the boat."

With a good stroke of his right oar he sent the boat's prow on the bank, and I clambered on the soft. It would bear me, I found, without mud-shoes, so I cut across very quietly, and presently I found I was just opposite the place where I had seen a large bird. I got within a few yards, and nothing appeared. Finally I stood on the bank, but could see nothing, when quack, quack! up flew a duck from behind an island of mud, about a yard square in extent. Bang! and the duck tumbles, toes over head, on the mud. I went to pick it up, but found this difficult, as it had fallen on the other side of the creek, and there was too much water as yet to allow me to wade across. I went farther on to look for a jumpable spot, when, to my astonishment, I found my curlew quite dead, flat on his breast.

On referring to my watch, I found that it was time to turn back if I wished to manage a little sea-fishing. The tide was getting out very quickly, and as we intended leaving the river and going out to sea, we had to take advantage of the tide in order to manage it comfortably. The creek we had been beating last was just opposite Grimston Hall, and as this was fully four miles from Harwich we had before us a tolerably long sail, for, according to the old man's experience, past the Cork lightship near the Lower Rough, and on the other side of the latter near the Shipwash, were the two best spots thereabouts; that is when the sea was willing to let you, for at times it is "uncommon rough" all along that coast—witness the *Deutschland*, and many other wrecks.

We turned the boat's head towards the Orwell, but scarcely had we gone down fifty yards when the boat stuck. The old man endeavoured to shove her off with an oar, but she would not stir. We had gone so high up the creek that the tide had nearly left us behind for good. Eventually the boatman got off and shoved her from the bank into the channel, and then resuming his oars, we got out as quick as we could. I shot another shank whilst going down, but it fell ashore; and for fear of being stranded if we went to fetch it, we had to leave it where it fell.

In ten minutes we were in the river, and as soon as we were clear of the flats we propped up the mast and hoisted sail. Then I took the tiller, whilst the old boy attended to his wet legs and muddy boots.

The wind was fair, and we had a very nice sail down the river. We passed the shipping, the Landguard Fort, the lighthouse, shaved the Point, and headed straightaway for the lightship, about four miles off.

We saw a good many birds, but they were so wild that

there was no getting near them. The sea was as smooth as the pate of a close-shaved heathen Chinee, so that we took our ease in every way. When the old man had done with his mopping he offered to take my place, but I employed him in cutting me a lot of bait ready for use. An old salt goes through the not very entertaining process with indifference, and arranges the whole lot with such tact that there is no waste. Every bit you pick up when he has done is fit to use, and is a good bait—no straggling bits hanging together with a shred of skin; his are compact morsels, and no fish can have a taste of it without gobbling the lot. I watched him through his operation, and when he swept the whole back into the tin, and sprinkled it with a few drops of salt water, I complimented him on his expertness. We had brought with us a long line of one hundred hooks, and the old man got all his line-bladders ready for inflating.

"Shall I bait the hooks?" he inquired.

"Will it be worth while setting the line?" I returned, answering his question by another.

"Yes, of course it will work well," he said; "but perhaps you would like to keep all the bait for hand-hooking?"

I told him if he would leave me enough bait to go on with my hand-lines for an hour and a half that would suit me very well, and he took three or four handfuls, placed them on the seat, and, glancing at the remainder in the can, declared there would be plenty for the long line to be set. This was cheerful news, for it is a pleasure in prospective to know that a long line is set, for some fish will certainly be caught, and there is an agreeable uncertainty as to the nature of the take. We passed the Cork lightship about half a mile, and when behind the Cork Ledge, prepared to set the long line. Joe took his thick bladders and blew into them until his face looked not unlike those painted heads of angels in Continental pictures. These bladders, when filled, are stopped in a very primitive manner, simply by inserting a wooden peg in the vent hole, and there you are with a mark plainly visible at a long distance, and safe to float until your return. Joe, of course, paid out the line. It needs a good deal of practice to do it tolerably well, and I always hook myself, the boat, or the basket, and once I hooked the bait-can and sent it overboard. I therefore declined the undertaking, but volunteered to keep the boat going. Between us we managed the affair splendidly.

"Now, that is done," exclaimed the old man cheerily, when he dropped his last bladder on the German Ocean, "let us go to the Shipwash. I was there the other day, and got two fish-boxes full all by myself."

It was 12.30 P.M., and the weather had kept bright and quiet, so we went on towards the narrow bank which rejoices in the highly-suggestive name of the Shipwash. Most of the places along the coast are queerly named. For instance: why was the place near which we had set our long line called the Cork Sand? Higher up there is a bank called the Kettle Bottom. Lower down there is the Goldmer Gat in the Wallet, then the Gunfleet, the East Knock, the East Swin, &c. The Shipwash is a long, narrow belt of sand, extending from south to north-east, some eight or nine miles, and it is about a mile broad the whole length. Such a bank always shelters the fish, from whichever way, east or west, the wind may blow, and there is always something to be done there, for it is rarely that the wind blows direct south or north with no mixture of east or west. We found that where we anchored we had seven or eight

Off the Shipwash. 197

fathoms of water, and the sea being smooth, with no wind worth mentioning, it did not matter which side of the bank we took, so we remained on the west side. We began by throwing overboard all the tails, heads, and etceteras of our bait as a sort of notice to the fish of our whereabouts, then we got three lines in order and began work. I remained astern, and fished over the starboard side. Old Joe sat forward, and, facing me, he let his line down over the port gunwale.

"I have had a shaker just now," he said presently, and after a few moments' expectation up went his hand and he brought up a gurnard.

He tumbled him into one of the fish-boxes, and then I got a crab on for a start, and several times brought him almost into the boat, but he was a cunning old one, and whenever he found that he was getting rather too close to the surface he unhooked his claws and went. At last I got the landing-net ready at hand, and the next few times that I brought up the line I looked over the gunwale to ascertain if he or any of his *confrères* were coming. After catching two or three whiting and a gurnard I thought the crab had taken his departure, when lo! as I was peering into the depths below, I saw him coming up edgeways, gnawing away, and holding tight one of my baits. I transferred the line to old Joe, and cautiously getting the landing-net in hand thrust it quietly into the sea, brought it quickly under the line, and when crabby let go to regain his domicile he found himself caught in the meshes. I brought him into the boat, and he was furious. He held up his pincers for my own private inspection, and the glance of his eyes plainly told us that he would have cheerfully subscribed a trifle to have a jolly pinch at me, anywhere. He spat too most venomously, but in spite of all his efforts he was dropped into my creel, and eventually he came with me to town, and was declared very tender eating.

Well, the Shipwash bank appeared to hold attractions for whiting and gurnard only, as, with few exceptions, we caught no other fish. We remained there about an hour and a half, and then prepared for a start. The old man set up the mast and sail, although the wind was not very fair for the line of road we wished to pursue, and with an oar over the starboard thwart he kept her going at an amazing rate towards the Cork Hole, where we had dropped our long line. We were a good hour and a half reaching our first bladder. The old man had commissioned me to look for it.

"I can't see so well as I used to do," he said; "and when I sets a line by myself I always stops by it until it is time to get it up. That is partly why I uses bladders. They are easier to see than corks or line-buoys when a fellow, like me, gets dim-sighted. There is an old man in the town who is nearly blind, and he sets up little flags on his buoys, but sometimes the flag-staffs get broken, and then he is nowhere."

At 3 o'clock we reached our first bladder, and got down mast and sail, stowing them forward out of the way. I went amidships and took the oars, whilst the old fisherman put on his oilskin leggings, and, clutching at the first buoy, began getting up its moorings. Then he took the line proper in hand, with a twinkle in his weather eye. "There be some fish on it," he said; "I can feel them." He got half-a-dozen hooks in, coiling up the line scientifically as it came, fish and all, when he said to me hurriedly:

"There be a large one coming, sir! Will you please bring the landing-net?"

Off the Shipwash.

I got the oars in at once, and proceeded to the rescue, when we found an enormous skate was the object in question.

"I don't want it," I said; "let it go."

"Begging your pardon, sir," said he, "but if you don't want it I will be glad to have it."

I had hoped, when he called for the net, that it might have been a nice cod, or some other valuable prize; and was disappointed to see the ugly brute winking at us, and opening its round mouth with indignation and splutterings.

"These fish," said the old man, "are very good eating when you know how to cook 'em, but it is precious few who do know how."

Our long line filled one fish-box very decently, and we should have had many more fish had there not been such a lot of crabs about the spot. These pests had actually gnawed many of our baits, leaving not a shred on the hooks. In fact, throughout the whole line, not a particle of bait was to be seen anywhere. On the other hand, those hooks that had no fish had plenty of rubbish on to make up for it. Seaweeds in all forms and shapes and colours were there in abundance, and a man might have made a collection of many varieties from the stock we brought up from the bottom of the sea.

"I thought the bottom was mud and sand," I said to Joe.

"So it is, sir," he replied, "but seaweeds travel about, and you find some almost everywhere. We always get our trawls choke-full of that sort of rubbish when we trawl along the coast, and a great nuisance it is."

Meanwhile he had got the bladder and end anchor up, and we resumed sailing, as I wished to be on the river in time for some popping at the birds before darkness set in. Fortunately the weather had kept bright, and now the tide had turned and served us well, as it was going up the river in grand style. We got in the haven by 4.20 P.M., and kept the boat under way, but steady, along the shore, in the hope of seeing some of the flocks coming our way. As I did not trust much to my old companion's powers of vision, I had to do nearly all the look-out by myself; and the way I kept turning this way, that way, and the other way, would have puzzled anyone stationed on the mud-flats watching my motions.

With the rising tide the wind rose, and birds of all sorts flocked up the haven. I shot a few waders and a diver, but when the "long crosses" began to appear in the sky, I looked up to them with solemn interest.

"Joe," I said presently, "there is a flock of at least two hundred birds on the wing up the harbour. They are now going over the coastguard-station."

"Then," he replied, "they are going over to the Stour, and will stay there unless a puntsman rouses them up with his swivel-gun, and sends them our way."

I kept my eye on the flock; they flew at a great rate over the town of Harwich, and I lost sight of them. I then turned round, and saw a score of ducks coming our way from up river. They were a long way off, but both of us crouched at the bottom of the boat, and I got the celebrated hammer up, and sighted the birds, following and covering the leader, as the lot kept well behind him in a line. When they passed parallel to us, I was going to fire on the spec of a chance shot hitting one of them at that awful distance, but at the moment of pressing the trigger I perceived two more birds coming down, and bound to pass much nearer to us than the first company. I shifted my

Off the Shipwash.

position slightly, and when the two ducks came within fifty yards I killed them both with one shot.

Thereupon several men came up on the decks of their ships at anchor, and said the shot had gone to them, but as some of the grumblers were behind us we paid no heed, and after picking up our birds went a little higher up to try for a creek. What particularly induced us to do so was that the sea had become perfectly rough on account of the tide rushing up the haven so fast, and the boat rocked dreadfully, so as to make a shot very uncertain. I told Joe we must keep her well on, and sail across the tide. She would then gather some steadiness as soon as she had some way on her.

It was then getting dusk, and the number of birds was simply bewildering.

Now, some friends and correspondents of mine ask me weekly, where can they go for a little shooting, &c.? They say they are told that wherever birds are to be had such multitudes of fowlers turn up as to make sport perfectly unattainable. Now, although, as a matter of course, many shooters are found wherever plenty of birds are to be had, they do not much interfere with each other's sport; on the contrary, they help one another, unwittingly, to make good bags. On such wide estuaries as the Blackwater, the Colne's mouth, the Stour, the Orwell, and Poole harbour, fifty puntsmen might be out and not meet each other. What are fifty shots fired on an extent of thirty square miles of water? Moreover, the shots of one man drive the fowl to another; and although no one can nowadays expect to make such monstrous bags as were obtained fifty years ago, yet anyone knowing what he is about, and who uses proper craft and proper artillery, is tolerably sure of making an average of at least a score of birds in three or four days. The only thing is, our amateurs of the present day are not so indifferent as the amateurs of the olden times to the state of the weather; hence so few of them pursue wildfowl when the weather is highly propitious for that sort of sport. There are hundreds of birds to be seen even when the weather is mild, so this may give an idea of the numbers to be met with when it is regularly cold. Statistics of the market must not be depended upon, simply because the market is provisioned by professionals only. Amateurs who kill wildfowl do not sell it. They eat it or give it away to their friends. This being so, the dealers are supplied almost exclusively from decoys and from the professional duck-shooters. There are far fewer ducks caught in decoys now than used to be the case years ago. The lands in the neighbourhood of the decoys are not such wildernesses as they used to be. They are drained, reclaimed, and pastured over by cattle, or cultivated. Men, dogs, horses, sheep, and cattle are about, and the ducks will not come.

As regards the puntsmen and shore-gunners, they are poor men who try to make a living of it. They cannot afford buying the heavy improved guns, and still use their old swivel or shoulder-gun; but these cannot well reach the fowl of our day, because these are more wary, precisely on account of the land being more thickly populated. Therefore, the average for each man is much smaller; and although the number of shooters has much increased, the quantity killed bears no comparison with what it would be were heavier guns and heavier charges used. An amateur who takes to that sort of thing spares no expense. He therefore meets with considerable success, and the professionals are jealous of that success. Witness the English wildfowl-shooters who go every winter for the duck season on the Dutch coast. Half-a-dozen English swivels on the Dutch coast bag as many birds as a hundred Dutch gunners put together. This I know for a fact, as I have shot there. Now, our principal amateur gunners go to Holland, because the fowl are very numerous there; but those who cannot afford the luxury of a yacht for such a lengthened trip can very well go to any of the estuaries on our coast, and are sure to meet, in suitable weather, with very respectable sport, notwithstanding the assertions of prejudiced or interested persons. I enjoyed my trip to the Harwich neighbourhood amazingly, and am certain that any of my readers who will give the place a thorough trial will thank me for the hint.

CHAPTER LVII.

EASTBOURNE AND SELSEA BILL.

I ARRIVED at Eastbourne one evening, accompanied by a friend, in the very mildest of weathers, and as soon as we had secured our quarters for the night, we went to see about a boat, and found the right sort of man with the right sort of craft, to take us out on the morrow. We had brought our bait with us, and this was fortunate, as it seemed that no bait was to be had there, either for love or money.

We turned in at a decent hour, and were woke up at an unearthly one. Now, I am a good hand at making arrangements overnight for the employment of the following day, but a very bad one at getting up early, in spite of all entreaties, threats, and promises. Quoth my friend, at some hour I am really afraid to state:

"Get up, do! That is a good fellow! The man is waiting below."

But I must acknowledge that it was in a very discontented frame of mind that I listened to his arguments.

However, I got up and dressed, and when we turned out I confess I rather liked it, for everything presaged us a very fine day, and already the pink tint of the rising sun appeared over the Royal Sovereign shoals. Our boatman was enjoying his morning pipe with evident gusto, and, *chemin faisant*, he enlightened us on the sporting capabilities of the neighbourhood.

"I have often thought," said he, "that it was a pity some gentlemen did not come to live for good about here. There is mostly always something to be done in sea-fishing and shooting, either on the shore or in a boat. There used to be a sea-fisher gentleman, two or three years ago, who cast lines from the shore at this time of the year, and he used to catch all sorts of fish; but he is gone now."

I then asked the man about the sea proper, and what sport we might reasonably expect to find there.

"I don't know," he said, "about ducks, and all them sort of birds; of course, we always do see some out at sea, but they are mighty 'cute, they are, and it is rare that they let you get near enough for a shot; but, still, with these guns of yours you ought to get a few, if there are any about. As for divers, there are always a dozen or so knocking about the bay, and they are easy enough to get at, because no one goes after them about here. So, if it be that you would like to get one or two, I think I could warrant taking you near enough to bag them."

"Well, and what about fish?" I then asked.

"Oh," he said, "we will go into deep water, about an hour-and-a-half's sail from here, and if you don't catch as many fish as you would wish, I shall be astonished, that's all."

On these words we reached the shore and found two or three men about, ready to lend us a hand. We took our seats, the man went to fetch a basket, a pail, and an anchor, together with the mast and sail of his boat; then he joined us, and our tide-waiters shoved us away.

With a glorious sea, a glorious sun, and a glorious sky,

I know very few things more entertaining than the start for a sea-fishing and sea-fowling excursion. The opening of the cartridge-bags, the loading of the guns, the getting out of lines, fixing them, rigging them out, scraping the rusty hooks with a knife, cutting up the bait, clearing up the tails, heads, &c.; all these details, however often repeated, lose none of their attractions. As regards the guns, a word of advice to young sportsmen may not be considered as out of place. I would earnestly recommend all boat-shooters never to allow a gun to be placed flat on a seat when loaded. If the boat should happen to give a lurch, it will send the gun down to the bottom of the boat; then the hammers may be knocked by the violence of the concussion on to the cap or on the cartridge, and the gun goes off and maims or kills somebody. A gentleman was shot thus a little while ago. He was out wildfowling with two friends. They placed one of the guns on a seat, and when one of the party got up to attend to the mast the boat gave a roll, the gun of course slipped, fell suddenly against the floor, and the owner was shot dead on the spot. Now, if you place the guns with the stocks resting on the bottom of the boat and the barrels leaning on either gunwale, should one of them by any chance go off, the muzzle being over the side and directed away from the boat, its occupants would escape injury. Why I have mentioned this is, because I have noticed the tendency to place guns on the seats by the side of the boats, not only in youthful sportsmen but also in older ones, who ought to have known better.

When we had all our things ship-shape, guns ready, lines out on the seats waiting to be baited, we looked about, and a pleasanter sight could not have met our eyes.

The golden rays of the sun had tinged the heights with brown stripes, whilst the few clouds that were about dotted the land and the sea with their shadows. My friend is addicted to writing verses, and when I saw him, with frowns on his countenance, gloomily scribbling on a seat, I knew he was having a poetical fit, and the Muses were at work within him, so I left him to his own devices and philosophically loaded a pipe.

The boatman looked on with an air of astonishment, and at last whispered to me, with an accompanying jerk of his thumb over his shoulder: " Noospaper writer ? " Nodding at the same time towards my friend.

"No," I returned in a stage voice, as he bent his ear to my mouth; and I then said the sacred word, " poet!"

But the man did not know what a poet was, and I think he considered the expression as being synonymous with "lunatic," for he looked henceforth with no remarkable favour on my companion.

In the meantime, the old boat had not been idle, and with its sturdy stump of a mast, square sail, and round prow, was making way very nicely indeed. It is surprising how quickly these clumsy-looking craft get over their ground. Much in the same way are the Dutch barges that come up to London Bridge with cargoes of live eels. Looking at their rig and cut you would imagine that they would stand the sea about as readily as a washing-tub, and make about as much way against a wind.

Well, when land became somewhat lower on the horizon, and Beachy Head appeared considerably less high than it was when we had started, I ventured to question our worthy Charon.

"We are ten miles anyhow from the shore now," he

said, "and in a quarter of an hour we will drop anchor and see if the fish I told you about are not somewhere very near."

My friend now woke up from his trance, and as he plays a good knife and fork when not in a poetical fit, suggested that we might just as well have our breakfast before beginning fishing. In the midst of our meal we arrived over our ground, and our man, looking very knowing over the stern, took his own bearings, which I noted carefully, and were as follows: Beachy Head, N.W.; Pevensey, N.N.W.; Hastings, N.N.E.; distance, about ten or twelve miles from Eastbourne.

We then anchored, shipped the mast, as it was a heavy bit of wood, and kept the boat rocking to and fro, besides being considerably in the way of everybody. I then went amidships, my friend took the stern-sheets like a rear-admiral of the fleet, the boatman stooped in the bows, and made a round back like a single-humped camel, much to our astonishment at first. But soon a sulphurous smell, not altogether unmixed with very rank cavendish tobacco smoke, told us his employment, and when he had lighted his pipe we had already caught a fish—a small gurnard.

"Now," said he, "you are sure to get lots of whiting here; but I should not bait freely, because the fish do not run very large, and if you put on your hook a lump as large as the half of a mackerel, of course they can't get it into their mouths."

This speech was delivered to the poet, who, being, I suppose, in another inspired fit, was placing on the bottom hook of his line a piece of mackerel as big as my inkstand.

We got on first-rate, but caught only half-a-dozen large fish, amongst which were a codling 4 lb. in weight, a couple of large whitings, a monster gurnard, and a large coalfish. The latter was a handsome specimen. What a pity these fish do not eat better! Their flesh is flabby and tasteless, whereas, judging from their appearance, you would suppose they would be capital just coming out of the frying-pan.

We stopped fishing twice, once for luncheon and again to change our ground. Barring this, we stuck to the sport like a couple of hungry leeches, and never thought of coming back ashore till the sun began to go down very fast, and we felt the chill of the evening fog.

We had during the day seen a few birds about, but we had not gone in chase of any, simply because those we had seen were only divers, which are hardly worth going out of one's way for; but on our way back several companies of ducks made their appearance, and we expended a considerable lot of ammunition—for nothing. The fact was, the birds were so shy that there was no getting near them in any way. The moment we got within a hundred yards or so of them, up would the long necks go, flap, flap, flap! would the short wings paddle, and up the red legs would appear. Of course bang, bang, and bang! at once, just with the faintest of hopes that a stray central pellet might tell on one of them, but it was all in vain. Nevertheless we kept up our spirits wonderfully well under the circumstances, but our trip was, after all, not very enjoyable.

This being so, I thought I would try some other station, and accordingly was glad to get a letter from a friend asking me down to Chichester harbour, for a trip to Selsea Bill; and, against my expectations—which were rather gloomy, on account of the very meagre sport I had met at Eastbourne—I found during this last trip an abundance of fowl and fish.

I went *via* Chichester town, where my friend, who had

left his little yacht at the entrance of the Chichester harbour, was waiting for me, and we drove in the evening to the harbour, some six or seven miles, and found the dingey waiting to convey us aboard.

During this very short journey my ears were pleasantly tickled by the sound of many birds whistling over the flats, and I felt quite enthusiastic over it. Early in the morning we began operations by loading the dingey with provisions and ammunition. To these were added a couple of rugs, our guns, and ourselves; one of the men took the oars, and we left the yacht in charge of the master. The estuary is not more than a mile at its broadest part at low tide, and more frequently a quarter of a mile would cover the interval from shore to shore. It would have been, therefore, useless to try sailing with the yacht, and better sport was to be obtained by knocking about with a small boat until it would be quite broad daylight.

We began by bagging a duck, but as we both fired together it was accounted a " common " bird.

Our man next stopped rowing, and said a file of ducks were coming along behind us. My friend, who was facing them, had a good chance of scoring, and placed one bird to the good. The rest of our barrels went nowhere.

Whilst reloading, some oystercatchers passed about eighty yards ahead across our bows. My friend fired one of the single 4-bores and killed two. Another one, probably hit in the head, flew our way, some thirty yards or so nearer, and I shot it; so that within a quarter of an hour we had three oystercatchers and two ducks.

As for waders, there were hundreds of them about, and we might have fired a cartload of ammunition at them had we been so minded.

Meanwhile the sun was rising fast, and soon its height

put a stop to any further sport, as the fowl left the river and went about the mouth of the estuary.

Quoth my friend, " We shall find them by-and-by ; I would not mind betting a 'fiver,' off Wittering, by the East Pole Sand, we see a couple of hundred birds in the course of the day."

We accordingly went back on board, and prepared to set sail for a trip out of the harbour.

Whilst sailing down we had several shots at divers, and bagged two—one a perfect beauty, in the very best condition. The plumage of its breast would have shamed snow for whiteness. The other diver was a smaller specimen, but it was not spoilt either. The fact is, big guns fired at long ranges somehow kill very neatly, as, at most, but very few shots at such tremendous distances find their way into the birds.

We picked up each bird under sail, and at about 11 o'clock we were hugging the east coast of Hayling Island. Already, with the Dollond, we could see small flocks of fowl here and there dotting the sea, and we held a council of war over a chart. My companion, who knew the spot well, opined that we should first try the fowl and afterwards see what sea-fishing was to be had off Selsea Bill. We accordingly went carefully about amidst the sand-banks, and, taking our positions forward with the big guns, we soon entered in earnest into the sport in hand. First of all, we got each a crack into a company of ten at about eighty yards. They rose one after the other instead of getting up tolerably compact, so that ours were rather random shots, and we only got one bird that time. The next shot was at a larger company ; and as we were more favoured by the fowl, and our guns pitched their shot right into the lot, we got three, and at least three or four of those which escaped appeared at first very doubtful whether they should proceed or not. Had another big gun been fired just when they were so taken aback, I believe our score would have been six or seven birds instead of three.

We then arrived opposite East Wittering, and there we saw the hundreds of birds to which my friend had alluded. We passed Bracklesham without being able to circumvent any of the hosts; but once past that little village the coast is bare for five or six miles, and we had more chances of success there.

During luncheon time one of the men was placed as watch forward, with orders to call out whenever birds turned up. His office was no sinecure, and our meal was a myth; as no sooner were we installed at the table than the man called out vehemently, "Birds ahead!" and we left the cabin hurriedly and then stopped on deck, for the sight was something surprising. We had a most entertaining day of it; and I could not help wondering how it was that off Eastbourne we could hardly get within cannon-shot of the birds, whilst off Selsea Bill we mostly got within a hundred and twenty yards of the wildest companies. The others allowed us to get much nearer than that; and in fact our best crack of the day was at a small bunch of seven widgeons that allowed us to come within seventy yards of them, and had not one of our men, in stumbling aft on a coil of rope and nearly slipping overboard, frightened them, I think we should have had to put them up. However, of the seven birds, four were killed and one wounded by the two 4-bore guns. It was then 2.30 P.M., and the men turned the boat's head Channelwards and set the trawl going. The first catch was simply tremendous. When all unsizable fish were removed, we had about a score of fine fish left, none of which were under 3 lb. weight. We then had a spin of three-quarters of an hour, and when we arrived in twelve fathoms we all rigged out lines and set to hooking. When we had been there about ten minutes we began to have plenty of bites, and the way in which fish came up over our gunwales was a "caution." The four lines caught quite as much as the trawl had done in its first throw, and we were so pleased with the sport that we never thought of removing until it was quite dark. I might enter into the details of the sport at greater length, but this chapter is already getting somewhat long, and I must now come to an anchor.

CHAPTER LVIII.

OFF THE TYNE BAR.

I ARRIVED at Newcastle late in the evening, and was met at the station by my three future sea-fishing companions. They had been out to sea the day before, had met with most glorious sport, and, the weather being remarkably mild, there was no reason why we should not, on the morrow, be made equally happy. We made our preparations after supper, and discussed our plans. My mouth, figuratively speaking, watered when I listened to what my companions had to say about our prospective success for the next day: According to their notions, the boat we were to take was bound to be loaded to the gunwale with our catches, but, what was more to the point, they said there was but very little rubbish to be caught; the fish were mostly good ones, and when anchored in a certain thirty-five or forty fathom spot, which they knew well, the sport, they averred, was quite first-rate. Of course I dreamt of immense fish being caught, and all that sort of thing, and accordingly woke up "seedy" on the next day.

The morning was dull and warm at first, but turned somewhat cold afterwards, when we landed at North Shields, where our boatmen were in waiting; and when we stepped into our craft and set sail to clear out of the river, the way in which all of us donned extra coats and turned up the collars was highly suggestive.

The boat that took us out was what I should consider an 8-tonner, though the men pronounced her larger. She was a strong, cosy boat withal; and the cabin, though roughly fitted up and upholstered, proved a comfortable crib, and a very pleasant dining-room.

It was about 8.30 A.M. when we left the estuary and passed the breakwater. The moment we got clear of the north shore cliffs we experienced a sharp gale, which bent our starboard gunwale clean under. Two or three of the guns which had been placed on the port cushions had been unceremoniously banged to the floor on the top of a leather trunk, which had averted any damage; and this again led me to think of the wisdom of never allowing loaded guns in boat-cabins under any consideration, unless there be gun-slings, racks, or hooks, with suitable accommodation for the reception of the weapons. Even then, in this epoch of breechloaders, there is no need in reality to keep a gun loaded on board, except when in expectation of having immediately to use it.

We had our first shot off the breakwater. There were several files of black ducks going northwards against a strong north-east wind, and they literally shaved the breakwater in their course.

"Look out!" I sang out, collaring a 4-bore at the same time; and we bolted helter-skelter, some forward, some aft, but all with a weapon of some sort. One of my companions had got jammed into the fo'c'sle hatchway, from thence he had got the barrel of a long gun resting on the gunwale, and was aiming all the while deliberately at a flock which was, as yet, at least two hundred yards off.

"For goodness' sake, Fred, don't fire yet," someone said to him.

"Not I," he replied ; "I am only getting ready."

And so effectively had he got ready with his aiming under the foresail that when the first flock, consisting of a score of birds, passed across our starboard at a range of some eighty odd yards, he blew up the three first birds into their happy feeding-grounds without so much as a shake of one of their feathers Up the twenty birds were coming, with necks well straightened, and their short wings flapping on madly, when the cloud of smoke issued forth from the barrel, and lo! the three leaders flopped down on the surface of the sea. The seventeen remaining unanimously bolted, broke their line of flight until we had fired our other barrels to no purpose, and then reformed themselves into a travelling column when half-a-mile away from us. Just there, however, two gentlemen were in an open boat with guns, and the blackies got another dreadful scare, leaving two more of their number behind.

After losing sight of them we looked for others, and saw a good many travelling at great speed in the direction the first company was originally taking. From this we concluded that a passage was taking place, and that if we came to an anchor off the mouth of the harbour we might hope to bag a few more birds. After a quarter-of-an-hour's waiting in vain, under easy sail, we kept on tacking towards the Long Sands, and then towards Frenchman's Bay, near the coastguard-station, until nearly 12 o'clock, when the passage stopped, and we gave up waiting any longer. We had nailed three more birds, all widgeons ; and, strange to say, out of these three birds the four of us claimed at least one bird to our individual guns.

We now went below and had luncheon, and then began

Off the Tyne Bar.

to get things ready, and the long lines made their appearance. The sea off the Tyne is abrupt in its depth. Immediately off the breakwater one finds five and six fathoms; half-a-mile farther, ten or twelve; and two miles away, twenty-four or twenty-five. Any distance beyond eight miles from the shore one may find depths to his heart's content.

Now, be it borne in mind, the lifting of a line thirty or forty fathoms deep is not quite a joke, when a heavy fish is on. Moreover, it requires an adept to detect a fish on at such depths the moment he hooks himself. The sea, always heavy and on the move, gives many false alarms to the uninitiated; but when a man has been thus deceived a dozen times, he begins to set his heart into his work, and makes no such mistakes afterwards. Still, too great caution does not pay. If you never lift up your line but when you feel a fish on, you may allow it to be down with bare hooks for a considerable time, especially when crabs abound. If, on lifting your line, you fancy it is a little heavier than usual, you ought to get it up and see to it. Moreover, sea-fishing lines have their peculiarities. One vibrates, one stretches, one is seemingly as stiff as an iron rod and about as elastic, one kinks, the other does not, &c. If you doubt it, listen to three or four desperate hookers as they get ready for the fray; each picks out the line that suits his ways best, yet seemingly the lines are all alike. Then again, hark at the hookers' recommendations of hand-lines. When hooking becomes so delicate a sport as it is when the lines are of considerable length, it behoves a professed enthusiastic hooker always to use the same line, if he wishes to thoroughly enjoy all the little incidents of his sport. It does one's heart good to see how heartily those fond of the sport of sea-fishing enter into it, and I am sure not one of us, on our excursion off Tynemouth, would have changed places with any potentate, however mighty. Fred, I must state, was fishing astern with me, and he had, besides his own line, shied another of his own rig at some distance from the boat. This second " string " was weighted exactly like ours, but it had only one hook on a long stout gimp, and besides, on the long line let loose a large cork, painted red and white, was floating on the waves. Subsequently, I pointed out to Fred the defects of that rig, and he remedied them, but of this more anon. We had not been more than a minute feeling our lines, when, simultaneously, two of our companions jerked theirs up.

"Got one!" they exclaimed, and Fred and I looked on with envy. Two whitings, a couple of pounds weight, were the result of their first try. Up went my hand then, instinctively, almost startling me with its suddenness, and I had on something rather heavy. Rush one way, rush the other! and I bring up a codling about 3 lb. close to the surface, when, just as I was going to heave him on board, another fish rushed up, and hooked himself on the bottom hook. This second fish was about half the size of the former, but both looked very well, and were in my estimation far better fish than were my neighbours'. Fred then began blessing his stars, *sotto voce*:

"Not an ounce of luck I haven't," when suddenly he brightened up, and jumping to his feet, " By Jove!" said he, with a thoughtful air, " I have got one on this time ;" and he gives another sly feel, then up comes the line, four yards at a time, and flop he bundles a large codling on to the floor of the cockpit.

He was triumphant, and voted a baptism of his fish. Carried unanimously, and sport was resumed with greater earnestness than ever.

We then bethought ourselves of the line Fred had sent out on spec, and looked everywhere for its little buoy.

"I believe the line is broken and the cork gone," said Fred, when he pulled it up; but it was not, and soon the red-and-white affair loomed in the depths, and came up, when he declared that there was a fish on the hook, and it turned out to be a dogfish about two feet long.

I pointed out to him that the cork had been perfectly useless, and fishing out of my creel a board and bell ready to be screwed on the gunwale, I explained to him its *modus operandi*, and he forthwith proceeded to try it. He re-baited his line, renewed his float, cast away the lead and hooks, and, making due allowance of line for the boat's sheering motions, gave two or three turns round the piece of wood, and the whole affair was ready.

We caught several fish, and then the bell rang desperately; Fred's brother at the time was hauling up his line, and declared he had a large fish on; Fred hauled up the floating line, and said he had one there also. He pulled, his brother pulled, and then they found that their lines were entangled together, and that they had no fish whatsoever on. Each one's lead had deceived the other.

At 4 o'clock we had a tremendous load of fish of the most varied description, weighing, more or less, a couple of hundred pounds. In fact, we were getting them in all the afternoon, as fast almost as we could haul up our deep lines and rebait them. At dusk we began to feel tired, and an indescribable longing came over us to feel *terra firmâ* under our feet once more. So out of the way we placed our gear, and our men, who during all the time we had been fishing had remained in the fo'c'sle, came up looking rather seedy and sleepy. Snow began to fall, and it was a perfect miracle that no one was pitched overboard during the hoisting up of the sails and anchor and general working of the boat, for the deck, owing to the sleet and snow "fixing" themselves there, was terribly slippery, and more like a skating-rink than anything else.

On our return journey we had a little amusement. A black duck was coming straight along for a broadside, and we were all ready for his reception. I was in the cockpit, and had the first shot. Bang, bang! Before the smoke of my two barrels had quite cleared away, I knew the verdict was "Missed," by the various exclamations of "Duffer!" unanimously and ironically given by my companions. Then bang! bang, bang, bang! bang, bang! You never heard such a row, and the fun was that all missed the blessed bird, and I had the satisfaction of grinning in return at my companions.

We re-entered the bar at about 6 P.M., all fairly knocked up.

We caught a train at North Shields, and found ourselves, at 7 o'clock, with our legs "under the mahogany," and a good dinner, well earned, before us. Thus ended our first day.

The next morning, according to my special request, we started a little earlier, and went for trips along the coast. The weather was a little colder, and some snow fell again part of the day. I was riled at having missed the black duck so stupidly, and the others were also anxious to show me that they could handle their "shootin'-irons" better than on the previous day. But we were destined to experience another snubbing at the hands of Fate, for the first bird that passed us we again collectively missed.

"That will never do," I thought. "Let us resort to the 4-bores." I quietly took one of the heavy guns, and loading it, placed it handy. Fred followed suit, remarking that the birds were so tough, that nothing short of a cannon, loaded with grape-shot, could tell on them.

Some dozen or so of ducks passed at about a hundred yards. Fred fired and they went. I fired and one fell. The next company I fired first, and none came down, whereas when he fired one was winged.

"It is a tie," said he; but, in reality, such work is no criterion of the driving capabilities of the guns. The birds flew wide of one another, so that there was no compact hitting into the leaders. It was either killing one or none. Of course the comparative mildness of the weather was the cause of this. When it is very rough and cold, it is astonishing how close the birds crowd one to another, even when on the-wing. We had considerable sport, nevertheless, with the guns, bagging seven birds, and losing one or two that fell too near the shore for us to venture near enough to pick them up.

Our first tack was past Tynemouth, along the Long Sands and past the Smugglers' Cave. We then sailed by Cullercoats and Whitley, went by the Whitley Sands, Briersden Burn, and the village of Hartley, by which time it was nearly 12 o'clock. We had been going on in short tacks against a strong head-wind all the way, hence our being so slow to cover such a short distance—*i.e.* not more than eight miles, I believe. Returning was a totally different affair, as the wind was directly in our favour, and we came back as if borne on the wings of a hurricane. When we passed the Bar on our starboard the men suggested that it would be wise not to go too far south, as the wind might have increased and precluded the notion of re-entering the harbour, and we agreed that we would not go lower than the Lizard Point. We then passed the Herd Sands, Frenchman's Bay, and coastguard-station, and dropped anchor opposite the Marsden Rock, some four miles south from the mouth of the harbour.

There we found lots of divers, and bagged one before the anchor was fairly down. This caused the men to grumble—they always do when a little extra work turns up. The bird secured, we came back to the spot where we had originally intended anchoring, and had a little sea-fishing. The fish naturally ran smaller than we had found them in the deeper water, but we got on very nicely indeed, and had it not been for the birds, which kept bothering us continually, we should have certainly trebled our score.

First came a line of ducks, too far. Then several widgeon and teal passed by, also too far off. Half-a-dozen black ducks came next, and we riddled one of them. Then, when we had resumed fishing, and were beginning to enjoy it, someone drew our attention to a large diver about a hundred and sixty yards away. Fred went below and brought back a small breech-loading rifle. The betting was lively at any amount to one on the bird. Fred was bothered at this, as he wished to shine in this particular line, and he actually drew a "bead" within a yard of the bird. Down went the diver, whilst the conical bullet was ricocheting far away over the North Sea.

"Now, where is he?" asked our inveterate rifleman, when he had reloaded.

"Stop," I said, "fire beyond the bird, Fred, it will bring it nearer."

"Will it?" he said, "all right;" and when the diver turned up he fired above it, and at the next turn-up the bird was, at least, forty yards nearer to us.

"This time you ought to kill it," the other fellows said, but he did not, and probably the bird will remain a living target for a good many years to come, if only rifles are fired at him. I have not much faith in rifle-shooting from a boat. I have seen thousands of bullets fired thus, and can safely say I never saw a bird killed under such circumstances. The motion of the craft, however slight, is sure to disturb the aim. When ashore, however, I have seen, and have performed myself, excellent shots with rook-rifles. One of my last acquisitions in the firearm line is a ·380 rook-and-rabbit rifle of Messrs. Holland and Holland, the celebrated makers, of Bond Street. With this instrument I have repeatedly knocked over rooks at above a hundred yards' range, and rabbits at a hundred and fifty. A better tool to draw a "small bead" with I have never yet seen.

To resume my narrative. At 2 o'clock we went away to sea for two hours, and fell to work in thirty fathoms of water. The sea was very clear, notwithstanding the few flakes of snow that persisted in falling, and we could see our fish a fathom or two before they reached the surface. We got some score of fish, half of which were certainly above 2 lb. in weight, and the rest about 1 lb. each. The whiting was extremely abundant; at one haul I had three on, and we repeatedly caught two.

Altogether my trip to the neighbourhood of the Tyne was most enjoyable. Birds were fairly abundant, and the fish positively swarming. The sea, however, was rough at the best of times, and I should not advise weak-stomached hookers to go and try hooking there.

At dark we were sailing back up the river in company with two or three screeching screw-steamers, and at 9 P.M. I was once more in the train speeding back to town, fully satisfied with the sport I had found off the Tyne Bar.

CHAPTER LIX.

SUNDERLAND.

WHEN I went to Sunderland I did not expect to find it such a fine town, and as for the harbour, it simply took me by surprise. I have a friend living in the town, so as soon as I landed I hunted him out—no very arduous task, as everybody knows everybody in Sunderland—and at 6 P.M. I found myself dining with my friend and his family.

I ascertained from my host that the fish caught in the harbour were mostly of insignificant size, but that some gentlemen of the town and neighbourhood were constantly in the habit of going out to sea in boats for fishing and wildfowl-shooting. He stated that a friend of his would place a boat at my disposal, with two men, who would take me wherever I liked; but laughingly declined my suggestion that he should accompany me, on the ground that he was a "poor sailor," and, to the best of his knowledge, had never fired a gun. I therefore made up my mind to be alone in my glory on the morrow. The weather, I may remark, was remarkably cold, although I had left London flooded with mud and steaming. Of course my friend knew all about the surroundings of the place, and he declared that any depths almost were to be had within twelve miles of the shore. The next thing to be done was to get bait. Lugs were not to be had; the shore is too pebbly for them. A few mackerel were purchased instead, and as they were tolerably fresh I was satisfied. One of the two men who were to take me out on the morrow agreed to call for me at the hotel, and we parted.

When he came in the morning he looked rather doubtful, and said it was snowing slightly. Evidently he thought this would put a stop to the excursion; but as I had only two days to spare, I was not going to be put off by a trifle, and away we went. It was about 7.30, and there was a moderately strong breeze blowing from the north, which made the harbour look very ripply. Nothing daunted, we set sail, and in ten minutes were clear and away. In answer to the men's inquiry, I had told them to shape our course towards the deepest water they knew, and the steersman turned her head slightly north, and said that thirty fathoms would be about the average of the part we were going to. I sat forward in the bows with my two guns by my side, muzzle upwards, and kept a good lookout for any stray birds.

The first two or three miles were traversed without anything coming within range, and no companies were floating about in our way. I began to feel dull, and fished out a briar-root pipe, but whilst loading it the men saw birds some distance ahead, and drew my attention to them. We shaped our course their way, and just then, to our astonishment, several ducks passed overhead, without our seeing them until it was too late to fire. I had collared a gun, and was looking disconsolate, when I caught a glimpse of another duck coming along singly, in the wake of his predecessors, and evidently trying to follow their line of flight. I turned round quietly, and when he arrived overhead sent him one ounce and one-eighth of No. 4 shot out of my

12-bore, and he almost fell in the boat. The men got the sail down, and rowed back to pick up the bird—a splendid mallard, in first-rate plumage and condition; and how lovely these birds do look to a sportsman who has shot them himself!

When our bird was bagged, we resumed sail, but before the boat had quite gathered way, we shipped a copious sea over the bows.

"It will be a rough day, sir, I am afraid," said one of the men; but I told him I did not mind that if we had sport.

We looked about for the birds we had sighted at first, but owing to the increased roughness of the sea could not, for some time, discover them, and then only when we were sailing past them. They were about four hundred yards on our port side, and the wind being hard on us from that quarter, there was but faint prospect of our being able to get up to them at all. We nevertheless made up our minds to try.

"It will take us two tacks with the boat, but that will do it," said the man at the tiller, and we went about at once, took a spin towards the Roker Battery, and when well abreast with it, tacked on our starboard, and I got ready.

We were then half-a-mile from the birds, but well forward of them, and with the wind we had we were bound to sail close by them, and within easy range. As we got nearer I saw they were widgeons, and told the men so. They crouched at the bottom of the boat, and the man at the tiller steered from the signals I gave him by hand. We passed within a hundred yards of the hindmost bird, and as the long gun alone could bear with some chance of success at that distance, I aimed above the last lot, and when they rose I pulled. Simultaneously with the report my two men jumped up to see what was the result. The birds were all flying away, and we thought the shot had been a clean miss. I was reloading disconsolately, when one of my companions jumped up on the seat amidships, holding on to the mast, and declared that one of the birds had fallen down, or else settled on the sea.

"Then," I said, "it is a cripple, and we will have him yet."

This was sooner said than done, for the widgeon had flown on with the others, and he was now four hundred yards away, necessitating two more tacks, and then, during the manœuvring of the craft, we lost sight of him several times. At last we spied him, and the moment he tried to rise I settled him. I fancy he had been at first but very slightly hit, and had I not been ready to stop him thus summarily we might have lost him.

I remember once firing a large gun at a company, and picking up, amongst four ducks, one—a mallard—that to all appearances was quite dead. He was placed under the stern-sheets with the others, and we had resumed our look-out, when someone remarked that the mallard was on the move. Sure enough there he was, standing on the planking, and rolling with the motion of the boat. We tried to collar him, but he then half climbed, half jumped on the seat, went overboard, set sail, and we looked on without a thought of firing, so that he escaped scot-free! Probably one of the large shot had struck him on the head and stunned him completely for awhile.

Our chase had taken us quite opposite the life-boat station, two miles north of the harbour, and we had already been over three hours out, much to our astonishment. I told the men that hooking was just as amusing as shooting, but they laughed and shook their heads incredulously.

They had seen boys fishing at Sunderland, and thought little of the sport. I promised that when we reached our ground I would lend one of them a line, and if he did not like it he could leave off. With this understanding we held away towards the open sea, but had strong doubts as to the advisability of going far. The sky looked very low and very dark. We had no compass, and should a heavy fall of snow take place the trip might have ended in a tragedy, which would have appeared in the papers, headed "Lost in the North Sea; dreadful sufferings," &c. We were content, therefore, to drop our anchor five miles from shore in some twenty-fathom holes. I had prepared my lines whilst we were under way, and it was with quite a merry feeling that I gave the men a line each, and told them how to use them. Now we began, and presently one of them caught a very large whiting. This excited his comrade, who, too, was soon rewarded, and the three of us remained hard at work until 3 P.M., when the sea got so bad that it was deemed advisable to get back as soon as possible. The whiting had been extremely abundant, and the men had a great pile heaped up forward as their share, and I had done equally well. One of the men hooked on his line a tremendous gurnard, which would have certainly broken away had he not played him quietly, allowed him a little line when needed, and taken advantage of the fish getting tired or lazy to bring him up with safety to the tackle. I complimented him on his angling craft, and he admitted that nothing would give him greater pleasure than to go out two or three days a week, and enjoy his outings at the whiting-banks.

On our way back we saw several companies of birds, but the sea was so rough that it was impossible to fire straight. The lighthouses were beginning to twinkle when we arrived off the piers, and we went in with a brig or two from abroad.

On our way up we fell in with the skipper of a Dutch boat, who had also been out fishing with three of his men, and they had a most tremendous load of fish in their boat. They had been fishing lower down the coast, and had seemingly hit upon good rocky ground, as they had a great variety of rock-fish, amongst which were four or five congers. I asked the skipper where they had anchored, and he told me half-way between the new pier lighthouse and the Salterfan Rocks, in about ten fathoms. We made a note of this for the morrow, and I told the men to make sure of a good bit of bait, as we had run so short that we had baited very parsimoniously for the last hour of our fishing. The next morning turned out quite bright and cold, the wind blew from nearly the same quarter, but not so strong as on the previous afternoon.

A cousin of my friend's joined me for this trip, and was very anxious to get a shot at some birds.

" It is not that I care to eat them," said he, " but I am making a collection, and every bird I shoot I get stuffed."

I thought to myself, if I were to get every bird I have shot stuffed, what a collection I should have!

However, his enthusiasm was infectious, and I caught it beautifully, and the way we strained our eyes in every direction to catch sight of coming birds would have done good to any *blasé* man.

The few birds we saw at first kept tantalisingly near, and yet surprisingly well out of range, so that we had none until we had quite passed the timber-pond, and entered the sort of bay formed by the coast between the new pier and the Salterfan Rocks. We there saw about two score of black ducks and divers, and near the rocks three widgeons.

My companion had not any black ducks or divers in his collection, and was anxious to secure, at least, a specimen of each. I placed the sweeps forward across the bows in such a way as to allow me to peep between them and the gunwale when getting near the birds, and my companion took his seat by my side at the bottom of the boat. The two men remained aft and sat out of sight; one of them, who was smoking, put out his pipe of his own accord, which showed his good sense, and we soon made way on the birds. I kept my eye on the first lot, five in number. Two or three were diving, and coming up every other moment. The others had fed probably, as they were pluming themselves and ducking their heads under water, shaking their wings, standing up on the sea almost, and apparently well satisfied with themselves. I whispered to my companion that one of them would be on our starboard, and therefore on his side. He nodded "All right," and when I looked through once more we were about a hundred yards from the birds, the boat gliding on fast and well with our stern-wind. I nudged my companion, and we took up our guns.

"Fire at him sitting," I whispered ; "it is a small diver, a grebe, I believe ; it is no use trying to shoot him flying. Pop your barrel quietly over the gunwale. Now at him!"

As I said the words, boom went the gun, and the grebe had been, but was no more.

The three black ducks that had been feeding got up together. I let fly the 4-bore at them, and got the "tailer."

We were then about half a mile or rather less from the shore, and had some popping at flocks of shore-birds that passed on all sides of us. Before we reached the rocks we had about a dozen birds, including the grebe and the black duck. My friend inclined to devoting the whole day to shooting, but I was anxious to see what the fishing would be like at the spot where the Dutch captain had been the day before, and the men were getting tired of rowing after the wounded birds. We had to sail out about a mile, and anchored nearly three miles from Sunderland, in a south-easterly line. I had brought a rod for this trip, and weighted the line with a 4-oz. lead, just sufficient to keep it taut, and not heavy enough to make it awkward to feel a bite. I baited my two bottom hooks with mackerel and the top hook with a strip of mackerel skin, which I cut to resemble a small fry. I begged my friend to take one of the lines, and the men had already begun when I made my first cast. I found the depth to be about seven or eight fathoms, and that was quite as much as I could conveniently manage with my light rod and tackle. I got a pouting almost as soon as my lead reached the bottom, the fish being hooked over the strip of bright skin, disdaining the more substantial bait underneath it. That was indeed clutching at "the shadow for the substance." The strip being uninjured, I let the line go again, and I believe it was caught before the lead fairly reached the bottom. This time it was a codling, and again the strip of mackerel had proved the attraction. I "promenaded" my line about along the bottom, and presently there came such a tremendous wriggling pull that the rod bent under the waves. I held on like grim death, knowing well that if I once let the expected conger get into a hole my line would be almost certainly lost.

"What is it?" asked my companions.

"It is something that will make you jump out of its way, or I am much mistaken," I said with a grin. One of the men picked up a board and got ready to settle the conger as soon as he came up, which he did speedily, as the elasticity of the rod tires the fish wonderfully, and in a minute I had the fellow in. He was about a yard-and-a-half long, and we had some trouble to kill him and get the hook out. On the next hook was a small pouting, almost microscopic in size. It was a marvel how it had managed to get the hook and bait within its little mouth. The other hookers were not idle. We got several rays, several congers, half-a-dozen good codlings, a dozen gurnards and coalfish, and a rare lot of pouting and whiting. The weather was lovely, though rather cold, the sea fairly smooth, and the sport quite exhilarating.

We had luncheon at about 1 o'clock, and as we were getting rather cramped with sitting up, we thought a half-sail, half-row would do us good, and took a tack towards shore. I removed my tackle from the rod, and substituted a whiffing-line, but I only caught one fish, and gave it up. When the circulation of our blood was restored we went northwards in a fifteen-fathom spot, and there my old rod came to irretrievable grief. It was the one whose top joint I had mended on my trip to Holyhead, and I felt confident that that top joint would stand a good deal, but, alas for human calculations! the *second* joint broke down very badly. I had on two fish, and was trying to feel their weight, when I heard and felt a crack was taking place in my apparatus. A glance showed me the seat of disorder, and I thereupon pronounced an *oraison funèbre* over the remains of the poor rod. Two joints out of four out of order, the concern must now be shelved, but it will have that place amidst my paraphernalia of sport which an old and faithful servant deserves. I may add that I managed to bring up my fish by trusting only to the line.

Towards 4 o'clock we packed up and came back. I had told my companion that as evening drew near many

Sunderland. 233

birds would be certain to turn up, and he had looked forward to the time with longing. But we were doomed to disappointment. Very few birds were seen, and only two of them passed near enough to warrant a shot. Of these we disabled one, chased it for nearly half a mile, and fired a dozen shots before it gave up the ghost. This brought my Sunderland trip to a worthy conclusion. The only defect I noticed was the bleak openness of the sea. There is no bay there, so to speak, and you are blown about by the winds from three sides of the compass. A fair sailor, therefore, is needed to do the place justice in the hooking line, and I daresay, in severe winter weather, a very fair bag of fowl could be made with large-bore shoulder-guns.

CHAPTER LX.

THE WALLET, ORFORDNESS, AND THE DEBEN.

I HAD three days to spare, and made up my mind to spend them at sea. A London friend of mine had arranged to pick me up at Maldon, and he accordingly sailed his 10-tonner up the Blackwater, anchoring in the river about a mile from the Heybridge basin, where he landed with his dingey to meet me. I arrived in the evening, and brought with me the most beastly weather that can be conceived. The wind was blowing a regular gale, and rain fell in torrents. We discussed matters at the Blue Boar Hotel, and after a sound dinner came to the conclusion that, since the "wine was drawn, we were bound to drink it," and forthwith set off for the basin.

No sooner were we in the small boat, and had shoved out in mid-stream, than there was another downpour, and in two minutes we were drenched to the skin, and the dingey had a foot or so of rain-water wandering over its planking. We dropped down the river for a good quarter of an hour, and the rain was falling so thick that we could not see the yacht's riding-light. At last we spied and made for it. My friend's friend helped me on board, and we changed our clothes, made ourselves snug in the cabin,

The Wallet, Orfordness, and the Deben. 235

and, whilst talking and smoking, listened to the roar of the gale outside. It blew terribly, and the whistling in the rigging promised us a treat for the night. By-and-by the tide rose, and then we got the full benefit of the war amongst the elements. No glass or bottle could stand, and the swinging of the boom told a tale. Of course we could not have set sail owing to the darkness, even if the coast had been clear, which it was not.

We turned in at 12 o'clock. Lulled by the noise of the waves and wind, and rocked by the boat, I was soon in the land of dreams.

At 7 o'clock I went on deck. The sky was clearing up, but the wind was still high, and the boat swerved very roughly. The river was riding white, but not so badly as to prevent us from sailing about, and we spread the yacht's wings after breakfast and sailed down the estuary, intending to go as far as the state of the sea would permit, and if the storm was really too bad in the Wallet we would remain in the Blackwater, or would run up the Colne to Brightlingsea and remain there for shelter.

We were not slow in reaching the Mersea Island. There we found that it would be but a sheer foolhardy trick to go to sea, so we turned her back, and went to knock about after birds. We had three very large-bore guns, one a muzzle-loader, into whose muzzle one could drop a half-crown, and the two others were single breech-loading 4-bores. The loading of the first weapon almost took my breath away. Nearly half a canister of powder and well-nigh half a pound of shot in a "shooting-iron" means earnest business, and I thought to myself, "The ducks or widgeons that are within ninety yards in front of the muzzle of that gun when it is fired will have to look out for squalls;" and I promised myself to keep an eye on the "sweep" of that gun whenever a chance turned up of seeing it perform.

We were about twenty minutes going, before sighting a company "on the squat." There were many on the wing, but all flying far away. The company we saw was about half a mile N.W. from Bradwell quay, and we found on getting closer that they were mixed birds—widgeons and ducks—about a dozen altogether, and as the sea was rough in the reach, they did not dive, but kept heading the wind and topping the waves. My host took the muzzle-loading instrument of warfare, and fixed it on a movable rest forward in the bows. A coil or two of rope lashed to the boom sheltered him against the spray, and hid him at the same time from the birds. I went by his side with one of the 4-bores, and the other man crouched in the cockpit with the other. When we were at a fairish range some of the ducks took to their wings, and the whole lot began to stretch necks and flap sides. Next moment I saw my friend's shoulder recoiling violently, and simultaneously the gun-barrel jumping up, these movements being accompanied with a cloud of smoke and a roar as of artillery. Three widgeons just leaving the water were cut down clean in the attempt, and a swimming duck, some ten yards farther, was also laid flat on the waves. The rest of the birds flew so wide of each other that there was no chance for the two 4-bores to hit more than one bird at a shot, and, as fate would have it, our companion and I fired at the same bird. It dropped, of course, and I was laying the soft unction to my soul that I had done the deed, when our friend entered his protest that he, too, had aimed at the unlucky duck.

Now that the birds were down came the question how were we to pick them up? The sea was bad, so that going into the dingey was, for the time, quite out of the question.

"We shall lose our birds," I said, "unless the skipper handles the yacht in such a way as to bring us within easy reach of the birds before they drift over the shallows."

We flew on at least a hundred yards ere we could bring her to and get her about. Then I went forward to signal the way, whilst the lad and my two companions stood by, one with a gaff, the next with a sweep, and the third with a landing-net, ready to pounce on our prey as soon as it came within reach. We missed the first bird, but kept on, and picked up the two next; came back again, and the landing-net again secured another; finally, on the third tack, we picked up the last but one. As for the last, we lost sight of it, and it must have drifted to shore in the course of the day. That is the first bird, to my knowledge, we lost during the season at sea; but then the day was really bad, and our ground too dangerous to indulge in any piece of recklessness.

When we had done with our birds we went to anchor in the large creek at Single Head Point, and the men went below to get luncheon ready. Meanwhile the wind abated gradually, the clouds went their way, and when our meal was concluded a most charming day it promised to be. The reach was smoothing down its roughened billows, and many smacks began to appear on the scene. As we had yet four hours' daylight I voted that we should go at once to the Wallet and try sea-fishing. We had a lot of bait on board, a pailful of lugs, besides mackerel and herring, and my hands itched to feel a line. We had a fine spin past the bar, and got into the Wallet at about 3.30. We anchored between the Gunfleet and the Buxey, in six or seven fathoms, and of all places commend me to the spot for a bit of fun with the hook. We frequently had three fish on each line, and though the majority ran small, we caught some very handsome fish, and interest in the sport never flagged for a moment.

At dusk the sea was quite smooth, the wind had dropped almost altogether, and the scene was lovely as we stood watching the shore-lights glimmering and flickering in the increasing gloom of the night. We remained fishing till 6 o'clock, when we tripped up the anchor; and the little wind that blew being fair, we undertook sailing to Harwich harbour and remaining there for the night. On we went, trying our best to cover our twenty-five miles' journey as soon as possible; but it promised to be a rather tedious undertaking, and when everything was made snug in the harbour it was 2.30.

We remained in our bunks until 10 A.M., when, on coming up, we found the day and the wind quite mild. We passed the Langer Point at 12 o'clock, and, heading north-east, and keeping within two miles of shore, soon left Felixtow behind on our port side, and reached the mouth of the river Deben at 3 P.M. We then came a mile or so nearer shore, and kept on the same tack all the afternoon, making the Orford haven at dusk. We were then very near some first-rate whiting banks, and prepared our tackle with glee for the next day's fray. We had still a lot of lugs, and by packing them with sand, seaweed, and a judicious addition of fresh sea-water every now and then, we managed to keep them in good condition. There are few baits which whiting will not leave for a piece of lug, so we looked forward to good sport on the next day.

At 10 o'clock we were all below and in bed. I was the first up in the morning, and before I got fairly on deck I became aware of the state of the weather by the appearance of the cockpit, which was very wet. There was a little wind, and we were about an hour and a half getting to the whiting bank, and there prepared ourselves for a lengthened stay. I went into the dingey by myself, with a tinful of lugs, two mackerel, and two fresh herrings as my share of bait. I had a gun with me, in case some birds should turn up.

It is astonishing how quickly the gull tribe especially congregate round a boat where any fishing is going on, and as some friends had asked me to get them specimens, I was wishful to bag a few. I then got two lines ready, using moderate-sized hooks, and baited with lugs to begin with, and found them answer admirably. The first line down was quite cleaned out of bait before I was ready with the other, and I had only one fish on. Still it was a good omen; but, to make matters safer, I thought one line would do to work at a time. My friends were equally diligent, and sat facing me, astern of the yacht. We got on capitally with our hooking. All the smaller fish were thrown back as soon as caught, and what I had expected soon took place. A lot of seagulls congregated to pounce upon our refuse, and I soon had my choice of the birds I wanted. There were about thirty birds around us, and amongst these were several blue-backed gulls, two black ones, and an enormous gray one. The latter was very shy, but keeping my eye on him he soon gave me an opportunity, and I bagged him and a black-backer. I then called out to one of my friends to cast the painter loose, and taking up the sculls I rowed to the birds and picked them up. The gray fellow was fully five feet and a half from tip to tip, and his head was the size of a baby's. As for his beak, it was a "caution." As soon as the other birds saw that there was something wrong they sheered off, and nothing would bring them near for a long time. The two I had were all I required; and nothing, I think, is more reckless and savouring of deliberate cruelty than firing at birds one does not want.

Whilst rowing back to the yacht I discovered that a breeze had sprung up, and as we had done very well at the south part of the bank, we thought after luncheon we would try the north point. Now, the bank proper is only three miles long or so, but the shallows around it at least double that distance, and we were about an hour reaching our new station. Several trawlers and shrimpers passed by, and from one of the latter we bought some splendid shrimps for the table and for bait. Opinions differed widely on board our craft. I said that live shrimps were best. My friend said boiled ones were "cocks of the walk;" and to put the matter to a test we tried both, but the fish were so well on the feed that they took anything. Mackerel strips, mackerel bits, herring pieces, bits of lugs, and shrimps, raw or boiled, seemed welcome to them; but, if anything, the lugs won the day.

By-the-way, the fisherman who sold us our shrimps told us that they were rather scarce, and that the shrimpers had in consequence to extend their field of action considerably. This man had been twelve hours out, according to his account, and had but seven or eight shillings' worth of shrimps; pretty fair pay, it is true, for twelve hours' work, but then something must be allowed for nets, and for the wear and tear of the boat and its gear. We remained off the bank until 2 o'clock, when we found that our catches amounted to scores of fish.

Now, my time drawing near, I opined that setting sail back for Heybridge basin, or any other landing-point, would be the right thing to do; but in yachting matters, to parody the well-known saying "*L'homme propose,*" &c., instead of heaven one must say the sea disposes; and although I

The Wallet, Orfordness, and the Deben. 241

had intended being only three days away—lo! my three days were already nearly spent, and I was sixty miles by sea from our starting-point. I yielded, however, with a very good grace to my friend's entreaties to stop for another day. This decision come to, I told my companions that we were not far from the river Deben, and if they had no objection we would go there to anchor for the night, and the next day could be spent shooting along the river.

At 5 o'clock we entered the haven, and went to anchor a little higher than the ferry. Early in the morning we were up and doing, and whilst breakfast was getting ready I went on deck with a couple of guns and kept watch over the water. There were a great many small waders about, and any amount of curlews, herons, &c., but all wild, and no ducks were to be seen. The only shot I had was at half-a-dozen companies of black ducks which passed over the bar in the offing. Just, however, when breakfast was laid, a lot of curlews came over to sit on the mud on our side, and I began well by flooring three of them.

After breakfast we got our ammunition and guns in the dingey, the lad undertaking to row us about. Acting on my advice, my friend has had his dingey fitted up with a small mast and sail, which we soon found very handy. He had also found it an improvement to alter the first seat in the boat according to the directions I gave in one of my papers; so we were all facing the same way, had plenty of room, and dispensed with the oars for nine-tenths of the way. The owner took the fore-seat, with his muzzle-loading implement; our friend sat amidships, near the mast; the lad was by his side, holding the ropes; and your humble servant was in the stern-sheets, with a 4-bore and his double 12-bore for cripples.

When we were off Falkenham, the biggest gun got its

first crack at two passing birds. Both were floored, and I saw the swan-shot cutting along the water and splashing the mud on shore at least fifty yards farther. The birds picked up and the gun reloaded, we set sail again up river, and, seeing no large birds, agreed to make a "mixed" bag. It was mixed with a vengeance. We got two pigeons, a tame duck, a wild ditto, at least forty oxbirds and sandpipers, three curlews, a diver, two grebes, and three crows. The latter were shot at the urgent request of the lad, whose skipper, it seems, was fond of that delicacy. As for the tame duck, it served him right. He had no business to be flying about like a disreputable fellow over that part of the river.

We had at least two hundred shots during the day. Every second almost a shot turned up, and more than once we all fired together at different birds. One shot knocked over a shank, the next shot laid an oxbird low, the third floored a sandpiper; then a flock of these birds was spied coming along at wonderful speed, and the rustling of their wings reached the ear like the sound of a heavy downpour of rain on the leaves of forest trees.

The local shooters along the Deben do not shoot at small waders. They say that it is not worth their while. Is it because the birds are too small to warrant the expenditure of powder and shot to a professional, or is it because the said professionals cannot hit them? It takes a good gun and a rather handy shooter to bag one out of two such shots, and the professional duck-shooters are at a loss when they have to cope with the tumbles and gyrations of a shank, for instance. There is a wide difference between bagging a duck, that comes to you as straight as a poker, and a lively little bird that, when in the air, seems dancing, or rather hopping, from one wing to the other, with jerks a couple of yards or so in length at each jump. I believe every professional who fires at a shank on the impulse of the moment generally swears at his folly as soon as he has pulled trigger.

During our trip we fell in with such a man, and we saw him fire ten shots for one bird.

We landed at the ferry at Ramsholt for a few minutes, and we boarded the yacht again at 1 o'clock, found luncheon ready, a long line ready baited, and the trawl fixed on by the port side of the boat. We went out in the dingey, and laid the line just outside the haven, and then returned to enjoy our meal. This settled, we set sail and cleared out of the river, anchored at the bar, and went to pick up the long line. We found almost every second hook occupied, but the fish ran small, although there were five or six very good ones. We next made the best of our way to a good trawling-ground about two miles from the coast, and there had three casts, averaging each very fair catches, but nothing wonderful in point of size. A little before dark we had a few shots at passing birds, but did not bag; and then we ran into the harbour, and sailed right up to the town at Harwich. The dingey took the three of us ashore, we had a parting meal at the hotel, and my friends saw me off by train. We arranged to go south in a few days, if the weather should turn right for a trip, and our mutual friend made us promise solemnly that we would not go without him.

CHAPTER LXI.

OFF THE TEES MOUTH.

THERE are few places along the coast where one may meet with the many varieties of sport to be found at and near the Tees mouth. Those who object to going far to sea for their fishing will find there all depths, and consequently all sorts of fish, within three miles or a little over from the shore. Moreover, when the wind and sea are rather rough, and preclude going away at all in small boats, the mouth of the Tees offers nice fun in the shape of a quiet anchorage, lots of small waders to fire at, besides an occasional large bird, and the hooking for dabs, &c., can be carried on there comfortably and pleasantly. When tired of boating, the sands from Saltburn past Redcar up to the Bran Sand, back by the lighthouse and Tod Point, are simply charming, and at this time of the year they afford no end of popping to the gunner, there being absolutely nobody to be seen there now, barring an occasional wood and odds-and-ends gatherer, plying his calling at each retiring tide. Besides all these inducements to the sportsman, the neighbourhood is very pretty, and the accommodation perfectly equal to all requirements. There is, therefore, no occasion to feel any *ennui* there, even during a fortnight's stay, and I recommend the spot to those of my readers who may now be in search of a quiet place, where they may enjoy their comforts, and find withal tolerable food for their sporting tastes and cravings. Two of us were on the expedition, and my companion had already been with me on several trips this year. We arrived in the evening, and at once sent for a man to take us out on the morrow and to secure bait. Fortunately the weather turned bright during the night, and we made our start the next morning under the best of auspices.

The Tees is not a very comfortable river to navigate, owing to the numerous sand-banks which almost block its estuary here and there, so that even with a small boat it needs a sound knowledge of the line, especially at high· tide, for when the sand-banks are covered over with the brine, then heaven and the pilots alone know where they are.

When we started, at about 7 o'clock, the tide was half-ebb, and running out right smartly yet. We made ready as soon as we passed Port Clarence, and hearing many birds calling on the shore, we loaded one barrel of our 12-bore with No. 8 shot, the other with No. 6, and our two 4-bores with the usual swan-shot.

By-the-way, I am happy to say that my experience of "choke-bores in the field" quite agrees with that of *Bell's* able contributor, "Peveril." Everyone who has fired the choke, or modified choke-bores, at wildfowl and seafowl will agree with me that they leave the old guns a long way behind in that particular line of business. First of all, they carry a good deal farther than the old guns; they also carry their shot more compactly, and their driving powers leave nothing to be desired. Indeed, a 12-bore, choke or modified, loaded with duck-shot, carries its load fully up to a hundred yards. If anyone doubts it, let him try it on a flock of oxbirds, and he will find that several birds will be killed, if the flock is compact, at a range at which an ordinary gun would produce just as much effect as if loaded with snuff instead of shot. I only advise this trial as an experiment, just to satisfy oneself of the state of the case. For regular shooting I like firing at single birds, because that is the only criterion of skill in the marksman, and the question for an amateur is not to kill many birds, but to exercise his knack in the handling of his weapon. That is why we had loaded with small shot both our double guns.

We began work soon after passing the Point. One of our men pointed out three curlews on the shore, stalking close to the water, almost opposite Lazenby station, but, of course, a good mile and a half or so from it, for the estuary altogether widens there considerably, and extends to four, five, and six miles respectively, from shore to shore, at sundry points. Well, we went down with the tide so quietly, that when the curlews thought fit to go they were well within range of the 4-bores, and we got two of them, the third starting at a run towards the bar. Tom's spaniel, however, bolted overboard at once, and after a smart chase captured the bird and brought him back.

Our two men had been somewhat astonished at the performance of the big guns.

"If you had been here, gentlemen, six weeks ago with these guns," said one of them, "you could have loaded the boat with birds. The estuary was full of them when it froze hard and the snow was on the ground."

The three curlews picked up and stowed away, we had a shot at some gray plovers. I saw them coming up the estuary a good half-mile off. There were about a couple of hundred together, and they flew so fast that in a few seconds they were upon us. Now, in such a case, one has no choice, and *must* fire at the flock. The two No. 8 barrels floored about a dozen, the two No. 6 only about half-a-dozen, on account of the distance; but Tom fired his big gun at about a hundred and twenty yards, and the swan-shot cut down nearly a score. Our men were perfectly enthusiastic.

"Well, that is what I call business," remarked one, with an undisguised admiration, which goes a long way to prove that, in his estimation, "success is the index of merit."

The dog got fairly bothered at this unexpected number of cripples and dead birds, and it was quite laughable to see how he behaved in the water. He swam to a cripple, then another bird would flutter energetically, and so attract his attention, that he would leave *ses premiers amours* to attend to the new one.

We, however, rowed to the different spots, and soon got the lot aboard. When we had done, we looked about us, and what I expected had taken place—several of the cripples had paddled to shore, and were there running about. The dog was sent in pursuit, and eventually we got them all. Whilst thus engaged the flock passed over us again, but we were so busy that we did not see them until it was too late to fire, and they escaped scot-free. The tide was then quite low, and the river very quiet.

"We had better make our way quickly out," our man remarked, "before the flow comes up strong, as we should find it almost impossible then to get clear away, there being so little wind."

They then got the sail up and took the sweeps, and in this wise we passed the Par Lighthouse and the floating light. At Snook Point, however, we met the strong tide full in the bows, and our progress was slower. We saw several small bunches of birds on the sea, and would gladly have gone in chase, but all our efforts were insufficient to bring us quickly enough upon the birds. The noise of the sweeps besides frightens them, and moreover the sea was too smooth and the birds too shy to give us the shadow of a chance.

When we reached the bay proper, we found a slight breeze awaiting us, and the tide lost a good deal of its strength against us, as we had left the channel. We, therefore, made far better way, and in about an hour and a half we anchored opposite West Scar, in about twenty-three fathoms, some three miles from shore. It was then about mid-day. There was no sun, but it was not cold. The sea was remarkably smooth, the boat scarcely moved, and fishing was very pleasant. I found that bait was not very abundant, and proposed to try a little whiffing of my own device. I rigged on my rod, and Tom hooked with an ordinary deep-sea line. I was some five minutes or so without getting a bite; and Tom, whose patience is none of the most enduring, was getting very uneasy when he caught a gurnard about 2 lb. weight, and had a large crab on the bottom hook. Of course he lost the crab, but the gurnard was landed safely. I fixed on my rod a large reel of about forty yards of good thin but strong line, placed a boat-shaped sinker above a bright spinner, supplemented this attraction with four bits of white flies, and, getting about thirty yards of my line loose and ready on the seat, I gave the rod a good swing from bow to stern, and sent the sinker just where I wanted it to go. Of course the whole line ran on pretty nearly, and I began hauling it up and along, as though I had cast for trout with a fly. I struck at the third attempt, and landed a lovely coalfish. Tom had caught several whiting in the interval, and finally he lost his line in, I believe, a cod. I had a glimpse of the fish, but it was too deep to swear to. Anyhow, he broke the line by sheer weight, and went off with the best part of it. My spinner took half-a-dozen gurnards and two more coalfish. Then there was a lull in the proceedings, and I was remarking to Tom that we might just as well "strike" and "go in" for luncheon, when I had a most tremendous snatch on my silver spinner. None of your shaking and hanging on with leaden weight there; it was a succession of most brilliant dashes to all points of the compass.

"Well," I said, "if it were not so early in the season I should say this is a mackerel."

Then I felt that another bite had taken place, and simultaneously I became aware that a new weight had been added to my line. I had at least thirty yards to get back before I could try to land my prey, and I found this a rather ticklish job. As soon as I had pulled back a yard or so the fish gave a start and pulled out too. At last they tired, and I brought them up. Both were mackerel—one a beauty, about a foot-and-a-half long, the other only a foot, and I made up my mind to look for them whenever whiffing was practicable, for I was told that the shoals had already begun to appear, and that along the north and west coasts some of the fishermen had already done well with their nets. My success put off our luncheon to an indefinite period, and we tried hard for at least an hour to repeat the deed. I only caught another gurnard and a small coalfish—my friend all the while getting on well, particularly with the whiting.

At 3 o'clock we had done with all the bait, and resolved to depart at once, as there might be a chance of falling in with large birds on our return. We certainly did see a few of them, mostly black ducks, but they were very shy, and there was a deal of long-range practice with the big guns for only one bird. The latter was with three or four more just in front of the Tees' mouth, about a mile from the shore, and a stray swan-shot settled him. The range was simply preposterous. The evening breeze was at first undecided as to which way it should blow, and it became a moot question whether we should land that night or not.

However, at 4.30 the wind increased, and turned tolerably fair, so that we managed to reach our starting-place, but it was very late when we stood once more on land. The men told us that in the estuary there is always a good deal of dab-fishing going on. Fishermen who are not quite seasick-proof are pretty sure there to escape this insidious inconvenience; and I daresay, at high tide, there are good fish up the river too. We were exceedingly tired after our first day, and, by way of a change, thought we would spend the following day on the sands.

We prepared our cartridges, game-bags, and 12-bore guns, and before 9 o'clock on the next day we were in the train bound for Redcar. We breakfasted at Redcar; then we secured the services of a strapping youth, and, loading him with our bags and gun-covers, we set out to show the Redcar birds a trick or two ere we had done with them.

It was low tide, and the sands were simply enormous in extent, reminding me somewhat of the shore from Ostend to Nieuport, in Belgium. The walking was superb, and most holes in the sands were tenanted with birds. We saw, to begin with, several flocks of ringed dotterel about, but had only a single crack at them, getting four. This took place later on.

We began with oxbirds, and bagged half-a-dozen very quickly. We saw only two or three redshanks, and could not succeed in circumventing them for a long time, in spite of our efforts. On such bare places as sands it is difficult to overcome the proverbial shyness of those long-legged birds; and try as we would, they would not look upon us as inoffensive beings. They persistently remained on the sands, and were unmolested by anybody, until the high tide drove them up to shore, when we managed to get one, and scared away the two others effectually. We first went northwards, and walked right up to the Point near the lighthouse. This was by far the best sport; and as there were several parties of shooters about in boats and on the shore, their firing sent the shoals to us, ours drove them back again, and between the two great was the slaughter. We had several sensations in the shape of large waders coming tantalisingly to the sands to feed, when we would divide our forces and try to get near them, but the weather was so open just then, and food so abundant, that the birds cared not about allowing anyone to stalk them openly, and we only killed a curlew between us the whole day.

At 12 o'clock the tide was about half-way over the sands, and we retraced our footsteps, with the wind in our backs, and had about a dozen satisfactory shots at passing birds.

At Redcar we had luncheon, and when after that meal we bent our footsteps towards Saltburn, the tide was high, and we had then the very best sport of the day.

I had started with a bagful of Schultze cartridges, loaded with No. 8 and No. 5, thinking that such stores would be amply sufficient for my needs, but I had reckoned without "the hosts" of birds, and before we were half-way towards Saltburn I had fired all my cartridges but about a dozen. It was quite a treat to see the birds coming, and how tough the little rascals are too! Ordinary game-birds retain somehow their handsome appearance even after death, but such is not the case with oxbirds and sandpipers. They stick up their feathers all over their bodies before giving up the ghost, and their wings and legs take all sorts of angles, so that anyone wishing to preserve some of them for stuffing has a troublesome task when he comes to smoothing their feathers. For difficult shots these birds "lick creation into fits." An oxbird who has allowed his steam to bring him within fifty yards of a gun, no sooner perceives his mistake than he describes all sorts of figures in the sky, and it takes some judgment and a quick calculation to make out where the bird will be at a given time, and to send one's shot there just in the nick of time to overtake him. Tom is a very good hand at that game, owing to his great practice at snipe, but he declares that sea-birds are more difficult to hit than snipe, and take more hard hitting to bring them down.

When we reached Saltburn the sea was on the ebb, and evening was near. We had done very well during the day, and were quite done up, so declined walking back to Redcar, and booked ourselves at the station for Middlesbrough.

The next day was to be our last, and we had arranged to spend it at sea with the men we had engaged before, on the understanding that they should provide plenty of bait for our use.

We started the next morning in good time, but the weather was simply disgusting. Fitful gusts of wind blew, and in the interval rain fell steadily. The two men were silently coiling up the painter, and getting in the anchor, sweeps, masts, and sail, and as they did not seem to object to the trip, why should we do so? They had their oilskins, and we had our ulsters, but no waterproofs. One would have thought the shore-birds would have appeared in strength on such a wet morning, and there were many of them about, as we could hear them away on the banks, calling or whistling, but not many took to their wings, and we had but a few shots at stray birds. The drizzling rain increased, and the sail and the boat looked very damp and slimy altogether. Tom, who was in the bows, called out at last that there were four or five birds to leeward. We went forward, and crouched there until such time as our steersman should motion to us that we were near enough to rise. When the man winked and nodded to us we peered over the gunwale, and perceived that the birds were still a good hundred and fifty yards off.

"Too far!" I whispered to the man.

Thereupon he raised his eyebrows with surprise. I suppose he thought the guns would kill, like rifles, up to a mile or so, more or less. He was getting nervous evidently, for he lost ground, and actually could not bring us nearer than a hundred and twenty yards at least from the birds, which were now to windward. We sat up and looked disconsolately at the widgeons, which did not seem to mind us much. The rain bothered them, I imagine.

"I will have a shot at the lot," said Tom at last, "and when they rise you give them the other barrel; there is nothing else to be done."

Away went his load, splashing well around the bunch, and the birds rose, one looking very queer indeed. I fired, and the queer-looking one fell. On rowing up to him we found a shot in one of his legs, and besides that he had a broken wing, evidently the result of my shot, which had totally disabled him.

The rain then stopped and the wind increased. We took advantage of this to go out farther than on the first day, and when we anchored I found over sixty yards of line were needed to reach bottom. After ten minutes spent in waiting we suggested shifting our quarters. We were discussing the matter, when on getting up my line I found it heavy, and brought up no fewer than three fish, two whitings and a gurnard. The fourth hook was bare. We countermanded orders and remained, doing well, but what tumbles we had! Pulling up sixty-odd yards of line when you cannot sit or stand still for a second is something terrible. Just when you have managed to run up ten yards, up goes the stern of the boat, and you have to clutch the gunwale or a seat; then you watch for a lull, and haul up another twelve or fifteen yards, when slap go the bows on to the waves, and you are sent neatly on to your neighbour's lap, with perchance one or two of his hooks in the fat of your legs. As to our luncheon, it remained untouched as far as the eatables were concerned. We gave those to the men, and contented ourselves with an occasional glass of wine. Our total of fish was monstrous, both in weight and in numbers, and comprised two mackerel, coalfish, codlings of good size, gurnards of all sizes, and whiting in immense variety. Thus ended an excursion to the Tees mouth, not the worst trip by a long way of all those I have undertaken. In fact, all in all, I vote it to be unsurpassed except in the matter of large birds, with which we did not fall in.

CHAPTER LXII.

JERSEY.

CHARLIE had written me word from Kingstown that he was coming back to the river Thames, and I heard from him afterwards, when he was at Southampton, that he had an invitation from a friend who had gone to Jersey to visit him, and would I join him in the trip? I telegraphed back that he might expect me by one of the evening trains.

We met at the terminus, and at 6 o'clock the following morning set sail for our one hundred and forty miles' journey on the sea. The wind was very fair, and the way the old boat spun along down the Southampton Water presaged a speedy passage down the Solent and across the Channel. I got the guns on deck as soon as ever we were clear of the shipping. "Wildfowler" is never happy but when he has a gun by his side, and as the season was virtually on its last legs, he clung to his weapons with the desperation of a drowning man.

We reached Calshot Castle, on our starboard, at about 8.30 A.M. I could not get a shot at anything, owing to the straight course we held in mid-channel, so as to get the full benefit of the ebb tide. Round the point, however, opposite Eaglehurst, I just popped on three ducks, and killed two with the 4-bore. That was the only shot I had during the day. We were then in the Solent, and the spanking breeze gave us plenty to attend to.

At 12 o'clock we passed Hurst Castle, and made for the Needles. At 3 o'clock we had lost sight of land, owing partly to the distance we had covered, and partly to the thickening haze of the atmosphere. At 5 o'clock we just caught a glimpse of land on our starboard, and Charlie announced it as St. Alban's Head. When the said St. Alban's Head had disappeared astern, it was getting dark, and several lighthouses began to twinkle in the deepening gloom. Many steamers and sailing vessels were about, and, altogether, our sail was a most glorious treat. When I took my turn at the tiller, and was left alone on deck, Charlie having gone below to turn in, and Cook being busy in the fo'c'sle, I could not help thinking of the grandeur of my surroundings, and I acknowledge that a certain feeling of awe crept over me. Cook came up in the midst of my reflections, and handed me a glass of grog with a grin.

"I think you will like *that*," said he; "at least *I* do."

"Then you have tasted it, you rascal," I replied.

"Of course, sir, I have. How is a cook to know the taste of what he is cooking unless he tastes it?"

And the fellow smacked his lips as I handed him the glass—empty. Then he wished me good-night, and I was left alone for a watch of three hours.

At about 3 A.M. a steamer passed us, quite within a hundred yards, and they shouted out something or other. I secured the tiller, and went forward. Our red light was out. I called up Cook to see about it, and he then relieved me.

When I went below, I found the fire roaring lustily, and Charlie playing a duet with it. He woke up when I entered, and asked sleepily about the weather. I replied "Lovely," turned in, and didn't wake up till breakfast-time, 8 o'clock.

"Where are we now?" I asked of Cook.

"In sight of the French coast," he said, "and close to Alderney. The governor says we shall make St. Helier by 12 o'clock for certain."

I got up and went on deck, and thought the view lovely. We had Cherbourg astern, a lot of villages on the rugged coast, and several islands round about us.

"Do you know your way well?" I asked Charlie.

"Never been here before," he replied.

At 2 P.M. we saw several boats, and hailed one. They sailed near us, and entered into a deal of gesticulation. At last we caught the words, "*Suivez nous!*" so we took in sail to keep up with their "slow coaches," and lay in their wake. Thus we made our *entrée* into harbour. Jersey, from its appearance, seems an awkward place to land in, and the harbour is neither remarkably large nor easy. As soon as we had anchored we went ashore, and Charlie soon found his friend at an hotel, with his wife and son, the latter a lad of some fifteen summers; and then, to my astonishment, I found that they were a French family. In a minute we were as deep in our plans as if we had known each other for years. The son was a very intelligent-looking lad, wonderfully sharp in his questions. Thus, when we went on board, he examined, amongst other things, some Schultze powder (which looks like sawdust, by-the-way) I had in a canister, and when told that it was gunpowder he looked incredulous, said nothing, but at the first opportunity he took a pinch of the stuff and threw it in the stove, where, of course, the grains crackled like so many harmless and diminutive fireworks.

"Now," said the father, "why did you do that, Charles?"

"Well," said Charles, who, having been brought up at a séminaire, was evidently fond of showing off his Latin "Bonum est omnia scire, father."

"Granted," replied paterfamilias; "it is good to know everything, but had you 'turned over the page' you would have found et non uti ('and not to use it'). Now bear that in mind."

Now it stands to reason, that with two such clever companions, our hooking on the morrow was bound to prove something quite out of the ordinary run of such trips; and so it did. I do not think I ever laughed so much for the last twelve months.

"I have a large bucketful of bait," said the old gentleman when we were arranging an excursion, "and several lines of the most approved Jersey material; and when the sun rises to-morrow," he went on, "we will start for our fishing excursion."

We nodded assent.

"This place, Jersey, is the fatherland of the hooks; all the world here know how to fish, you will see."

This I did not doubt. The very smallest "brats" in Jersey take to hooking as naturally as a duckling takes to water, simply because fish abound there in all seasons, and fishing is, *de facto*, the staple amusement and trade in the place.

We started at about 9 A.M. on the following day. We had on board a man named Pierre Somebody or other, who was an adept at sea-fishing, and a clever pilot to boot; but then, when a man has spent his life hooking amidst the sunken rocks of a particular coast, if he does not know how to hook and where to go with safety to the craft, he must, indeed, be a noodle. Of course our friend and his son were our guests, and altogether we numbered six persons, of whom five were likely to enter into the sport. Charlie does not care for it, but likes to look on. Our French friends were very jubilant, and made no pretence to hide their opinion that they would show us a trick or two before we parted. We went about a mile and a half from the harbour, near some sunken reefs, and there came to a full stop. The sea was tolerably smooth, and the wind hardly worth mentioning, whilst a bright sun shone. Pierre, who, it seems, had been our friends' attendant during their stay in the island, placed a line in their hands ready baited, and it was with an artistic flourish that they had their first cast. The "old 'un," as Cook irreverently called him, was the first to hook, and he brought up a small conger, some 3 lb. weight, on his bottom hook. When he hoisted him over the gunwale he could not help calling out triumphantly, "*A la Française!*"

This watchword was, of course, taken up by his son and their man, and every fish they caught they looked at us and called out triumphantly, "*A la Française!*"

As good luck would have it, I caught two fish at my first cast—viz. a large conger, 7 lb. or 8 lb. weight, and a fine pouting. Thereupon Charlie called out, "*A l'Anglaise!* by Jingo!" and Cook, hoisting a monster over the gunwale, glanced wickedly at our neighbours and roared lustily, "English style, this is!" which set us all laughing. We had a very glorious time of it. The fish came up fast, and we filled a hamper to begin with; and just before luncheon, Cook caught another enormous conger. He hit it on the head, hit it on the side, hit it everywhere he could think of, yet the brute *would* wriggle and snap.

"*C'est le diable!*" said our friend.

"The devil!" said Cook, astonished; "yes, sir, I believe it is!"

We had nothing to pierce its head with, so Cook at last cut it off.

Well, after this execution we all struck, and went below to discuss some cold fowl and Bass's ale.

Everyone who has been on a yacht, and was not accustomed to it, must have noticed that so long as one remains on deck and has something to occupy the mind, there is but little need to fear an attack of sea-sickness; but the moment one pops below in the cabin and has the mind at rest, then qualms begin to appear. Cook was passing us a bottle of sherry from aft, when he significantly drew my attention to our youthful guest. A glance was sufficient, and we assisted him on deck, and presently his father suddenly jumped up, rushed to the door, gasped frantically for air, bolted outside —and Charlie and I looked at one another. They were soon better, though, but their woebegone countenances told a tale when we went up to resume operations. The father was the first to recover, and when we offered to get up our moorings and run back to the harbour, he held up his hands and protested that he would not hear of it. Cook then made the son an extempore bed with the cabin cushions, covered him over with a rug, and in a quarter of an hour he had forgotten all his troubles in a deep slumber.

We then resumed operations, but some little time elapsed before our worthy friend could look with composure at his bait.

Wishing to try for mackerel, I told Cook to put away his gear and get the dingey ready for a row. He, with an eye to sparing himself trouble, got not only the oars into the boat, but also its little mast and sail. I stepped into the dingey, and we left our comrades with a cheery good-bye. We went towards a small island called Ecrehou, or something of that sort, and I put out my spinner for a try. We went very easily, and soon had a gurnard in. That was not what I wanted. Gurnards don't give such good play that one should trouble to catch them. In the midst of our sail we caught sight of a shoal of fry rippling the surface of the sea. At first I thought it was a breeze that had sprung up. Presently Cook cried, " They are fish, sir, very tiny ones, and here they are ! " They passed quickly, but not so quick that we could not follow their motions. Some almost flew through the water, others jumped out an inch or two in their hurry. Evidently the shoal of fry was being hotly pursued. " They are mackerel ! " I said, after a moment's silence, "and there is a dogfish of some sort about. At any rate, since the fry are here, there are sure to be some big ones about, and we must get some of them." The words were hardly out of my mouth, when switch ! the line slipped for a yard or two through my fingers, just as I was hauling it up and letting it go in the usual style. Up came the first, a pound fish, looking extremely brilliant in the sun. I speedily unhooked him and cast out again, caught another in a moment, and for a quarter of an hour I was very busy, landing no fewer than nine or ten in that short time. I lost three or four through their hooking themselves so very slightly that they escaped, and two I struck too sharply, thereby breaking them loose. Such a thing rarely or never happens where one uses a rod. The elasticity of the rod deadens any too violent motion of the hand, and it gives way when the resisting body offers too much sudden dead weight or contrary motion. Unfortunately I had no rod. When the shoal had fairly passed away, I began to be idle and to feel dull, so I looked about me, and saw, about half a mile away from us, several small black ducks, called there *macreuses*.

"Hand me the gun and some cartridges," I said to Cook.

"These birds," said Cook, "are just like those we had so much trouble with near Boulogne, some years ago, do you remember, sir?"

Yes, I remembered it right well, for we nearly got the very identical dingey we were then in smashed on some sunken rocks. It seems that those small divers feed on mussels, and of course they swim above the rocks whereon the mussels are to be found; so that one is apt, when not carefully watching where the boat is going, to bump on some of the rocks that are almost on a level with the sea. For eating, the birds taste exactly like leather dipped in fish-oil. It was not, therefore, with an eye to a subsequent meal that we went in chase. The fact was, I wanted a few specimens for a friend; but what very wide-awake customers these 'cute divers proved to be! We went slap into a dozen of them, but when I popped up for a shot I could not see one; they had gone to the bottom. "All right!" I thought, as I stood in the bows, with my finger on trigger, and my eyes on the alert; "the first that turns up now will get it." But in this I was mistaken. One cropped up very quietly, but no sooner did I shoulder than up went its stern, and it was gone; and they all played me the same trick; it was like a game at bo-peep. Still, as the birds were sure to get sick of that game, if we only stuck to them long enough, we kept about, and finally I bagged two at one shot, and had a single shot at another. We then perceived that we were a considerable distance from the yacht, and the sea beginning to rise with the tide and the evening breeze, we turned our thoughts homewards.

Cook took the oars, and we kept the sail up until we had cleared the island, when Cook turned the dingey's head to the south, straight for the yacht, and we began to spin from crest to crest, with the pleasurable motion of a swing. Sometimes the little cockleshell of a boat stood almost hesitating on the top of a big wave; then down it would glide, and we could see nothing but water on either side of us; then, with the acquired impetus it would climb the opposite crest, and again seemed to stand still when it got there. Fishing was quite out of the question, and shooting was a thing of difficulties under the circumstances.

We had several shots at widgeons, but owing to the suddenness with which we caught and lost sight of the birds, it was not astonishing that none were bagged. We were a long time coming back, and glad at last to clamber on board and rest after our fatigues. The youngster was in the cockpit, looking very disconsolate, and entreating to be killed or thrown overboard, much to Charlie's annoyance.

"I would have taken them ashore," he said to me, "but that we were waiting for your return. Now, off we go!"

As soon as we got within the bar our friends began to feel better, and when we landed together, they looked quite like two seafaring and tough customers, for whom the sea had no terrors. Before we reached the hotel, however, to make matters doubly sure, our elderly companion came to us confidentially, and said, after a preliminary cough in his hand, "Respecting our malady on ze boat, er, er, you not speak of it, *enfin le plus grand silence*, eh?"

We promised that we would be as mute as fishes on that dreaded point, and accordingly our friends made their *entrée* with beaming countenances, and declared that they had never enjoyed themselves more in their lives!

We had caught during the day over three hundred fish of all sizes and of almost every species. We had skate, turbot, gurnard, whiting, conger, mackerel, and several fine pouting. Pierre had also brought up a lobster, located in an empty shell, and this specimen was very wonderful in its appearance. The left side of the crustacean had no elbow-room, and consequently its left claw was extremely diminutive and puny, whereas the right one, being just in the opening of the mollusc, was enormous, and very wild in its evolutions. I have caught myself just such another lobster at Kingstown, behind the West Pier, when fishing for dabs and plaice, near the Baths; and I consider such unexpected events extremely interesting, because they show us so vividly how Nature works in the deeps. Our young lobster was voted to an aquarium, but I believe it was found dead the following morning, much to the grief of our youthful friend.

The next day was very lovely and quiet, but our two friends debated seriously whether they should join us or not. Charlie settled the question in the following manner: "Come with us," said he, "and the moment you feel bad we will leave the others fishing in the dingey, and I will bring you back with the yacht."

This proposal met with universal approval, and taking up our anchor we set sail, and this time headed south, intending to try the belt of rocks which makes the bay a thickly populated one with fish. We went about four or five miles, Pierre holding the tiller, and when he gave the word he turned her head to the wind, and we came to an anchor.

"Lots of lobsters about here," he told us. Our two friends astern, and Pierre and Charlie forward, were quite enough for our boat.

"You and I, Cook," I said, "will go into the small boat.

Bring some bait and a box of lines. We will rig them out and try our luck."

"But," he remarked, "what shall we anchor with?"

"Oh," I rejoined, "go below and bring up a stout bar of pig-iron from the ballast; that will do."

He brought up a bar that nearly capsized our small craft, but we thought it would do nicely; and with a long and stout line for our moorings, we arranged the affair comfortably, and settled ourselves about fifty yards astern of the yacht. Cook then cut some mackerel for bait, and I began. I had caught about half-a-dozen fish, when I suddenly bethought myself that we were seemingly much farther from the yacht than we originally were. A glance at the painter, which was quite limp, revealed at once the state of the case. We had slipped our moorings, or rather our moorings had given us the slip.

"We are drifting," I said to Cook; "I believe our iron is lost." He jumped forward and felt the painter; it came so easily, that there was no doubt about the matter. So we had to run back to get another bar, and rig on another more substantial apparatus. The fish then began to be well on the feed, and we had two or three hours of unmitigated fun.

"Are you coming aboard to luncheon?" shouted Charlie, at last.

"Rather!" I called back, and we went.

Our friends declined to come down with us, alleging that they would prefer having their meal on deck. They remembered the treat they had had the day before, I presume, and did not wish to be once more bundled out so unceremoniously. Luncheon over, we resumed our stations, and I had half-a-dozen shots at birds, bagging two widgeons and a coot. Our friend expressed his astonishment at the little smoke and little noise the Schultze powder produced, and when I suggested that I would give him some cartridges to try when he went home, he declared that the Customs officers would confiscate them if they found them.

"Our Government," said he, "has the monopoly of manufacturing gunpowder, and in order to prevent competition, they forbid the importation of gunpowder under any pretence whatsoever."

We remained near the rocks until 5 P.M., when we came back to harbour, and early the following day we left our friends and set sail once more for "merrie England."

CHAPTER LXIII.

HOLYHEAD.

AFTER our trip to Jersey, Charlie had gone back to Kingstown, and I felt, figuratively, all at sea. Most of my shooting and fishing things were on board his boat, so that I had to shift on sundry occasions with second-rate tackle. Next, the fact that the yacht was away compelled me to resort to hiring boats and going by myself occasionally on my trips, and, of course, it is not so pleasant as when, on my arrival at the scene of action, I had the old boat with whose nooks and corners (especially the corners — oh my head!) I am thoroughly acquainted, waiting for me, and its owner ready at all times to welcome me. Judge, then, of the pleasure I experienced when a letter came from Charlie informing me that the weather being by some wonderful chance very nice, he was going over to Holyhead, and would I join him there? Would I go? Would I eat a bun? I would eat twenty buns, and I would go forty times. Perchance, methought, the poor fellow is lonely too. Hurrah! Now for a start! I lost no time, and, like a fellow going to meet his sweetheart, I was all in a flutter. Bless the boat! Many happy moments have I spent in it, and now I was going to tread her deck once more.

The journey was quick and uneventful, until we entered Wales, when the aspect of the country thoroughly enlisted all my attention. I had seen it before, but one always likes to see spots where imagination can picture a good deal of sport likely to take place. Especially when nearing the coast, the line runs amidst a lot of fine marshes, and I would give a trifle for the privilege of perambulating their bogs with a gun and Rover. Imagine what a state I was in—confined there in a railway carriage, whirled along at top speed, and a seemingly never-ending panorama of lakes, streams, and rough ground passing continually before my eyes, with a hare here, a couple of rabbits there, a heron flapping his heavy wings along the bank, another fishing in a melancholy manner in a pool, a file of ducks going over the valley, and yonder a bunch of teals rising from a river, as we thunder over the bridge.

Well, I had two fellow-travellers in my compartment, neither of whom had opened his lips since we had taken our respective seats at Euston. But when we came to the above-mentioned scenery, one actually said to me with sparkling eyes :

"This seems a likely spot for a shooter to make a bag in, does it not?"

"Rather," I said; "I was just thinking how pleased I should be if I were there."

The ice was thus broken between us two. As for the other, he looked at us through his monocle, and, though he said nothing, his glance expressed the most unutterable contempt. Poor fellow, perhaps he is afraid of a gun, even when it is not loaded. At any rate, after a good look at us, he picked up the left side of his ulster, which was hanging on the carpet, with the air of an old woman putting her skirts out of the way of contamination.

Holyhead.

Now, it is an astonishing thing how powerful a sort of freemasonry the common love of sport is between men. My opposite neighbour no sooner found out that I was that way inclined than he grew wonderfully chatty, and we spent half-an-hour in a pleasant interchange of ideas. He was intelligent and very amusing. In sober truth, there are but very few sportsmen that are dull and stupid.

Well, when we arrived at Holyhead, somewhere about 2 P.M., we had to part, as my new acquaintance was going over by the Kingstown steamer to the Emerald "Oisle." We shook hands very heartily, much to the astonishment of our quondam companion, who had not yet recovered from the shock we had given his system, and I looked about me for some known faces.

There was Cook blocked up behind two trucks, and making frantic efforts to get at me.

"Ah, sir," said he, rolling his cap in his horny fingers, and his face beaming with real pleasure, " this looks like old times, does it not?"

Then I asked him the news, he shouldered my traps, and away we went towards the harbour. The yacht was there, within a hundred yards of the wooden jetty, and on deck I saw Charlie and another fellow looking out our way. Thereupon great wavings of hats take place, and we get into the dingey. A dozen pulls and we are aboard, when we exchange warm greetings. Our new companion's nationality soon oozes out, for—

"Sure," says he, "I am glad at making your acquaintance."

And he squeezed my hand with such a pressure that there was no mistaking the genuineness of his feelings. Besides, I like Irishmen awfully; they are always ready for anything.

Whilst lunch was being got ready I went on deck to have a look round, and we discussed the course we should have to pursue. Charlie thought that a sail across the Channel to Dublin Bay would be just the thing.

"My dear fellow," I remonstrated, "of course it would be the best if I could afford the time for such a lengthy trip, but I cannot; I must be back to-morrow evening without fail."

He looked astonished, so I explained to him that I was preparing for the press, to be published in book form, my wildfowling trips of last year, and my sea-fishing excursions of this, besides many other articles on sport at home and on the Continent, which have appeared in *Bell's Life* and other papers; so that I was literally head over heels in work.

"Consequently, as regards sailing to Kingstown now, *that* is out of the question. I will tell you what we will do, if you and your friend are agreeable. We will sail and fish about here. I have never tried sea-fishing in this part of the world, and I should like to now, since we have the chance."

All right, they replied, we would do so. The next thing was to get bait. After luncheon we went into the town, but neither of us could make himself understood. Welsh is, no doubt, a very fine language for those who understand it, but as concerned us, we were nonplussed by it. At last, after a good deal of perambulating, we met a man who understood us, and he promised to bring us some bait. Where he got it I do not know, but I strongly suspect he went on board a Dublin smack and purloined the lot, as there was no one on board. Anyhow, he brought us seven mackerel, pretty fresh, and with that we were content. He asked us a shilling for them, and went his way.

At 3.30 P.M. we got up anchor and ran out. The wind was very quiet and the sea smooth so far, but there was an ominous look of dark clouds gathering behind the Welsh hills which boded no good, and we, therefore, made a note of it, and did not venture so far that we could not run in if anything wrong took place. We went south for a couple of miles or so, and anchored there. We all lent a hand to the manœuvring of the yacht, getting down her wings, letting go the anchor, clearing the deck, &c., so as to have plenty of room for our evolutions; then I got a camp-stool from a locker, and sat down on the port side with my creel and lines by my side.

Quoth Charlie, "How long shall we stop here? It will be dark in an hour's time, you know."

"Well, but you know your way into harbour?" I inquired.

"Oh yes, there are lights, and I know the bearings well."

"Very well then, we need not hurry ourselves; we will stop until 6 o'clock if you like."

My companion told me he had read my Kingstown trip.

"Yes," he went on enthusiastically, "Kingstown and Dalkey for hooking, and the Bay of Dublin for long lines and for trawling, are not to be surpassed anywhere. You can always catch fish there, no matter when you go. At the same time this coast is not bad either."

"Then you have been fishing here before?" I asked him.

"Not at the spot we are at," he explained; "but I have done a good deal in that line all along the Welsh coast, last year."

"And you did well?"

"Very well indeed, but not so well as along the Irish coast."

Well, we got our lines ready and began. Where we stood the sea was, owing to the proximity of the shore which protected it against the wind, extremely quiet, and this soon suggested to us the desirability of trying our rods. Not that hand-line fishing is without its charms, but it has certain inconveniences which a rod has not, and amongst these stand the fact that hand-lines in November keep your hands continually wet, whereas with a rod you only wet your fingers when unhooking a fish. Finding our first trials cold work, we therefore fell back on our bamboos. When we had caught five or six poutings, a dozen codlings, and a whiting, we rigged out our rods, and experienced very fair success indeed. I only broke three hooks and one line, which must be considered lucky when fishing over a rocky bottom, where the hooks may catch in weeds, &c., without mentioning what may happen when a large fish takes a fancy to one of your bait. We took there some of the best fish I had as yet caught that season. Three gurnards weighed nearly 8 lb. between them, and some of the codlings, pouting, and whiting were excellent specimens of their kinds. We also caught half-a-dozen skate, which we returned to the sea, as we do not care for them. And a very pretty sight it is, too, to see how delighted those fish are when they find themselves once more in their element. Of course you do not see them very long, but in the short space of time which elapses between the moment they are thrown back on to the water, and the instant they recover consciousness and avail themselves of the opportunity thus afforded them to make good their escape, one sees very well the whole affair. There they are, lying flat and motionless on the top of the water, then a sort of wave, beginning from their noses and ending at their tails, undulates along their bodies very gracefully; they

Holyhead.

then bend their heads, give a twist with their screw, and down they go like a flash of lightning.

At dusk the lighthouse began to shed its rays over the sea, and rather gloomy the dark waves looked. The Irish Channel is always more or less on the loose at every tide. The boat began to roll very uncomfortably, the wind rose too, and the waves, nothing loath, began to ride white, seeing which we put away our utensils and got up our anchor. A twenty minutes' sail brought us back in harbour, where we anchored for the night.

Holyhead is a wretched place to a stranger in winter time. In summer weather, I daresay, walks over the hills, and rows out to sea or in the harbour, may offer some inducements to visitors to while away their leisure pleasantly; but in winter the hills are bleak, rugged, and bare ; the wind blows as though it meant to spend all its strength over that particular spot; and walks and rows are, moreover, out of the question. There are several inns, and one or two hotels, but no society ; in fact, Holyhead is but a mere place of passage for people who are bound for Ireland. All these things considered, we were very glad we had the yacht to roost in. After all, there are few places more cosy than a yacht's cabin at night when the evening meal is over, and the chatty smoke is entered upon. My most pleasant reminiscences date from evenings thus spent on board that and other yachts.

Well, as our time for fishing during the afternoon had been so short, we had been content with trying bottom-fishing with hand-lines and rods ; but as we were aware that bass and pollack were to be had, it was an understood thing that on the morrow we should try a little whiffing for these most desirable fish. This being settled, we set-to to prepare our whiffing-lines beforehand. Mine were in a sad mess, on account of their being tumbled anyhow into a locker, no one having looked at them for three weeks or a month. In fact, one of these I had not had time even to wind up on the reel, but had placed it in the locker just as it had come to hand. Now, I have found that whenever a knot or any other kind of protuberance exists on a running-line, it is long odds that the said line will eventually come to grief, through the knot sticking into one of the rings when it ought to jump through it; and as I have, in my time, thus lost three or four scores of good lines with silver spinners, I am getting somewhat more careful, and I consequently revised each of my whiffing-lines with very great care, instantly condemning any one in which I found a defect. I had plenty of fresh line, and I rigged it on the reels whenever wanted, so as to have everything ready for the morrow. The reels themselves ran stiff. I use brass ones with ivory handles. Some folks use wooden ones, but that is only when their lines are thick; and I don't like them, they kick up such an awful row when you get a good throw. They creak away then, and snore like so many hand coffee-mills run mad. On the other hand, the brass ones are heavier, and occasionally bother one's fingers with some verdigris, but that is one of the inconveniences of the beast; and if one fixes it well on the rod, there is no occasion to touch it except at the handle, and this being covered with a small ivory cylinder keeps it in tolerably clear condition. As to the brass reels getting stiff, this sometimes happens through their getting verdigrised inside, between the outside and inside plates. Sometimes, also, it arises through sand or grit getting between these plates. Finally, it may happen that when knocking them about one of the outside plates gets bent, and jams one of the inner ones. In that case, a pair of pliers and careful inspection of the diseased organs will soon effect a remedy. In the case of grit or sand, a good shake does a deal of good, and a drop of oil on either side makes the concern run as smooth as—the settlement of Turkish debts.

Well, fixing on new lines, oiling and cleaning four or five reels, splicing the top joint of a weak rod which had given warning in the course of the day of its declining stanchness, took me a good hour and a half, with the filling-up of an occasional pipe and the emptying of an accompanying glass; so that it was nearly 12 'o'clock (midnight) when we bethought ourselves that Cook in his fo'c'sle was mighty quiet, and had been so for some time.

" The fellow is asleep," said Charlie, with a yawn, " and I think we had better turn in too; what say you ? "

We agreed, and went on deck to glance at the landscape. The wind had moderated, and the moon shone occasionally. Had it not been so late it is probable that we should have set sail there and then, for the fun of the thing. We went down again, and bed-making was the next question. I took the port cushions, Charlie took the starboard side, and our long-legged Irish friend gloried in occupying the whole of the floor. We cleared the table, got it out of the way outside, lit the night-lamp, and turned in. Cook then began to snore so outrageously behind the partition that I went to give him a hint to moderate his transports. In my shirt I went on deck, and lifting the hatch I dived below. Cook was there, with his mouth wide open, just under his lamp, and he was giving vent to the most unearthly groans.

I shook him, and he said: "G'lon, d't bather ! Led fellow schleep ! "

Then he turned on his starboard and went off peaceably this time.

Shivering, I returned to my berth, congratulating myself on the peace I had thus obtained; but judge of my dismay when, on re-entering the cabin, I found both my companions snoring! I administered Charlie a kick and our Irish comrade a dig in the ribs, and all fell into oblivion.

We slept peaceably until 2 or 3 o'clock in the morning, when I was awakened by a most astounding knock on the head. This was caused by a cartridge-bag that had fallen from the rack, owing to the boat's unruly motions. I thought at first it might have been a steamer passing by that had caused the turmoil; but as it kept on I ventured to lift up my head, and then became aware that my companions were, like me, listening. Charlie was nearly pitched bodily out of bed on to the top of our Irish friend; then at the next swing my turn came, and as I was "grinning and therefore powerless," I was bundled out unceremoniously. Then on deck we heard the boom swinging heavily, through not having been made perfectly taut overnight.

Quoth Charlie, jumping out, "My friends, this is the beginning of a storm. Let us turn out and make all safe."

And he knocked at the partition for Cook to wake up. This worthy was also listening to the roar of the gale outside, for he replied at once, " Ay, ay, sir, coming ! "

And we presently heard him removing the hatch, crawling out, and his bare feet pattering on deck. He then began securing the boom and taking in the bowsprit, when we went to lend him a hand. The wind was blowing then with a vengeance. Rain came down at intervals in perfect sheets, so that in two minutes we were drenched. Fortunately our riding-light was still burning to help us on our labours. When everything was done we went below again, and, sleep being out of the question, Cook made a roaring fire in the stove, and then went to light his own in the fo'c'sle, when we stripped to the skin and passed him our things to be dried. I had brought no change, as I intended staying only a day and a half, and did not expect having to turn out suddenly in a storm; so I had to put on some of Charlie's things, wrap myself in a blanket, and smoke philosophically until my underclothing and clothes were dry.

Meanwhile the wind was, if anything, increasing; and at 6 o'clock all boats that had been out, that could manage it, had turned into harbour for shelter.

At daybreak the Channel was like a seething caldron, and our fishing at an end. It was annoying, especially after we had spent the best part of our vigils the preceding evening mending our lines and getting them ready; but one cannot command the elements, and seeing that the barometer was still going down, and that everything foreboded a beastly day, I packed up and came back to town, thoroughly "riled" with the *fâcheux contretemps*.

Altogether I had only a couple of hours' *bonâ fide* hooking, near Holyhead, but those two hours had been thoroughly enjoyable. There are all sorts of fish to be caught, and shoals of them too. I was sorry I had not been able to try whiffing for the big bass and pollack amongst the rocks; but in such matters the elements are supreme rulers, and, when they say nay, kicking against their decision is not of the slightest use. Such, then, was the experience I could glean of the fishing capabilities of the Welsh coast round about Holyhead, and with this meagre narrative I must now take leave of my readers.

CHAPTER LXIV.

THE NORTH-EAST COAST OF THE ISLE OF WIGHT.

THE snow was on the ground and it was freezing hard when I arrived at Portsmouth for my intended trip to the Isle of Wight. The snow was not deep, but the frost, by hardening the ground and covering with ice the inland pools and marshes, necessarily drove birds seawards for feeding, so that fair sport might reasonably be expected.

Of course I am aware that to hunting-men and coursers this state of things is not cheerful, but I would suggest that they should join our ranks. I like hunting as well as any man, and I dote on coursing. But when neither hunting nor coursing is available, I am glad to undertake anything else that comes handy rather than be idle. The days are so slow when one is confined indoors! It is so dreary to be smoking and drinking all day. Now, sea-fishing and sea-shooting are as entertaining as any other sports, and as they are available at all seasons, and are at their best just when other outdoor sports fail, I advise all frozen-out hunting and coursing men to try them.

The talented writer of the *Bell's Life* leaders lately remarked, very truthfully, that no man who had tried sea-fishing at a well-populated bank has ever given up the sport. I can thoroughly endorse that remark, and point out the daily increasing number of sea-fishermen as a proof. Were all the charms of seafowl-shooting, too, revealed by a gifted pen, people would wonder at the pleasures which may be found therein. Seafowl-shooting demands the possession in its pursuers of some eminent qualities, of which indomitable pluck and endurance are not the least. It needs, moreover, good sound practical seamanship, knowledge of the haunts of the birds, which practice alone can give and the fire of sporting enthusiasm alone can induce one to thoroughly investigate. I have tried almost every sport, and I like them all, but none so much as that which brings one face to face with the sea—its whims and its furies.

As an instance of the fondness with which men get imbued for that sport, I may mention the tenacity with which the common fishermen of our coasts hold to it. See how, every winter, when the frost is so intense that traffic is suspended, when the snow-storms are covering nature with a thick white cloak, and most people think only of their bodily comforts, these men leave the shore in their thin-ribbed little punts, and are thoroughly happy in their pursuit of the fowl. When fowl are to be had, no puntsman will take a stranger with him ; he wants to enjoy the sport undisturbed by the companionship of anybody. Of course when a good batch can be brought to bag so much the better, but it is not the £ s. d. value of the cargo that the man considers so much as his own pleasure and the opinion of his *confrères* and neighbours. Now, if the sport of wild-fowl-shooting takes such a hold on the minds of rough, uncultivated men (none the less estimable if they are honest and straightforward in their dealings), judge of the fascination it must exercise over refined and well-educated sportsmen, who can indulge in all the pleasures of the pursuit and suffer few of its drawbacks.

Our trip to the Isle of Wight was a very fair specimen of what could be done in both the fishing and shooting line. Had the snow, however, been a little thicker it would have been still all the better for us. As it was, we had very fair sport indeed ; not that we made a monstrous bag, but we had plenty of firing, saw plenty of birds, had a lively sail on both days over the sea, and barring a slight fall of snow and a somewhat cold wind all went well.

We had arranged to sail in a decked boat this time, as we intended going to Cowes and staying there for the nights, instead of returning to Portsmouth to sleep each evening.

I arrived somewhere about noon, and found my friend and Frank waiting for me at the station.

At 1 P.M. we went to the pier and found the dingey waiting for us. We rowed aboard, and then set sail. The boat my friend had provided was one of those which take out fishing-parties during the summer. It had originally been a private gentleman's yacht, and was sold by auction at his death, when our skipper secured it for a mere song. It had paid its cost over and over again, and probably will do so yet for many years to come. Why ? Simply because both the skipper and his son are handy with tools, and can mend her without trusting her to strangers, who might knock her about. The boat is a roomy, comfortable one, rides well to a rough sea, and, for a fishing-boat, she is all one could wish. We found it very cold on deck, but a roaring fire was kept up below, and we enjoyed our trip wonderfully. The sea was lovely in behaviour and bright green in tint. The wind blew from the north quarter with a dash of west, so that we had it fair for about half the distance.

Leaving Portsmouth, we kept about half a mile from the west shore, passed the Haslar Hospital, then the fort a mile from it, and flew past the Gilliker Point like a mew on the wings of a gale. Once there, we turned her head due west, and this somewhat moderated her speed. Still she kept on at it steadily, and we covered the thirteen miles that separated us from Cowes in three hours. We then headed south, and got into the harbour. Once there we got up our riding-light for the night, went ashore for a visit to the old place, came back at 11 P.M., had supper, a pipe, a glass of grog apiece, and we all prepared to turn in.

The night was lovely; the moon had risen, and the prospect from the yacht's deck was charming. We slept comfortably until daybreak, when the creaking of the deck under the old man's seaboots announced another day at hand. Presently Frank popped his head in, and began clearing away the lamp that had been burning on our table all night, the glasses, tobacco-ashes, pipes, and so forth, and we went on deck to wash. There were many craft about then, and several of them were getting under weigh.

We cleared the harbour, and my friend taking the tiller, I got into the dingey with a railing-line to while away the time. I tried my most alluring hauls and slacks for awhile without any success, and was going to give it up when, by some wonderful chance, a fish came by, gobbled up my spinner, and literally caught himself, for I did not strike at all. I was deep in thought when I felt the welcome stranger hanging on like a log. "What is this?" said I, and I gave it a gentle lift, when it darted away, and I hauled it up at once. A large plaice, by all that was curious! I fancy that during my musing I had allowed the sinker to get a little lower than I thought. In fact, it must have gone to the bottom, or very near it, for plaice, as a rule, do not travel much above the bottom of the sea.

Opining that since one was there others might be about keeping it company, I proposed that we should have a "go" into plaice-hooking. We had a bucketful of bait and plenty of lines, so I went on board and altered several lines, rigging two of their whalebone projectors quite near the weights, and another one about a yard above these two. The lower ones would do for all mud-fish and sand-fish, and the top one for a codling, or whiting, or any other denizen of the deep who might be wandering thereabouts. Whilst this was being done we came to an anchor, and I resumed my former seat in the dingey, and began operations capitally. I was swinging one of the lines previous to casting it away, wishing it to go a long way off, and when I let it go one of the bottom hooks caught in the seat, broke the snooding, swung the line round and round, nearly pulling one of my eyes out, and entangling the concern in a most desperate manner. A look at the line convinced me that a quarter of an hour would be needed to set it right, so I put it away, and was content with fishing with the two others. I baited with lugs, and got a bite directly, but the hook was too large presumably, for when I brought it up the bait was gone. I told my friend then to rig me a line with smaller hooks; he handed me one ready, and I caught two flounders at once. My friend and Frank were equally successful, but most of our catches were such very small fish that we had to return them to their element, as they were not worth keeping for eating. We got about five score of fish. There were a few dabs, plaice, small whiting, .&c., intermixed, together with crabs, anemones, &c. At the end of an hour we got tired of it, and voted for a removal.

"Skipper," said my friend.

"Halloa, sir," replied the old man from the depths below.

"How is the barometer?" inquired my companion.

"The what, sir?"

"The barometer."

"What does the gentleman say, Frank?" we then heard him ask his son.

"He wants to know how the brometcher stands," replied the latter.

"Oh, be that it? All right, sir. Let us see. The brometcher, sir, is fair, sir."

"Well, then, we will be off, if you have no objection."

Of course he had none, and we went.

I came aboard once again, intending to have a good warm at the cabin stove, for it had been very cold work standing or sitting in the dingey all the while, but before going down I glanced round, caught sight of a single bird coming straight towards us and flying just above the waves. I said nothing, but picked up the first gun that came handy. I found, by its feeling, that it was a 4-bore gun, and would willingly have put it back and taken another, as it was hardly worth while firing a 4-cartridge for a single bird; but there was no time to lose, and so I cocked the gun and placed the barrel over the gunwale. This attracted the men's attention, and they both squatted forward. I then covered the bird's head well and smashed him. We picked him up by sailing the yacht to him, and found it was a widgeon. His death must have been very sudden, for his head was riddled, both wings were smashed, and he never moved a feather after I had pulled trigger.

When we had bagged our bird, we went down along the shore, but keeping about a mile from it, and passed thus the Old Castle Point and Osborne Bay, without any incident.

I tried whiffing, or railing, with sundry averages of speed, but could get no fish. Past the first creek, whose name I now forget, we set the trawl going. The bottom, it seems, is there very good for some distance, and I rather liked the trawl being tried, as it gave us a prospect of ascertaining what sort of fish frequented the shore. All the time that the trawl was out we watched for birds, had two shots at black ducks from the deck, and I went in chase of a diver, in the dingey. I was in such a hurry to go that I went alone, but I soon found out that it was impossible for me to manage the rowing and the firing. Just when I ought to have fired, for instance, I had to put the oars in. This frightened the bird, and down he would dive at the very first motion of the oars. Once he actually rose within fifteen yards of the boat, but on my right side, and in a line with my shoulder. I put the oars in safe enough that time, because I had already got them out of their rowlocks, but, to fire I had to turn round, as I cannot shoot from the left shoulder. The consequence was the bird again went to visit the bottom of the sea. I then went back to the yacht, and besought Frank to look sharp and come with me.

"I do not see him just now," I said, standing up in the stern-sheets, "but I shall spy him the moment he shows himself. Ah! There he is! Pull away! Starboard, starboard again," I whispered the man, whilst I clutched the gun.

But we were not to have him so easily as all that, and it took seven shots to bring him to book. Every time we got almost near enough for a try, Frank would dodge to

evade the gun's muzzle (just as if I would have shot him);
but still I could not blame him for so doing, so that it was
awkward, very, to manage the job.

How stupidly dingeys are built. They all have some
planking forward, making a kind of little deck for the
painter, just as if the painter (a piece of rope, value three-
pence, perhaps) needed such attentions for its preservation.
Then, the next seat is for the rower; finally, the stern-
sheets are for the shooter—the very place from which he
cannot shoot. Why not do away with the forward planking
and make a seat there for the shooter, so that he can face
the quarter towards which the boat is proceeding and have
plenty room for his legs and feet? Then the rower's seat
might be a little farther aft, so as to evenly trim the boat.
This, with the rudder-lines handy near the shooter, would
be simply perfection. I had my own dingey some years
ago fitted in that style, and a capital plan I found it to be.
If more than one shooter care about the fun, let room be
made for them all forward, and let the oarsman, or oarsmen,
be seated proportionally farther astern. By the time we
had bagged the diver the trawl had been down about an
hour, and it was time, on our return aboard, to get it up.
Now, this job is a joke to the men, because they put on
their oilskins (both trousers and overalls), and in that wise
all the splashing in the world does not affect them. But it
does affect amateurs who are unprovided with those water-
proof coverings. I knew that of old, having been caught
in my age of inexperience; so I remained by the tow-rope,
and hauled on with the men, but took good care not to get
near the dripping meshes. My friend, however, did not
seem to mind, and went on like a professional fisherman,
in spite of my warning and the men's caution.

"Oh, it won't matter," he kept on saying. But it did

matter! and when he had quite done he was drenched to the skin, and the cold wind acting on the wet part of his clothing rendered his position perfectly untenable.

We had, fortunately, brought a few things, in order to change our clothing should we meet with storms, &c., and he gladly availed himself of the opportunity, and turned up in a few minutes with a new rig on, and then joined us in clearing up the trawl-bag. We had very many flatfish, about thirty whitings, and other round fish, and a rare lot of sand-eels of many colours, crabs innumerable, and an assortment of many seaweeds, which we "chucked" overboard. Our edible fish we kept in a hamper, and the rest were returned to the sea; but amongst those we kept, most annoying to relate, several of the flatfish remained alive and kicking until the next day. I suppose their being covered over by the other fish kept them alive somehow. Cruelty of any sort I abhor. I will catch with pleasure a million fish if possible, but to see one lingering in death like that is dreadful. I am aware that professionals rather like this state of things, as they fancy it keeps their fish fresher, but I think it is a mistake. A fish caught and killed there and then is always better eating than one whose agony has been protracted. I would, therefore, suggest that all fish should be killed as soon as caught in some expeditious manner, just as, when shooting, we at once kill our wounded birds the moment they come to hand. Round fish, as a rule, are very easily sent to their happy feeding-grounds. A blow on the head settles them quickly. As for flatfish, I confess I am puzzled to make out what is to be done.

We kept religiously every sand-eel and every shrimp that came into the trawl, for we intended setting a long line during the afternoon. As soon as the sorting of our fish was concluded we came to an anchor, had luncheon, and then set about laying the long line; a very tedious job preparing it, too, at the best of times, but especially so when it is freezing. We set down the line at about 1 P.M., and went after a company of ducks that we had seen settling a mile or so from us in mid-Channel. We sailed to them in the yacht, but got only one bird, although two or three appeared considerably hampered in their flight. Our bird bagged, we tacked back towards our buoys, and I went in the dingey with Frank to get it up. I did not fancy wetting my hands, and preferred rowing, so I took the oars, whilst he got up our first buoy and anchor and hauled in the long line. It had been down about an hour, and had about a hundred hooks baited with sand-eels, shrimps, mussels, lugs, herring, and mackerel, and we found about twenty good fish on—a fair average. All our bait was gone, moreover, but this might have been effected by crabs and anemones, or by the sea itself. In its perpetual motion it rubs the line and hooks at the bottom, and even if no fish or crabs attacked the baits, these would all get rubbed off the hooks.

Very well pleased with our catches, we returned to the boat, and it being then nearly 4 o'clock, we went to anchor opposite the Wootton Creek, and waited there to see if any ducks would come by at flight time. We saw about a hundred, but all passed very wide, except a small company of seven which crossed our bows within eighty yards. We fired every gun we had at them. Frank swore that his old musket had brought one down, at any rate, out of the three we got, but I very much doubted it. I fancy the 4-bore gun did all the mischief.

Our birds collected, and no more appearing, we got up anchor and headed for Portsmouth, much pleased with our sport.

On our way back I busied myself packing up what birds and fish I was to take home, and found that only four birds would go comfortably into the net of my game-bag. I had, moreover, about a dozen fine fish in my creel, and though my friend insisted that I should take more birds and more fish, I did not "see it in the same light." He then gave to the men a brace of birds and what remained of the fish after he had strung half-a-dozen for himself, and we arrived at Portsmouth in good time for our evening train.

CHAPTER LXV.

KINGSTOWN.

A FRIEND from London (a rare man for sport of any kind, though a City man) had come over to see me and spend three weeks with us in Kingstown, and it was naturally my duty to bestir myself in order to show him some sport. As my friend was a good sailor, we thought that what would suit him best would be an excursion in which sailing should be combined with fishing and shooting. Accordingly, as soon as he had unpacked his portmanteau and got his gun and traps out, we repaired to the West Pier, where my boat was located. Having got on board we found her in sad want of a good baling out. This we set ourselves to do without further delay, and as the day was fine and warm I put up the mast, and hauled up the sails so as to give them a good airing and stretching. My boat was an open one, with a 6-inch keel, and cutter-rigged, easy to sail and easy to row, roomy and comfortable; and had she been fitted up with a small cabin wherein to take shelter when needed, she would have been as near perfection as anything of her kind. When the boat was clean and in proper working order, we left her with the sails up, and I recommended her to the care of one of the watermen who were always to be found loitering on or about the pier, and we went home to get things ready against the morrow.

The deep-sea lines, as they are used in Kingstown, consist of a bell-shaped leaden weight, more or less heavy (according to the size of the line and the depth of the water to be tried), fixed at the bottom of the line. About a foot above this weight a piece of whalebone is fixed on the line at a right angle with it, and to this piece of whalebone the gut of the hook is fastened. There are generally two such contrivances to each line, but the lines are not sold thus readily made in the shops; the amateur fisherman arranges his tackle himself according to his previous notions and experience. Thus, for bream, the pieces of whalebone are selected remarkably long and fastened high; whilst, for flounders, they are short and placed low on the line.

As we intended fishing at or near Dalkey Island, we brought rather strong tackle, the fish there being heavy; and as the bottom is covered with rocks, overgrown with long, rough weeds, we expected to lose a good many hooks, and accordingly secured a goodly number of different sizes—a wise foresight this, as events subsequently proved. The next thing to be procured was bait; somehow we did not readily get any. The fishermen kept their bait for their own use, and not only money but persuasion also was required in order to coax them into parting with their worms.

Before daybreak my waterman called, and it was still very dark when we reached the pier; the breeze was a stiffish one, so that the black waves of the harbour were somewhat angrily dashing against the pier, some of them even leaping over the steps of the slimy stairs, making them still slimier. We got safely aboard, stowed away all that we had brought, and, hoisting sails, made a start. We

Kingstown.

flew under a collier's stern, passed half-a-dozen ships and as many fishing-smacks; finally, we stood between the lighthouses, whose lights now were but dimly burning, owing to the increase of the light of the new day. The stars were fast disappearing—a few only flickered hopelessly—and by the time we had rounded the East Pier lighthouse the dawn had appeared over the Killiney Hills, and already a rosy tint was gilding the horizon; Dalkey Island appeared clearer and clearer before us, and ere long we were enabled to see well enough to shoot.

A lot of birds had already passed, screaming and whistling, over our heads. We loaded our guns; I went forward under the jib, my friend remained amidships, whilst our waterman kept the tiller; and thus we sailed on for some time without any incident whatsoever, when I spied, right ahead of us, and coming towards us at full speed, what seemed to me, in the gray light of dawn, to be a duck; however, as it drew nearer I perceived my mistake: it was a cormorant, evidently on his way to his feeding-ground, either in Kingstown harbour or in the Bay of Dublin, where great numbers sometimes congregate. As I wished my friend to have as much fun as possible, I called him near me and pointed out the bird to him. On it came as straight as an arrow, just as if our boat had not been in its way, till it came within thirty or forty yards, when, instead of keeping on its course, which would have brought it clear before the guns, it inclined suddenly towards the other side, and we had to scramble round in order to get a shot; we dodged, however, quickly under the sails, and a broadside tumbled our bird. It was not killed outright, and I was afraid lest it should recover and dive out of our reach; so, when we got nearer, as it began to look up, I told my friend to give it another barrel, and this time it had enough.

Whilst on our way a flock of at least thirty widgeons passed across our bows, but rather far out of range. Nevertheless, we tried four cartridges, but without success, as the birds only swerved from their route on hearing the report, and evidently the shot had not affected any of them in the least. Soon after a number of seagulls appeared, and we picked up two or three for stuffing. Then another cormorant came by, but he, wiser than his *confrère*, sheered off when a hundred yards away, and thereby saved himself from getting peppered with large shot. Two others, however, who were sailing in company, thought themselves perfectly secure, and got knocked over. One of them gave us a rare tussle with his divings, and although we fired at him again and again he invariably dived at the flash, and would have escaped if we had not resolutely tacked to his lee and waited for his coming up, when he got his quietus without knowing from what quarter it came.

This pursuit had caused us to lose time, and when we got to Dalkey, three boats, loaded with amateurs, were already at work fishing. However, a good station being still untenanted, we sailed up to it, then turned the boat's head to the wind, dropped anchor, hauled down our sails, put down our mast, and, all being snug and comfortable, we began fishing. The wind had dropped almost completely, the sun had risen, and the sky being clear, the water was as smooth as could be, and we could (by looking over the gunwale) clearly see the fish swimming round about the boat, amongst the seaweeds, and between the rocks. I was the first to "hook," and I hauled in a beautiful bream of about 1 lb. weight. This catch was followed by another from my friend; then the waterman hauled up one too, and the sport became very lively indeed, and we all three had a fair share of success for some time, when it

suddenly, and apparently without cause, came to pass that
my friend's line got all the bites and ours none. Then he
ceased to have any bites, and I had a lot. Finally our man
had his turn. By 10 A.M., after four hours' fishing, we
had enough of it for the time being, and accordingly we
bethought ourselves of doing something else. We landed
on the island, the sight from the top of which was beautiful
to behold. The Wexford valley, Killiney hills and strand,
Dalkey itself, finally Kingstown, Dublin and its bay,
Howth lighthouse, and the north coast were a most magnificent panorama to contemplate.

After luncheon we went down towards our boat, when
we found that, according to our boatman's prognostications,
the tide, when receding, had left it high and dry. This,
however, was but a slight *contretemps*, as we shoved it over
the pebbles without difficulty, and soon launched it again
in its element. We re-embarked, but we found the tide
so strong that fishing was quite out of the question, and, in
self-defence against the stream, we set sail and went up
towards Killiney strand, where I knew that birds were to
be found.

We landed opposite the fishermen's cottages, and
leaving our man on board to keep the boat afloat, we
stalked forth in the pursuit of a flock of sandpipers. We
bagged three. Then I shot a curlew, and my friend fired
at a wood-pigeon and tumbled it over on the railway line.
The strand then appearing apparently deserted by birds,
we went under one of the railway arches, and on the other
side of the line we found ourselves near a small marsh,
over which a large bird was slowly and heavily flying.

"That is a heron," I said to my friend, "and if he land
in the marsh we will bag him for certain."

We accordingly watched the bird intently, keeping ourselves well out of its sight behind a low hedge, and, to our satisfaction, after a very solemn survey of his domain, he unsuspectingly went down near some willow-trees, thickly surrounded by tall reeds and brambles. We ran round with all speed, but silently, for nearly half a mile, so as to get well under the wind, and behind the trees that concealed us from the bird. Then we had two or three ditches to jump over, a hedge or two to crawl through, and finally we found ourselves in a bog, wherein at the first step I went up to my knees, and was thankful to get out without any worse mishap. This unforeseen *contretemps* compelled us to seek another route, when, by shirking the bog, I spied a plank placed across the dangerous part, and leading to a sort of bank whereupon grew the willow-trees, and behind which was the bird. We walked silently across the plank, and crawled up the bank noiselessly as we thought; but, evidently something had startled the bird, for before we were fairly on the top of the bank its great heavy wings were already flapping, and he was going off. I jumped up quickly, as further concealment was perfectly useless, and with one barrel I floored the unlucky heron; a snipe rising, I brought it also down with my second, although it was loaded with very large shot. On investigation we found that the snipe had been hit by one single shot. As for the heron, he was not spoilt in the least, and was apparently a very old bird, judging from his plumage.

We sought for more snipe, but found none. When we had carefully beaten the open marsh we went along the banks of a small stream hard by, where we shot a teal, a moorhen, and a water-rail. When we got back to the sea-shore the tide was quite low, and the weather had altered for the worse. Heavy clouds had gathered over the sky the wind was fitful, and a few large drops of rain began to fall, so we went towards the boat as fast as we could, and were very glad, after two very hard hours' rowing, to reach the harbour again.

Our spoils consisted of one curlew, a lot of oxbirds and sandpipers, three cormorants, a diver, five gulls, a heron, a moorhen, a wood-pigeon, a teal, one rail, one snipe ; fish —one carp, and about two score and a half of bream.

Not bad for one day's sport.

CHAPTER LXVI.

SEA-FISHING AT KINGSTOWN AND DALKEY.

I WENT fishing two days running, at Kingstown, some years ago, and enjoyed myself so much that I cannot help giving my reminiscences of the sport.

Everyone knows what a deep-sea line is, but everybody does not know how to set it, according to the kind of fish one may reasonably expect to fall in with. Well, then, as I intended to go behind the West Pier for plaice and flounders, I provided myself with suitable lines—*i.e.* lines on which I had set the hooks on whalebone sticks very close to the lead, so as to insure the bait lying on the ground, or at least very close to it. It stands to reason that, had the bait been floating half-way up in the water, very few of the flatfish tribe could possibly have hooked themselves; yet many fishermen, or rather would-be fishermen, attempt to fish anywhere or everywhere for any kind of fish, without thinking of altering their apparatus. This is the greatest possible mistake; and if they, with such unsuitable arrangements, succeed in catching a few fish, let them think what they might "bag" if they paid proper attention to the fishes' propensities. Now flounders, and such like, invariably lie on or in the mud (generally

Sea-Fishing at Kingstown and Dalkey. 297

they are half-buried in it), and they must be hard pressed, I imagine, before they will condescend to leave their normal hunting-grounds for the sake of reaching a bait floating high above their heads; therefore a fisherman worthy the appellation must use his brains, and lure the fish in their own domains. Now, for flatfishes dreamily lying at the bottom of the sea, a bait temptingly placed, straggling to and fro close to their mouths, and sometimes even rubbing over their noses, proves a sore, and altogether an irresistible temptation; they gobble instinctively, dreamily, without thinking about it, and up they come to swell the "basket."

It was about 10 A.M. on a Wednesday when I made my first start. I was alone, for a wonder. I rowed out from among the other skiffs, then hoisted sail, and went skimming along. I passed the lighthouses, turned to the left, tacked along the West Pier, and when about a hundred and fifty yards from it and a hundred yards from the baths I took in mast and sail, threw the anchor, made all snug, and now the fishing began in earnest. I had provided myself with sea-lugs, a not by any means very cheap commodity in Kingstown. The reason for this high price of the lugs is obvious: they are collected by professional fishermen, who, of course, know very well that the more fish are caught by amateurs the less do they sell themselves; therefore they sell their bait to amateurs as dearly as they can, so as to prevent them, as far as possible, from indulging too much in baiting their ground well, and thereby reaping too great a harvest. However, there is a knack in everything; and if intending fishermen should come and pay a visit to that town, they must use their ingenuity if they are parsimonious. At any rate, any man ought to get for sixpence enough of lugs to last him for a whole day's fishing; but if one intends to have some fun, and does not mind a few coppers more or less, let him buy a good quantity of bait, and as soon as he is settled for a " try " let him throw overboard a few whole worms. This will draw the "shoals" to his neighbourhood, and the fish will take his bait (and hooks) quite readily.

I proceeded thus, and the result was most satisfactory: I heaved two lines, one at the stern and the other amidships; the latter I held between finger and thumb. The lead had hardly reached the bottom when " Tug, tug, tug!" three rapid and distinct pulls were had at the hooks. I hauled in, and a fine plaice came up. I heaved the line over again, and meanwhile I went to look at the stern line. I hauled it up a foot or so. It felt rather heavy, but there was no "wriggling ;" however, I pulled it in. A crab had convulsively clutched at one of the lugs, and he too, being a large one, came into the basket. Over again went the line ; back I went to the other one, where I found that considerable pulling and wriggling were going on. On due investigation of the phenomenon I discovered a flounder and a crab, each being in possession of a separate bait ; and thus it went on, reader, till the tide went down, when the bites became scarcer, and then ceased altogether, in spite of my very liberal baiting. I understood that the water was getting too shallow, and so I removed about fifty yards farther away from the pier, and there again I met with success. I must not forget to mention a very curious catch I made. It was a young lobster, hidden in a large shell ; it had collared a bait with its claws so tenaciously that I hauled him bodily in before he was able or willing to let go.

At about 2 P.M. I stopped " business " and went home

for lunch. My basket—a very large one—was as full as could be, and contained seventy-five fish, all of them plaice and flounders, barring two gurnets.

The next day I went to Dalkey. There was a strong head wind all the way, and we had to tack considerably before we reached the spot where we wanted to fish. There we caught nothing but bream, some of them very large ones. The ground there is extremely rocky and weedy, so that the breakages of lines and hooks were, to a certain extent, most annoying, but the sport was of a first-class character. We hooked such tremendously large fish that repeatedly they broke away, and smashed the hooks when nearly hauled in; therefore I should advise intending fishermen to provide themselves with extra strong tackle, in order to cope successfully with these monsters. I should also suggest that no anchor should be used for mooring the boat, as we nearly lost our own. It caught amongst a lot of craggy, hollow, and heavy rocks, and we had hard work to get it up again; in fact, we had given up all hopes of extracting it, when, by a little manœuvring and pulling ahead, we succeeded in freeing it. But it was a "caution;" and next time I shall certainly procure some large stone, and use an old rope for our anchorage, so that if it comes to the worst, and we have to leave our "moorings," at any rate the loss won't be much.

We caught altogether on that day fifty-six bream. We were two, with only one line each at a time; but we broke at least three; and certainly, from one cause or another, we smashed at least a score of hooks. Our bait was again sea-lugs. Our hooks were placed at about two feet from the leads, and on long, light sticks or whalebones, with long strings.

The current between Dalkey Island and Dalkey is

extremely strong, according to the state of the tide ; therefore great caution must be used when mooring the boat, so as to make sure that it will not drift ; not that there would be any danger for those in the boat, but their hooks would catch in the weeds or rocks ; and, at any rate, it would prevent them catching anything, if it did not break their lines altogether.

On the last day the weather was middling, but the wind at times was rather strong ; fortunately it was fair for our return journey, and we came back in a jiffey, delighted with our day's sport.

CHAPTER LXVII.

THE MOST AVAILABLE STATIONS.

FOR a long time I have had the pleasure of contributing to the sporting papers articles on the subjects of sea-fishing and wildfowl and seafowl shooting. I have visited all the best and most available sea-fishing stations on the east and south coasts, and now think that a review of all the spots I have tried will prove acceptable.

The most northern point I reached being Newcastle, I will begin with that town. Little shooting is to be had there, except under most favourable circumstances. The fishing is good in season, but for large fish it is necessary to go out. The depths are as follows: Ten miles right out of the Bar, from thirty to forty fathoms are to be found; within five miles of the Bar, twenty fathoms will be the average; within a mile, ten fathoms; five fathoms within half-a-mile, and the same depth will be found immediately past the breakwater. The usual deep-water fish are to be had in the open sea. For rock-fish and conger, towards Marsdon Bay will be found the best spot. Occasionally ducks, widgeon, and black ducks are to be had in the bay or on the wing, but it needs a strong easterly wind and a nasty sea to get them there in any numbers.

Sunderland has pretty much the same sort of fish, and

the same depths, as Newcastle. The sands, however, in frosty weather give tolerable sport with the gun, as shore-birds are apt to shelter themselves in the bay, past the Timber Pond. For rock-fish the neighbourhood of the Salterfan Rocks is about the best. Large birds are always to be seen there. Divers particularly abound in cold weather between Ryhope and Sunderland.

A walk along the shore from the harbour to Seaham will mostly prove an entertaining trip. There are some professional shore-shooters at Seaham, and the best spot to ambush in is amongst the rocks that spread out to sea some mile and a half or two miles from Seaham. Seafowl-shooting from a boat is good when there is no artillery practice going on from the cliffs, and in hard weather a stay at Seaham harbour is sure to repay the trouble. The sea, however, is very open there, and except when the wind blows from shore, or when there is no wind worth mentioning, the motions of a boat are apt to be rather rough. The sea-fishing is generally good, but for very large fish one must needs go a good way out. Within five or six miles, however, a twenty-fathom line will answer very fairly.

I now come to the Tees mouth. This is the place *par excellence* for any man who is fond of shooting and fishing. He may there take his fill of both. The shore-shooting, from the Tees mouth to Redcar and Saltburn-on-the-Sea, is admirable. The sands are firm, large, and always afford sport. Large birds, such as curlews and oystercatchers, are to be met with, more especially on the shores of the harbour, but a few flocks also patronise the sands. The duck tribes are only to be found within the harbour, and are unapproachable, except with a boat, the flighting being insignificant at most times. The sea-fishing comprises the ordinary run of open sea-fish. The only difficulty lies in the fact that the bay being shallow, one must needs go far out to meet with tolerably large-sized fish. Howbeit, taken all in all, for a man who can pick out his days, and is in no hurry, there is very good fun to be had at the Tees mouth, and shore-shooters who care not about dangerous mud-flats will find the sands firm, and affording some excellent walking and fair shooting practice.

Yarmouth gives good fishing only in winter time. The piers are usually tenanted by some score or so of enthusiastic sea-anglers, and the sport is at times simply first-class. Those anglers who prefer going out in boats will find the north side of the sea very good indeed, and on the south side, near the lightship, perfect shoals of whiting are caught periodically. The river-angling is also very fair. Eeling is carried to a considerable extent by professional spearers, and a trip or two with such fishermen will always prove entertaining to the amateur. The Broads are also noted for their sporting capabilities. The Fritton Decoy, one of them, is perhaps the best, and more easily reached from Yarmouth. The next in order, as regards being come-at-able, is the Oulton Broad Fishery. Leave must in all cases be obtained, and a good creel is occasionally to be managed. The other Broads are all more or less enjoyable, but they are so numerous that a description of each would require almost a full chapter. The northern bank of the river Yare runs along the railway line; there is, therefore, but little to be done there. The southern bank, however, is good. In ordinary weather one may find plenty of popping at small shore-birds, with an occasional shot at a stray duck, teal, widgeon, or curlew. Lots of herons are about in the adjoining marshes, and invariably come to the flats at low tide, so that by hiding and watching it is easy to bag a few of them. In winter time, however, the number of shots to be had along that shore may be multiplied tenfold, but then many of the Yarmouth professionals turn up and almost line the bank. An amateur at such times will fare a great deal better if he hires a punt and goes up the river in it with the flood, coming back at his leisure with the ebb tide. Care must be taken in this case never to undertake such a trip without the assistance of a man thoroughly acquainted with the river, for the Yare is so shallow everywhere but in the navigable channel that one may lose his reckoning and get stranded. If one prefers walking on the bank, the shooting there is free, as far as the vicarage of the village near the lime-kilns; in fact, as far as one can walk. Of course, private lands must not be traversed without leave. As regards the seashore-shooting, from the jetty at Gorlestown down to Lowestoft the sands are tolerably firm, and afford a little firing at small waders, but that is all. The land there is high and dry, and offers no enticement to the larger species. The other side of Yarmouth is a little better, the land being flatter, but there is not much to be done. At sea there are always a few companies about, but they never remain long, and are only worth going after in rough weather.

Lowestoft is fair for fishing right away out to sea, but the sea-shooting is next to *nil*, and the neighbourhood is dry in the extreme as regards sport with shore-birds.

Orfordness gives fair sea-fishing in season; whiting specially abound there, and the best banks are within three miles of the shore. The shore-shooting is fair, and a good deal of popping may be carried on in the estuary. The flighting, at times, is good, but very fickle. The best spot for it is at the mouth of the river Ore, and near the Havergate Island. A boat would be a *sine quâ non* there, for the lines of flight vary with the wind, and anchor-

The Most Available Stations. 305

ing in the lee of the island will, at most times, answer well.

The river Deben is noted for its shooting capabilities, and the neighbouring sand-banks are good fishing spots.

The Shipwash, the Kettle Bottom, and the Bawdsey Bank, when the whiting are on, will give plenty of sport, and in winter time many ducks will be seen about the mouth of the river. It needs a boat to do it justice, and it will be well also to secure' the services of a professional, until the best points on the river are known.

Harwich is decidedly one of the best stations for the sea-angler and seafowl-shooter. It stands at the mouth of two very fair wildfowl rivers, the Stour and the Orwell. The Orwell is the better of the two; it is not so wide perhaps as the Stour, but is quieter, and therefore is better patronised by the birds. Still, the Stour is not to be despised. Neither river can be tried thoroughly without a boat. Moreover, the softs are treacherous on both. Some of the flats will bear a man fairly, but in their midst he may come suddenly on a rotten piece, and go down to his armpits if he has no mud-shoes on. When snow is on the ground, and the wind blows roughly and cold, birds swarm over the flats and in the creeks. As regards sea-fishing, there are countless banks about, and the shallows are rather awkward to thread through, but when a fair depth is to be obtained, there, as a rule, fish will be found. When the weather is mild I advise the sportsman to go sea-fishing, and as soon as matters alter, go up the rivers and try his luck.

Brightlingsea is another fair place to put up at, especially for shooting, as it commands the river Colne, and is near the mouth of the Blackwater river. The fishing is tolerably fair in the season; whiting come up quite opposite Brightlingsea, and reach occasionally very large sizes. There are, moreover, plenty of plaice, dabs, and flounders about the estuary of the Colne, and a trawl will always answer very fairly. The shooting is first-rate. In cold weather curlews teem, and ducks, widgeon, teal, and divers come up as far almost as Wivenhoe. In fact, I fancy Brightlingsea would just suit several correspondents of mine, who have been keenly inquiring as to what places would suit best their sporting requirements. For shooting small birds on the Colne, any place and any season will do (barring the breeding season, of course). When the large birds turn up, the biggest companies will be found along the Mersea Island, at the estuary of the Colne proper, and at the mouth of the Pyefleet Channel. The sea-fishing proper may be carried on in the Wallet, but large fish are not the rule there, except under special circumstances.

The Blackwater river is undoubtedly "cock of the walk" as regards wildfowl-shooting, but the fishing is generally poor, excepting when the mullet are in. For shooting ducks no better spot nearer London can be found. Bunches of the birds in winter weather will be found in the river and creeks. The companies are mostly off Bradwell, Sales Point, and along the St. Peter's sands. West Mersea, with its two neighbouring large creeks, is also a good place to put up at. The professional element is very strong everywhere about the Blackwater. At Heybridge basin, near Maldon, at Mundon, Bradwell, Goldhanger, and both Merseas, shoals of wildfowl-punts are to be seen, and many wildfowling-smacks are about, anchored in the creeks. The amateur, provided he has the "wherewith to smooth the path," will experience no difficulty in getting accommodated with boats, punts, and men. I need not add that the sport is rough and arduous, therefore none but very enthusiastic men are likely to stick to it. Hence the extraordinary ignorance and misrepresentation displayed in some quarters respecting the sport to be met with there. It seems queer, to say the least, to see it stated that duck-shooting is not to be had anywhere ! This originated probably with the professionals, and is served up again by reporters on the look-out for hearsay information. I could bring twenty men to back my assertion that there is always sport to be had on the Blackwater, and I would back myself to bag at least ten ducks between sunset and sunrise, with a shoulder 4-bore gun, on any suitable day, blessed with winter weather. By-the-way, I would recommend wildfowl-shooters to try one of Messrs. Tolley's 4-bore guns. They have made me one, central-fire, single, full-choked, with which I am tolerably certain of killing birds, in a " company," up to a hundred and twenty yards, and a better performer than that no man need wish to have.

To resume now, about the Blackwater. In my opinion it is quite as good for duck-shooting as the celebrated Poole harbour. Its punters make a good thing of it occasionally and this being admitted, where do they get their birds from, if, according to the aforesaid authorities, no birds are to be had ?

Those shooters who like sailing in yachts and shallow-draught smacks, will do well to try the Dengie Flats and to beat well the mouth of the river. They will see hundreds of birds any suitable day in winter.

The sea-fishing off the Blackwater is moderate in quality, the fish being mostly small, but this is made up for in quantity, and I shall not forget what a load we caught with our trawl once, on a tack from West Mersea to the Sales Point.

The Crouch River is fair for shooting, but moderate for fishing. The Anchor Inn, at Hull Bridge, is a fair " roost-ing-place," and everything in the way of boats and information is procurable there. The train from Fenchurch Street only goes as far as Benfleet. If, therefore, a sportsman wishes to patronise the Anchor, he must write to the proprietor. He will meet his customers with his own trap and drive them to the inn. There are shoals of shore-birds on the Crouch, and the sport is good when the shooters are not too many, and when they know what they are about.

The Bridgemarsh Island, three or four miles below Hull Bridge, is always well tenanted with shore-birds, and past Burnham large birds are occasionally to be bagged.

The fishing and shooting at Southend are not worth much. The fish run small, and consist mostly of plaice and dabs. In mid-channel, however, whiting, gurnards, &c., are to be had during the season, and they generally run fair-sized. From the end of the jetty a nice fish is sometimes caught. As for shooting, a few birds are to be had, but when the artillery practice begins at Shoeburyness it drives them away instantly. A few old stagers soon return, but they are not easy to be got at. It can be managed in stormy weather only, and I have done well there at times, whereas at others I could only just scrape two or three birds together.

Sheerness is about on a par with Southend for fishing, except that deep water being available in mid-channel, larger fish may be caught. The shooting is incomparably better than at Southend.

The shores of the Thames, of the Medway, and of the Swale work together to make the place a general rendezvous for all shore-birds on the look-out for a feed. If a man, well versed in the use of his weapon, ascertains the hours of the tide, &c., he will probably fill up the stern-sheets of his boat with birds.

Whitstable, the next station, is too cramped with shallows to give good fishing, except for flatfish. The shore-shooting, on the other hand, is fairly good.

Herne Bay is better for fishing, but worse for shooting. The sea being deeper, pouting and whiting are to be had; but owing to the shore being pebbly, few, except passing birds, are to be seen unless one goes with the gun towards Whitstable, or takes a boat towards the Island of Sheppey, where birds are generally to be found.

Margate is too much frequented to afford sport for the gunner.

In the Channel fair fishing at times rewards the sea-anglers, and the laying of a long line is occasionally a very remunerative process.

Broadstairs is much quieter than Margate or Ramsgate, but the shore rarely gives sport except in uncommonly cold weather. The fishing I found good, and from what I heard there seems to be always something to be done in that line.

Ramsgate has a nice stretch of sandy flats, running south, where in winter time many birds are to be shot. There are a few professional shooters, and they mostly resort to boats when the companies appear. The fishing is very nice, if one does not wish to catch "monsters of the deep."

From Cliff's End, near Ramsgate, to Sandwich, and from Sandwich to Deal, the shore is bare, and even in the mildest of weather a good bag of birds can be made.

At Deal the sea-fishing is generally very good. In 1876, however, it did not reach the average, on account of the whiting not turning up in such numbers as they ought to have done. Whiting-fishing used to be a staple sport at Deal. It was almost a failure that year.

Dover has no shore-shooting worth mentioning, although

the sea-shooting is sometimes, but rarely, worth looking after. Fishing, as a rule, is good.

Folkestone is almost similar to Dover as regards both sports.

Sandgate is not up to much either way.

Shorncliffe is also indifferent.

Hythe is worse than either, and Dymchurch very poor. All that shore is bare shingle, therefore no birds come to it, and the sea is shallow, holding only small fish.

Off the Dunge Marsh ducks are to be shot at sea in daytime, at daybreak, and when night sets in. The sea-fishing gets there tolerably good, on account of the depths to be found.

Rye is only noted for its marsh, a very bleak and desolate one, which requires a deal of tramping, together with a nose-freezing wind, to make it fairly remunerative to shoot over.

Hastings is a jolly place for fishing. Congers and pouting abound in the rocks, and one need not go very far from shore to meet with sport. The shooting is *nil*, except when a stray bird or two fly over the boat whilst one is fishing.

St. Leonards-on-Sea is exactly like Hastings—same fish and same absence of shooting.

The Royal Sovereign Shoals afford good sport at times, so do the Bexhill Reefs and Coxheath Shoals; but, the bay being very open, one must choose the weather to venture out as far as the first-named.

Eastbourne was not up to much when I went there.

Beachy Head is undoubtedly better, on account of birds congregating round the head, and, as the sea runs deep within a mile or two, good sport is to be had with the lines. Unfortunately, the nearest harbour is six miles away.

The Most Available Stations.

Seaford has good fishing, but no shooting.

Newhaven is "in the same boat," but, the harbour being easily accessible, it is not a bad head-quarter when a few ducks are on the sea.

Brighton offers first-rate sea-fishing and tolerable sea-fowl-shooting.

For the latter the Black Rock is a good station. The fish comprise codlings, skate, brill, turbot, gurnard, conger, whiting, &c. There are plenty of boats and boatmen to be had, but the sea is very open and rough when there is any wind.

At Shoreham there are shore-birds, and in the harbour a duck may occasionally be picked up; fishing tolerably fair.

At Worthing the Brill Rocks stand prominently as pleasant spots to visit. The Kingston Rock is also attractive to fish.

From Preston to Littlehampton the shore gives good sport to the guns; I mean, of course, when the weather is sharp and cold. Many ducks are bagged there as well as at sea.

Opposite Littlehampton are the Kingmere Rocks, where lobsters abound; the staple fishing, in fact, at Bognor and Littlehampton appears to be the laying of pots for lobsters. There are several good places for this work, and besides "potting" lobsters one may get a good many rock-fish as well with the lines. Large birds are not common, except divers and black ducks, which are mostly everywhere.

The Middleton Ledge, the Bognor Rocks, the Barn Rocks, and The Park are favourite spots for hookers and for pot-men.

At Selsea Bill many birds congregate in the daytime; they come, presumably, from Chichester harbour, close by.

A yacht, well handled and equipped with men who know how to circumvent the fowl, will do well there from November to February. The depths of sea are six fathoms within two miles; a sail out is needful, therefore, if one wishes to fall in with fish worth catching.

The same may be said of Chichester harbour. For shooting, this harbour is very good. From West Itchenor down to the East Pole Sand I have seen a thousand birds at least, two years ago, during the frosty weather. The usual shore-birds also abound there. The best places to put up at would be West Itchenor or West Wittering. At either of those villages, boats and men are readily procurable. The harbour is tolerably easily sailed about in a small boat. The tramping in some parts is perfectly impracticable, except with mud-shoes. In other parts the mud bears well. Those shooters who like shore-shooting can walk from Appledram, a distance of five or six miles, along the harbour, when at high tide the shore-birds will be easily got at.

At Portsmouth itself there is not much to be done, but in the deepest part of the sea at Spithead a good deal of fishing may be had all the year round; and as regards shooting, the Longstone harbour and the shores of Hayling Island are always very interesting to the gunner.

The Southampton Water is a very good wildfowl resort, where professional punters abound, and amateurs may also glean a tolerable bag of fowl. The shore-birds are very abundant, and the fishing in summer and autumn attracts many visitors to Southampton. The best way to "do" the Southampton Water is to hire a four or five ton yacht, in which a party can make themselves comfortable for two or three days. By anchoring at night in one of the numerous creeks that line both shores, much unnecessary sailing will be saved. Boats are numerous, and may be had for from twelve shillings to a sovereign per day, according to the season; this will entail the services of a man and a lad to work the yacht and dingey.

The same terms generally apply to hiring boat accommodation at Plymouth. In this case, however, the boatmen rarely agree to stop out overnight, the coast being a rocky one, and therefore somewhat dangerous, where anchoring at night might turn out anything but a saving of time. The fishing there is quite first-class, and all sorts of fish are to be had all the year round. In fact, there is no better station for an enthusiastic sea-fisherman. As for ducks, they are, in stormy weather, numerous; many companies being seen about in winter time. Concerning divers and black ducks, there are generally some to be found round about the Eddystone, in Plymouth Sound, and by the Rame Head, but, except for a collection, these birds are rarely shot at; and, on the whole, Plymouth is more of a fishing than a shooting place.

This brings my review to an end; but I cannot come to a conclusion without thanking cordially all my correspondents for the many expressions of approval which my papers have elicited, and with my best wishes for their success, I now drop the curtain over my series of "Sea-fishing and Seafowl-shooting Excursions."

THE END.

CHARLES DICKENS AND EVANS, CRYSTAL PALACE PRESS.

CHARLES DICKENS'S WORKS.

THE ILLUSTRATED LIBRARY EDITION.

Complete in 30 vols., demy 8vo, 10s. each.

This Edition is printed on a finer paper and in a larger type than has been employed in any previous Edition. The type has been cast especially for it, and the page is of a size to admit of the introduction of all the Original Illustrations. No such attractive issue has been made of the writings of MR. DICKENS, which, various as have been the forms of Publication adapted to the demands of an ever widely-increasing popularity, have never yet been worthily presented in a really handsome library form. The Collection comprises all the Minor Writings it was MR. DICKENS'S wish to preserve.

SKETCHES BY "BOZ." With 40 Illustrations by GEORGE CRUIKSHANK.
PICKWICK. 2 vols. With 42 Illustrations by "PHIZ."
OLIVER TWIST. With 24 Illustrations by CRUIKSHANK.
NICHOLAS NICKLEBY. 2 vols. With 40 Illustrations by "PHIZ."
OLD CURIOSITY SHOP and REPRINTED PIECES. 2 vols. With Illustrations by CATTERMOLE, &c.
BARNABY RUDGE and HARD TIMES. 2 vols. With Illustrations by CATTERMOLE, &c.
MARTIN CHUZZLEWIT. 2 vols. With 40 Illustrations by "PHIZ."
AMERICAN NOTES and PICTURES FROM ITALY. 1 vol. With 8 Illustrations.
DOMBEY AND SON. 2 vols. With 40 Illustrations by "PHIZ."
COPPERFIELD. 2 vols. With 40 Illustrations by "PHIZ."
BLEAK HOUSE. 2 vols. With 40 Illustrations by "PHIZ."
LITTLE DORRIT. 2 vols. With 40 Illustrations by "PHIZ."
A TALE OF TWO CITIES. With 16 Illustrations by "PHIZ."
THE UNCOMMERCIAL TRAVELLER. With 8 Illustrations by MARCUS STONE.
GREAT EXPECTATIONS. With 8 Illustrations by MARCUS STONE.
OUR MUTUAL FRIEND. 2 vols. With 40 Illustrations by MARCUS STONE.
CHRISTMAS BOOKS. With 17 Illustrations by SIR EDWIN LANDSEER, R.A., MACLISE, R.A., &c. &c.
HISTORY OF ENGLAND. With 8 Illustrations by MARCUS STONE.
CHRISTMAS STORIES (from "Household Words" and "All the Year Round"). With 14 Illustrations.
EDWIN DROOD and other STORIES. With 12 Illustrations by S. L. FILDES.

LIBRARY EDITION.

In post 8vo. With the Original Illustrations, 30 vols., cloth, £12.

THE "CHARLES DICKENS" EDITION.

In 21 vols., crown 8vo, cloth, with Illustrations, £3 9s. 6d.

HOUSEHOLD EDITION.

In crown 4to vols., now publishing in Weekly Penny Numbers and Sixpenny Monthly Parts. Each Penny Number contains Two Illustrations. 15 volumes completed.

CHAPMAN AND HALL, 193, PICCADILLY.

THOMAS CARLYLE'S WORKS.

LIBRARY EDITION COMPLETE.

Handsomely printed, in 34 *vols., demy 8vo, cloth,* £15.

SARTOR RESARTUS. The Life and Opinions of Herr Teufelsdrockh. With a Portrait. Price 7s. 6d.
THE FRENCH REVOLUTION: a History. 3 vols., each 9s.
LIFE OF FREDERICK SCHILLER AND EXAMINATION OF HIS WORKS. With Supplement of 1872, Portrait and Plates. Price 9s. The Supplement *separately*, price 2s.
CRITICAL AND MISCELLANEOUS ESSAYS. 6 vols., each 9s.
ON HEROES, HERO WORSHIP, AND THE HEROIC IN HISTORY. Price 7s. 6d.
PAST AND PRESENT. With a Portrait. Price 9s.
OLIVER CROMWELL'S LETTERS AND SPEECHES. With Portraits. 5 vols., each 9s.
LATTER-DAY PAMPHLETS. Price 9s.
LIFE OF JOHN STERLING. With Portrait. Price 9s.
HISTORY OF FREDERICK THE SECOND. 10 vols., each 9s.
TRANSLATIONS FROM THE GERMAN. 3 vols., each 9s.
GENERAL INDEX TO THE LIBRARY EDITON. 8vo, cloth, price 6s.

CHEAP AND UNIFORM EDITION.

In 23 *vols., crown 8vo, cloth,* £7 5s.

THE FRENCH REVOLUTION: a History. 2 vols., 12s.
OLIVER CROMWELL'S LETTERS AND SPEECHES. With Elucidations, &c. 3 vols., 18s.
LIVES OF SCHILLER AND JOHN STERLING. 1 vol., 6s.
CRITICAL AND MISCELLANEOUS ESSAYS. 4 vols., £1 4s.
SARTOR RESARTUS AND LECTURES ON HEROES. 1 vol., 6s.
LATTER-DAY PAMPHLETS. 1 vol., 6s.
CHARTISM AND PAST AND PRESENT. 1 vol., 6s.
TRANSLATIONS FROM THE GERMAN OF MUSÆUS, TIECK, AND RICHTER. 1 vol., 6s.
WILHELM MEISTER, by Goethe, a Translation. 2 vols., 12s.
HISTORY OF FRIEDRICH THE SECOND, called Frederick the Great. Vols. I. and II., containing Part I.—"Friedrich till his Accession." 14s.—Vols. III. and IV., containing Part II.—"The First Two Silesian Wars." 14s.—Vols. V., VI., VII., completing the Work, £1 1s.

PEOPLE'S EDITION.

In 37 *vols., small crown 8vo, price* 2s. *each vol., bound in cloth or in sets of* 37 *vols. in* 18, *cloth gilt, for* £3 14s.

CHAPMAN AND HALL, 193, PICCADILLY.

www.ingramcontent.com/pod-product-compliance
Lightning Source LLC
Chambersburg PA
CBHW030754230426
43667CB00007B/967